SPACE AGE BATCHELOR PAD MUSIC

THE STORY OF STEREOLAB IN 20 SONGS

BEN CARDEW

JAWBONE

For Alexandra, Francesca, Nicolau, and my parents, with love.

A Jawbone book
First edition 2026
Published by
Jawbone Press
7 Orlando Road
London SW4 0LE
England
www.jawbonepress.com
books@jawbonepress.com

ISBN 978-1-916829-32-9

Printed by PBtisk

1 2 3 4 5 30 29 28 27 26

contents

INTRO
'THE WAY WILL BE OPENING'
TYPICALLY ATYPICAL

Most bands are relatively simple. You come to them knowing what to expect, more or less, and if they *do* serve up the odd kink or wrinkle, it tends to be the exception.

Not so Stereolab. Stereolab are one of the most fascinating groups of the last fifty years, a source of constant reinvention and illuminating contrasts, where political ideology meets the sweetest pop melody and driving guitars rub along with space-age jazz.

You can't even get down to brass tacks with Stereolab. What kind of band are they? What genre of music do they make? You'd probably call them an indie band if you lived in the UK, or 'alternative' in the USA. But Stereolab signed a major label deal in the States, which makes them not exactly 'indie' in the classical sense of the word. (Although, as you'll see, autonomy and independence are incredibly important to the band.)

And what, exactly, are Stereolab an alternative to? Everything? Stereolab's spread is so wide, their musical leanings so immaculate, that they encompass genres from country to jazz, hard rock to hip-hop. They are simultaneously in harmony with and in opposition to pretty much everything: Dadaist punk rockers in tune with the sound of the lounge; jazz swingers with a love of outlandish electronics; and so on.

'Be different,' Stereolab co-founder Tim Gane told me when I interviewed him in June 2008, for *The Stool Pigeon*. I had asked him whether he still subscribed to the idea that it was better for a band to be interesting than to be good. 'Be unique,' he continued, 'be something new and then try and make that something good, as opposed to being very proficient. Attempt things. Try things. That is at the heart of why I like creating things.' To this day, it sounds like a manifesto: for art and also for life.

To be eclectic in music is to be fundamentally *inefficient*. And Stereolab have suffered for their eclecticism. They have had success, of course, over their initial two-decade run and subsequent revival. But nothing like the kind of grand commercial breakthrough that some of their records merited, the band hovering somewhere in between cult fame and actual, bottom-of-the-chart, mainstream-bothering renown.

People like things that are easy to classify. Musicians don't like to hear it, but it's true. Sure, when pressed, we all like to say that the only types of music are good music and bad music, but why do you think record shops are divided up into so many different sections?

Stereolab are hard to understand and difficult to classify. It has been a constant source of pleasure seeing people I have interviewed for this book tie themselves in knots trying to explain the appeal of Stereolab, as contradictions pile on top of inconsistencies.

I've been listening to Stereolab since around 1992—I'd like to mention a lightning-strike moment of first contact, but I honestly can't think of one—and I still don't fully understand them. What Stereolab album would I recommend to a friend who had never heard them? It changes from day to day. What song is their greatest? I could give you twenty songs today and a different twenty tomorrow.

This book is an attempt to address that. This is the story of Stereolab in twenty songs, each of which illustrates a certain facet of the band's abundant personality. It's not a comprehensive list, and it's not meant to be; it's a guide, a weak torch with dodgy batteries to light up your trip into the yawning Stereolab cave.

But, perhaps you protest, why would you *want* to explain the magic of Stereolab? What is a magic trick when the art has been explained away as a clever con?

I disagree. Maybe it's because I am a journalist, maybe it's because I am a nerd, but I find that burrowing deep into a band only makes me love them more. What I want, with this book, is to enhance your love of Stereolab, so that you, too, will come away in awe at one of the greatest bands of the twentieth century and beyond.

And if you don't, well . . . I *tried*.

I did approach the key Stereolab duo of Tim Gane and Laetitia Sadier, via the band's manager Martin Pike, to see if they would be interested in taking part in this book. The response was a polite but firm 'no'. And that is entirely their prerogative. I later spoke to Laetitia about the book when I interviewed her for *Line Noise* in May 2024. She wished me good luck and said that it sounded like an interesting idea. Not good; *interesting*.

I was slightly sad that I didn't get to interview Tim and Laetitia. Then again, on some level, I am *attracted to* the fact that they don't want to give everything away. Why would I want to write about a band that wants me to know everything about them? Where's the fun in that? Where's the mystery?

Stereolab are, to quote Shakespeare, 'of infinite jest, of most excellent fancy', where every layer peeled back reveals yet more intrigue. Their music gives layer upon layer of fresh insight, of strings to be followed and threads to be unspooled. This isn't a definitive Stereolab story, and I made a decision early on not to include every Peel session, flexi-disc, and B-side. But it is *a* story. Maybe no more relevant than the rest, but one I have worked hard on. (And, in the end, I did speak to more than fifty people for the book, some of whom I have quoted, some of whom I haven't.)

I have written about twenty Stereolab (and Stereolab-adjacent) songs, one per chapter. I could have written about two hundred. Maybe someday I will. My first task in researching this book was to listen to every single Stereolab song I could find—an incredibly deep and rewarding task I undertook over the 2023 Christmas holidays, my festive period soundtracked by the disturbing wooshes of 'Simple Headphone Mind' and the overloaded jazz of 'Free Witch And No Bra Queen'.

I picked twenty songs, but I wanted to add one more for the intro: a song to be chosen at random as an example of Stereolab's almost casual greatness; a song to stand for the fact that, almost everywhere you look in the band's thick and convoluted catalogue, brilliance lurks. (And, yes, I also added another song for the outro. Sue me.)

And so, this introductory chapter finds its musical companion in 'The Way Will Be Opening', track three of the *Super-Electric* EP, Stereolab's second release back in 1991. The selection isn't *entirely* random. I chose the song for its name, which sits snugly with an introductory chapter, suggesting something of import—and even of possible greatness—to come. It's also a song I mention in the book's first chapter.

All the same, this *almost* random musical choice does serve my point. 'The Way Will Be Opening' is an early Stereolab song that *feels* like an early work by a band still scrabbling to find their sound. And yet, still, isn't the very essence of Stereolab in there? In Gane's guitar, where droning technique meets jazzy chord sequences; in the nonchalant beauty of Sadier's vocal; in Gina Morris's intricate harmonies, which wend their way about Laetitia's voice like a rose around a lattice; in the simple drive of Martin Kean's bass and Joe Dilworth's drums?

My point is that 'The Way Will Be Opening'—a song I chose for its title, with no regard for its musical content—*could* be the perfect introduction to Stereolab. And yet it sounds little like the towering 'Super-Electric', which opens the same EP, let alone the band's excursions into micro-jazz loops on *Not Music*, a record released in 2010, after the band had announced their hiatus and their last studio album until *Instant Holograms On Metal Film* in 2025. Such is the wonder of Stereolab. They are, as former keyboard player Mick Conroy told me, the kind of band where people will debate their favourite era.

As I said, Gane and Sadier didn't want to be interviewed for this book, but I hope that if they ever read it, they will tolerate my tale. It comes from a place of love and respect, and if I have made any mistakes, I apologise for them in advance.

I hope, too, that Gane, Sadier, and all the other members of Stereolab are well and happy in the re-formed band, as they bring such joy to others. One of the things I always loved about Stereolab, as a crazed Francophile kid, was the way that Sadier brought a wealth of French cultural references to Stereolab, and how they ran headlong into Gane's English-born artistic thirst.

Nowadays, post-Daft Punk and all, French music is loved around the world. But that really wasn't the case back in 1991, when Stereolab released their first single. It felt so daring back then, so different, and yet so entirely natural.

And, yes, I saw Gane and Sadier, the great romantic and musical couple, as the embodiment of a grudging but deep-seated cross-Channel love affair, the greatest Anglo-French collaboration since Concorde. It gave hope to me, in small-town England, that there was more to life than British norms and customs, that there was a whole world out there of French poetry, avant-garde art, and obtuse musical angles that I could one day enjoy if I just kept my eyes open.

Gane and Sadier split up as a couple in the early 2000s, and their rare interviews today sometimes show a certain tetchiness. But still they continue to work together, touring the globe as Stereolab, recording new music, and carefully curating the band's musical legacy with a run of compilations.

So, who knows—maybe, despite Brexit, despite right-wing buffoons stirring up hatred, despite the constant social media signals that we should all despise each other, there is hope for us all. Because if the world can produce a band as judderingly brilliant and shockingly original as Stereolab, there must be *something* going for it.

I hope you enjoy this book. If you do, please get in touch. Tell me your favourite Stereolab song, and we can reminisce together.

•

As I was writing this book, I read The Jesus & Mary Chain's excellent autobiography, *Never Understood*, in which William Reid mentions that he used to read three or four musical biographies a month until David Cavanagh's Creation Records story, *My Magpie Eyes Are Hungry For The Prize*, was published, and his own band featured.

I understand where Reid is coming from: seeing your story written down in black and white can be a sobering experience, with all the nuance and different viewpoints of a particular tale reduced to one perspective. As we all know, human memory can be problematic, and if you ask ten different people about one event, you're going to get ten wildly different stories.

I've tried my very hardest to be accurate in this book, but it is inevitable that some people will disagree with some readings of events. At the same time, some of the things I've written here are very much *my opinion*. At points, this book runs closer to a very long review than a biography. Generally, I've tried to mix the two.

Hopefully, in writing this book, I won't forever wreck the joy of a rock biography for Tim, Laetitia, and the rest of Stereolab. If I do, you have my humblest apologies.

01

'SUPER-ELECTRIC' PROPULSION

Propulsion, movement, pace, energy: this is the rocket-rush feeling that lies at the core of so many of the greatest Stereolab songs. The whooshing surge of movement; the joy of progress; the chest-thump of excitement as the self-styled 'Groop' picks up the pace, drums beating like a lusty heart, guitars roaring like nuclear blowback, keyboards itching with passion.

You can hear this in dozens of Stereolab songs. And you can feel the same propulsion in the actions of the group themselves, in the incredible creative wave that drove them toward ten albums, seventeen EPs, three mini-LPs, and handfuls of split singles in just two decades of life, from 1990 to 2009, before their 2019 reunion put them back on the circuit.

Stereolab are endlessly creative, the music charging out of them like they have to expel it or die trying. Tim Gane, the polite-looking English guitarist who formed the band with French singer Laetitia Sadier, never looks back. When an album is done, it is there, on the shelf, and the band move ever onward, toward new territory. This white-heat creativity is one of many things that makes Stereolab so incredibly special. For more than two decades, they have been *driven* in a way that few bands can sustain over more than a couple of years, their prodigal output making other artists look like lazy-bellied sloths.

You can feel this momentum, too, in the way that Stereolab rushed out of the traps in their first few years of life. Gane and Sadier met in Paris in 1988, at a concert by Gane's previous band, McCarthy, their music a seditious mix of Marxist politics, jangling guitars, and post-punk vitality.

David Callahan from Essex noise-pop band The Wolfhounds, a contemporary of McCarthy's, says that Gane's old band were 'fantastic': 'Tim's music got better in Stereolab. But I still really rate [McCarthy singer] Malcolm Eden as one of the best lyricists in the 80s,' he says. 'Especially when they started, they were kind of crossing Joy Division with The Byrds, which sounds like a weird hybrid, but it worked.'

Speaking at the Red Bull Music Academy in 2015, Sadier remembered both the terrible support group at McCarthy's Paris gig and a big spot on Gane's nose. She introduced herself to Gane, offering to be his guide around Paris; he agreed, and the two ended up as a romantic couple, the creative fulcrum around which Stereolab would pivot.

Gane and Sadier's creative relationship would start almost as soon as their romantic one. Sadier moved to London in September 1989, joining McCarthy on backing vocals in the year before the band split.

'I think it was vital for me to escape France,' she said when I interviewed her for *Line Noise* in 2024. 'And for the longest time, I did kind of really hate the French, which meant probably that I hate myself, but I'm working on that.' (Later on in the interview, she said that her dislike of the French was waning, and that she is making peace with her origins.)

Escaping France helped Sadier to start making music. You can hear her voice on McCarthy's final album, *Banking, Violence And The Inner Life Today*, but by the time the record was released, in August 1990, McCarthy were history, and Gane and Sadier were working on new music.

'It just kind of happened,' says Callahan of the transition from McCarthy to Stereolab. 'McCarthy and The Wolfhounds finished at about the same time, but there was no question of not doing music. It happened osmotically. We were out around each other's houses, drinking coffee and going to gigs and swapping records and tapes and things. And it just kind of happened.'

Laetitia, he says, had become a familiar presence by this point. 'She would often be backstage at Wolfhounds and McCarthy shows, and she was always trying to find out how I wrote lyrics and how we went about making music. She was very keen to get involved herself, and more power to her.' Stereolab was, Callahan explains, 'a thing that just kind of grew . . . it was a fertile period, and there was fertile ground for it to grow on.'

In the first few months of Stereolab, Gane would come to Sadier with song ideas, liberated by his departure from McCarthy's creative tension and his new artistic relationship. She would put words to the songs and sing them—a way of working that has endured throughout Stereolab's career.

'When we formed, it was more important for us to be unique or different than it was to be really good,' Gane told journalist Mike McGonigal for the sleeve notes to the 2006 Stereolab compilation *Serene Velocity*. 'The conceptual side to the music was to try to find something that other people weren't doing at the time, which obviously involved German Krautrock music to a certain degree.' Gane said that Neu!, one of the pivotal Krautrock bands, 'had a great idea, but it could be taken further, involving melodies and so on.'

While Stereolab were an unusual band, they were also—at least in the early years—very much a product of the environment in which they formed: alternative London of the late 80s and early 90s. 'There were gigs every night!' Sadier told *Tone Glow* in 2024. 'Bands . . . all the time! And they played a lot. We'd see Th' Faith Healers maybe three times a month! So there was a lot of activity, and the scene was really thriving. I didn't realise it; I took it for granted. But, wow, we did not know which gig to attend, and sometimes we'd go to two in a night if we strategised.'

What was important in London, Sadier continued, was a collective spirit. 'There was this community and I think it was a healthy one because we helped each other—we supported each other, we went to each other's gigs, we lent each other gear. There was this healthy sense of collaborating. And there were very different bands as well—there were Gallon Drunk, who were more rockabilly. And there were also the

Riot Grrrl bands. That opened doors for people to fight together, to do things collectively—collective action.'

'It was kind of an underground scene there,' Callahan says of London in the early 1990s. By this point, he had formed Moonshake, an experimental rock band who would become lynchpins of the London scene. 'Lots of bands hung out together: people in Lush and Stereolab, and people like Moose and My Bloody Valentine; we're all at the same parties, in the same shows all the time.'

Bands, he explains, 'used to cross-fertilise, ideas-wise . . . but it was more just hanging out and having a good time, with everyone who found a whole bunch of like minds, who were relatively hedonistic but also making good music.'

Miki Berenyi is a founder member of Lush, who formed in London in 1987 and frequented many of the same venues as Stereolab in those early days. She says that London was a very productive place for music in the late 1980s and early 90s, largely thanks to the freedoms it offered.

'We had cheap rent. Even when it wasn't cheap, you had housing benefit, you had student grants, you had the Enterprise Allowance Scheme [a Government scheme to help unemployed people create their own businesses]. You had the dole [unemployment benefit]. Transport was cheap. Beer was cheap, food was cheap, it was shit, but it was cheap. All of those things were shit, but they were cheap,' she says.

This, she explains, allowed people the time and space to set up bands, create fanzines, promote gigs, and generally live beyond the day-to-day grind of normal working life. 'It was kind of a non-elitist melting pot of all different kinds of people, any one of whom, at any point, could suggest that you join a band or get involved with a fanzine or just go and look at guitars on Denmark Street for an afternoon,' Berenyi says. 'A lot of people with that dole culture had plenty of time on their hands and plenty of places to go that don't cost much money.'

Live music, in particular, blossomed. 'People were opening venues,' Berenyi says. 'You would get the Falcon [in Camden] . . . Jeff Barrett was putting on gigs there; Jon Beast was putting on gigs at the Bull & Gate; whoever the fuck was putting on gigs at the Dublin Castle. It didn't seem like such a big deal; it was quite easy to do. So it meant there was a lot of space and opportunity for people to play and rehearse.'

Gane and Sadier's finely weighted creative process bore *almost* immediate fruit with the release of their first EP, *Super 45*, in May 1991. Before that, though, the duo recorded a demo with Wolfhounds guitarist Andy Golding and McCarthy drummer Gary Baker, with the aim of releasing a single on Midnight Music, home to both The Wolfhounds and McCarthy.

Golding says that he spoke with Tim and Laetitia about doing something musically after the demise of their respective bands. 'I remember driving over there to Brixton [in South London, where Tim and Laetitia lived] about five or six times,' he says. 'I don't remember if we actually played any music. I think we just talked about what we were going to do. And then Tim got an offer from Nick Ralph, who ran Midnight Music, to put out a single. So I said, Yeah, come over and we'll get it together.'

The makeshift band, who Golding says didn't have a name, recorded one song, a cover of Serge Gainsbourg's classic 'Bonnie And Clyde'—not, at the time, a particularly well-known song in the UK—with Golding on vocals, bass, and keyboards; Baker on drums; Gane on guitar; and Sadier on vocals. The song is *interesting* without being anything particularly special—a scratchy-guitar, vaguely post-punky take on the song, with Sadier in fine Gallic voice. You could imagine it sitting alongside The Wolfhounds on Midnight Music. But it doesn't sound much like any of Stereolab's myriad phases.

Golding wouldn't hang around either. He was twenty-five years old and too old—in his mind—to be living with his parents. When an offer came in to work on an IT help desk, the same day he recorded 'Bonnie And Clyde', Golding took the job and abandoned the idea of working with Tim and Laetitia. The demo never made it to record, although in 1995, Sadier would guest on a cover version of the same song with US guitar band Luna, with whom Stereolab shared an American label.

While the 'Bonnie And Clyde' cover wasn't bad, the leap forward toward *Super 45*, Stereolab's first release, was startling. The four-track EP was recorded in November 1990 and released on Duophonic, a label created with the band's manager, Martin Pike.

'Martin [Pike] used to sell T-shirts for McCarthy. We first knew him in 1986 when he used to do a fanzine in England called *Diana*

Rigg,' Gane told *Chunklet* magazine. 'After McCarthy stopped, me and Laetitia wanted to do a group and Martin wanted to help us, so we decided to do the group and the label ourselves all in one go.' In the sleeve notes to *Serene Velocity*, Gane explains that the label's initial idea 'was to scatter loads of small seven-inches and ten-inches—to just do one a month and keep doing them in small editions.'

Super 45, which the band sold via mail order and the Rough Trade shops in London, was a moderate hit on the indie scene. John Peel played it on his Radio 1 show on May 5, 1991, and Leeds band The Wedding Present—at the time very much a *big thing* in indie music—offered the band their first gig, supporting them at the Birmingham Institute on July 15, 1991.

'I heard John Peel playing Stereolab's debut single, and it blew me away,' Wedding Present leader David Gedge explained on X in 2020. 'I contacted them to see if they fancied supporting The Wedding Present. They said yes, and it turned out to be their first ever gig.'

Rough Trade's Sean Forbes says *Super 45* sold well. 'Years later, when they started doing Cavern Of Anti-Matter [Tim's post-Stereolab band], they went back to selling it themselves and through us, and I swear that Martin said that's because of what they did originally,' he explains.

Forbes's initial reaction to Stereolab was that they resembled 'a fast Spacemen 3. Just because it was repetitive,' he adds. 'Honestly, Stereolab were the first wave of people stealing from Krautrock. But at the time, no one knew anything about Krautrock, especially people my age.'

In the first few years of Stereolab, the band's line-up could be quite fluid, as David Callahan, who occasionally played live keyboards with the group, explains. 'If you look at the Wikipedia entry, there's about fifteen members over [Stereolab's] history. But, in fact, there were probably about ten more in the first year or two,' he says, adding that Tim liked the idea of working with 'non-musicians' and people with only basic musical skills.

'It had a very *floating* kind of membership—like, Russell Yates from Moose played with them,' Callahan adds. Mick Conroy, the bass player with Modern English and a sometime member of Moose, also played keyboards with Stereolab, while Tim would sometimes appear with Moose, cementing the crossover between the two bands.

Conroy says that this fluidity suited him. 'I was also kind of in Modern English at the same time, so I didn't think, *Right, this is it. This is my job for the next . . .* you know? It always was completely obvious that it was Tim and Laetitia's band. Tim knew exactly what he wanted to do, and he was quite unashamed about it.'

'There were a few people coming and going that were only involved for a couple of gigs, including me,' Callahan continues. 'He [Tim] just borrowed people from other bands because they had a couple of gigs at the Falcon or whatever. But there was always a core line-up.'

That core line-up, at the time of *Super 45*, consisted of Sadier on vocals; Gane on guitar, Moog synthesizer, and Farfisa organ; Martin Kean, formerly of New Zealand indie band The Chills, on bass; and Joe Dilworth on drums (when Th' Faith Healers weren't too busy). As promising as *Super 45* was, the band hadn't *quite* clicked on their first record, even if many of the Stereolab hallmarks were there from day one.

'The Light That Will Cease To Fail', which opens *Super 45*, is the record's most notable song. The EP's three other tracks—'Au Grand Jour, Au Grand Jour" (or 'Au Grand Jour Apostrophe Version') and 'Brittle'—all employ the lightly shambling indie-dance drum beat that was de rigueur among British bands at the time, giving these songs a slightly dated, even derivative sound.

'The Light That Will Cease To Fail' is different. The song sees the group lock into the Motorik groove that would serve them so well in their early years, Dilworth laying down the pulse-racing but metronomically steady four-four bass drum rhythm favoured by Krautrock pioneers Klaus Dinger (of Neu!) and Jaki Liebezeit (of Can). To this Gane adds a driving two-chord chug, like The Velvet Underground's 'Sister Ray' if it had been brought up with more art and less heroin, around which Sadier winds a dazzling web of vocal harmonies.

Today, Neu! and Can have become common reference points for countless adventurous guitar bands, from Radiohead to LCD Soundsystem. But that wasn't the case back in May 1991, when *Super 45* was released. To further complicate matters, 'The Light That Will Cease To Fail' has a dangerously alluring whiff of the Gallic artiness that Stereolab would later make their own. In an era when indie bands were more likely to sing about getting high as kites and having their spindly hearts broken—*NME*'s singles of the year for 1991 included Primal Scream's 'Higher Than The Sun' and Spiritualized's 'Feel So Sad'—'The Light That Will Cease To Fail' borrowed its title from French poet André Breton's *Second Manifesto Of Surrealism*, while the song's mantra-like lyrics suggest the seductive intellectualism of Gallic erudition, particularly when delivered in Sadier's impeccably restrained, lightly accented tone.

Sadly, 'The Light That Will Cease To Fail' is also slightly muddy in its production, something that Stereolab, a band of sharp edges and bright lights, should *never* be—and rarely were after their first album. This was remedied—and so much more—on *Super-Electric*, the band's second EP, which was released in September 1991 by the London indie label Too Pure, best known as the early home of PJ Harvey.

By this point, *NME* journalist Gina Morris had joined the band, coming on board soon after the release of *Super 45*. Morris, who had briefly been in a group in Manchester with Jon Ronson (later an acclaimed writer) and Saul Davies from James, was living with Tim, Laetitia, and Laetitia's friend Susanna in their grotty Brixton flat.

'It was all very new,' Morris says. 'They wanted to tour. They realised a lot of the vocals they couldn't do together, and it was literally just in the kitchen. I think I said, I'll do it. Or they asked, Can you sing? And then, next minute, we were up in the bedroom [rehearsing].'

At this stage, band practice was a pretty basic affair. 'I would sit on the end of the bed and Tim would play a bit,' Morris explains. 'Laetitia would say, *Do this*, and I'd start doing the *doobie-doos*.' Morris was also on board for the band's first radio session, for John Peel, in July 1991, where they recorded four songs: 'Super-Electric', 'Changer', 'Doubt', and 'Difficult Fourth Title', which later became 'Contact'.

Again, the *Super-Electric* EP isn't perfect, the planets still aligning for the group. The third track, 'The Way Will Be Opening', has that indie-dance beat again, and 'High Expectation' has the faintest whiff of the shoegazing bands that were then all the fashion in indie London. But this was almost the last time that Stereolab could be considered to sound like they were following trends.

Paul Cox, who formed Too Pure with Richard Roberts, says he knew Stereolab were different as soon as he heard them. 'There are elements in their sound that were present in some of the indie scene that was around at the time, I guess,' he says. 'But nobody was doing repetition like Tim had set out to do. He knew exactly what the musical thinking behind the band was, and I don't reckon anyone else was into Krautrock like Tim had become.'

Roberts says there was something about the band that made you sit up and pay attention. He compares them to Th' Faith Healers, another Too Pure signing. 'It's this huge wall of noise like nothing you had ever experienced. But I remembered the songs. And it was the same with Stereolab,' he says. 'Stereolab, in my head, were writing great pop songs.'

Super-Electric's title song feels like the golden moment when a band discover their destiny, their individual sound emerging from their hodgepodge of influences with the regal purpose of Excalibur being hauled from the stone. Some bands never get there, other bands take years; Stereolab hit on their sound with their second-ever record. Which is not to say that *all* Stereolab sounds like 'Super-Electric'—it doesn't, by any means—but 'Super-Electric' exemplifies the raging, driving force that propelled their early releases, and which is littered throughout their career.

It's one thing for me to say this, as an outside observer. But the idea of propulsion was important to the band, too. '*Propulsion* works,' Morris says of 'Super-Electric', when I suggest my take on the song. 'I would probably go for *revolution*, though. It really makes me feel revolution, uprising. There was a lot of talk about revolution around a kitchen table . . . it's very uprising, for sure, in some form.'

Melodically, 'Super-Electric' isn't that far from 'The Light That Will Cease To Fail'. Cox claims that Gane told him—perhaps jokingly—that he set out to write a second single with exactly the same chords as the first. But the small yet vital differences—in brightness, tone, purpose, and harmony—between the two songs all multiply up, sending 'Super-Electric' into orbit while 'The Light' remains earthbound.

'We thought "Super-Electric" itself was the track, the best one that we'd heard so far,' says Too Pure's Paul Cox. 'It sounded slightly more hi-fi, which might just be down to them getting their momentum going. It's like, Oh, *this* is what Stereolab is.'

Roberts was equally impressed by the band's Too Pure debut. 'I think that the challenge to them was that thing of [us] saying, Okay, here's an opportunity for you to turn around and deliver. They saw that opportunity too. It was like, Okay, well, how big do we want to be? How big can we be off a first properly distributed record?'

Importantly, 'Super-Electric' starts with a squiggle of Moog synth, a sonic amuse-bouche that places the listener firmly in the Stereolab world. Insignificant as this ten-second doodle may appear to be, it cleanses the palate and sets the listener up for what is to come.

Neither Teenage Fanclub nor Nirvana nor Chapterhouse nor—in all likelihood—*any* of the big indie bands of 1991 would have started their record with ten seconds of Moog, still then a borderline-obscure modular synthesizer favoured by 1970s prog-rock giants. But this—the Moog is saying—is *Stereolab*. This is *different*. 'No one else was using Moogs, that's for sure,' says Cox. 'So that was a clear thing that differentiated them . . . that was probably almost more radical than Tim's guitar, which was just chiming and repetitious.'

The Moog is interrupted by a single guitar chord: strident, fuzzed, triumphant, a six-stringed monolith announcing the birth of a new guitar era, before the band kicks in, Dilworth again riding the Motorik beat. This time, though, his cymbal taps are freed from 'The Light''s distracted murk as the band lay highly controlled waste to another two-chord rush. On the face of it, guitar chords and drum thump might sound like the ingredients of traditional rock and roll music. But 'Super-Electric' is far from classic rock; this is Stereolab music, where economy of change meets propulsion of texture. A single guitar chord remains drifting over the top of the group's impeccable rhythmic chug, buzzing with the dangerous allure of an electricity pylon, its prickly texture more important than its melodic progress (or lack of). Two-thirds in, the same guitar explodes over the top of the mix, its latent menace unleashed with the force of a rocket, in the static-electricity rush of a one-note guitar solo.

Debbie Ball, who played guitar in the indie group Electrelane—a band often compared to Stereolab—describes Gane's guitar playing as 'really textural. Sometimes he has sort of a metallic effect on it. So it sounds a bit like shards of sounds,' she explains. 'I loved his guitar playing so much that when I went and saw them—I think I probably saw them a couple of times in that [early] period—I would look at what he was doing and try and work out how he was making the sounds that he was making.'

It's tempting to think of the group's repetitive assault as akin to a drone. And maybe it does constitute one, in the Velvet Underground sense of the word. But for me, the term feels wrong. Drone music is often associated with a sense of relaxation, of letting the brain drift away on a series of sustained tones. 'Super-Electric' is quite the opposite. The two chords that the band play are *shocking*, the sound of pulsing electrical energy delivered straight to the brain in a way that jerks open the senses and sweeps away everything that has come before.

Contrast and restraint are key. When the band do eventually move on from their two-note attack, splashing out briefly on four new chords, it feels like 'Super-Electric' has snowballed into a rainbow universe of new colour and endorphin release, as if changing the chord has earned the listener a whole new perspective on the world. Four new chords feels like endless, shameless abundance, and it can't be sustained for long.

'Tim used to talk at this time about *endless boogie*,' says Callahan, when discussing 'Super-Electric'. 'This idea of playing one Status Quo riff for fifteen minutes, almost like a Krautrock riff. A lot of their songs were based on the idea that you could get this repetitive, wheels-going-around, propulsion, and it could last as long as you wanted it to, and it would be exciting the whole way through.'

The vocal melody in 'Super-Electric' pulls off a similarly obdurate trick. Stereolab have scores of brilliant vocal lines, many of which cascade around the octave like bouncing balls. But for a large part of the song, Sadier sings just a couple of notes, with the emphasis on the rhythm of the words rather than their melody, the vocal chattering away insistently like a musical Morse code.

In tandem, Gina Morris earns her place in Stereolab immortality with the brilliant two-part harmony, her voice alternately harmonising with and trampolining around Sadier's coolly executed melody. 'It started to get to the point that we were both taking quite lead-ish vocals,' Morris explains. 'You can hear I wasn't just doing *bubba-de-bons*. There was a lot more interplay with the two vocals.'

'Super-Electric' marks a high point of the propulsive force that was a guiding principle for Stereolab in their early years. It wasn't until *Emperor Tomato Ketchup*, the band's fourth studio album, that their frenetic energy slowed somewhat, as Gane moved toward new ways of writing songs built on interacting loops. But the band's momentum never went away.

Speaking to *The Ringer* in 2019, Gane talked about the band's 'intensity', adding, 'I don't want them just to appear as quite nice, possibly reasonably well-written, songs.' He was talking about Stereolab's first wave of reunion shows, but he could have been laying out the band's career as a feverish whole. 'Let's take that [well-written songs] as a given,' he continued. 'But it's in the interaction of all the players and the sounds and the intensity. And this has to be kept really hard-wired up. It's like wound up. It's just really important that it doesn't drift into a nice, presentable pop tune.'

The same propulsion was also present in the group's frantic creative output. In 1991 and 1992, Stereolab released three EPs, two standalone singles, two flexi-discs, and their debut album, *Peng!* The following year, these were joined by the band's second studio album, *Transient Random-Noise Bursts With Announcements*, a mini-album, two EPs, two non-album singles, and three split singles.

This productivity was a result of a relentlessly propulsive creative force in full flow, the pace only slowing temporarily in 1995 when Gane hit a bout of writer's block. Later on, Stereolab's momentum slackened again as the band entered its second decade of existence. But they were never slouches.

On a personal level, I see the same kind of propulsion in the romantic connection between Gane and Sadier, which lay at the heart of the Stereolab fire. This idea isn't too far-fetched: the propulsion of love sounds ridiculous, but the rush of love—which is essentially the same thing—is commonplace enough to be a romantic cliché. And this, surely, must have driven the Stereolab two onward in their artistic endeavours, as Gane and Sadier found their soulmates both creatively and romantically.

Following the death of Stereolab vocalist Mary Hansen in 2002 and the dissolution of the Gane/Sadier romance, it appeared inevitable that Stereolab would split, the band's creative impulse floundering on the rocks of personal difficulty. And yet they held on until 2009, when manager Martin Pike announced the group's 'indefinite hiatus'.

After *Margerine Eclipse*, which came out in 2004, Stereolab phase one only released two new albums, 2008's *Chemical Chords* and 2010's *Not Music*, which was made up of unreleased material from the *Chemical Chords* sessions and two remixes. *Fab Four Suture*, an album-length compilation of the six singles released in 2005 and 2006, should probably count as an album, too. Even so, three albums in five years was a significant slowing down for a band as ruthlessly productive as Stereolab.

You could, perhaps, feel a certain lassitude around Stereolab in the group's last half-decade before their hiatus. Their records remained strong—*Fab Four Suture* is excellent—but the group were working to diminishing returns. Reviews became lukewarm, with the journalists who had supported them so avidly at the start of their career running out of things to say. The band returned to the same concert venues they had played years previously, and some of these gigs were far from full.

Sadier herself complained of a certain jadedness during the band's later years in a 2019 interview with the *New York Times*, explaining, in no uncertain terms, that she felt that the ambience in the band 'was really crappy and very stifling'. All of which we will come to later.

Stereolab's reunion, from 2019, has restored both prestige and momentum to their career. The venues are bigger and fuller, and the band's first studio album post-reunion, *Instant Holograms On Metal Film*, was warmly received on its release in 2025. True, one album in six years of touring is a little tardy by Stereolab standards. But *Instant Holograms* songs like 'Electrified Teenybop!' and 'Flashes From Everywhere' suggest that adrenaline still runs strong in the Stereolab veins, as the band thunder artfully along like buffalo rampaging through a high-end gallery.

There remains, too, a propulsive spark in the group's recent gigs. Years have passed, and none of us have escaped the attentions of time. And yet when you see modern-day Stereolab tear into 'Mountain'—a song from a 1993 split single with Unrest—or 'Electrified Teenybop!' or 'Super-Electric', you can feel the band's propulsion come roaring back, their restless energy recalling two young lovers in the first flush of creative delight, all those years ago.

02

'K-STARS'
ROMANCE

Stereolab don't sing love songs, as most bands understand the idea: McCarthy singer Malcolm Eden once warned Laetitia Sadier never to write about heartache, and I don't think there is anything so simple as an 'I love you' in all of the band's four-hundred-ish songs.*

For all that, romance is written deep into the Stereolab soul. Maybe Stereolab *themselves* would disagree with that. But when bands release their music into the world, the actual intended meanings of their songs are perhaps less important than the ways in which those songs are perceived by fans. And this is how *I* see Stereolab.

Besides, this is a band that grew out of a romance, whose two leading lights, creative sparks, and undisputed leaders were a romantic couple for the band's first decade. How could Stereolab *not*, then, sing about love? And let Eden's warning be damned.

* The band's official 'Complete Chronological Stereolab' playlist has 368 songs at the time of writing, while Spotify user dylan^-^'s 'stereolab discography' playlists has 472, although these include remixes, radio sessions, and demos. So I think 400 songs is about right, if you include unreleased work.

Stereolab's lyrics are rarely straightforward, whatever the subject matter. The band set out their lyrical stall right from the start, French and English words meeting political ideas, classical references, and esoteric cultural references in a way that defies easy explanation.

'There was a lot of political talk and talk of French politics,' says Gina Morris, the band's first co-vocalist. 'They were not so much love songs. There was a point and a message, which I think Laetitia delivered, sometimes very directly and sometimes more subtly. So, they could be interpreted as a love song. She was very clever.'

We are talking about the *Super-Electric* EP, the band's second release, on which Morris contributed vocals. I had suggested that 'High Expectation', from that record, seems to be about the nature of love, albeit in a rather doomed manner, while the EP's title track is rumoured to be about a broken relationship.

Morris isn't convinced. In the end, we agree that romance was a *possibility* on *Super-Electric*, but the songs were not romantic in themselves, particularly for a couple still close to the first flush of love. For that, I suggest, the listener would have to wait until *Peng!*, Stereolab's debut album, which was recorded in April 1992 and released one month after—a sign of the group's breakneck creativity.

Peng! is a curious record on which it feels as if Stereolab are growing into themselves. Joe Dilworth continues on drums, his beats just a shade too complicated for a genuine Krautrock stomp and still prone to the odd indie-dance shuffle, while Sadier has no vocal foil to play off, Morris having left the band before the album was recorded. Morris puts her departure down to the group's unease over her work as a journalist and her own dissatisfaction with the way she was credited as 'second vocalist' on the sleeve of *Stunning Debut Album*, the band's amusingly named 1991 seven-inch. 'When that single came in, I was so devastated,' she says. 'Because we'd had a talk [about being credited as 'vocalist' on the sleeve] and that caused real friction in the household', where she lived with Tim and Laetitia.

'I guess the cracks were beginning to show a little bit,' Morris adds. 'There was also a review in the *Melody Maker* by Ngaire Ruth that called me the lead singer. And that didn't go down well, either.'

Morris would continue in music journalism after leaving Stereolab—

Beck, apparently, was very impressed with her Stereolab past—and she married Mark Austin from Australian band The Paradise Motel in 2002 before moving to Australia the year after.

After the great leap forward of *Super-Electric*, *Peng!* feels almost like a backward step for Stereolab, with songs like 'Orgiastic' and 'Peng! 33' a little too close to My Bloody Valentine for comfort. There's nothing wrong with MBV, of course, but a lot of bands were riding their coattails back in the shoegaze year of our Lord, 1992. It doesn't help that *Peng!* sounds like it was recorded at the bottom of a honey pot, with none of *Super-Electric*'s deliciously sharp edges.

Where *Peng!* comes into its own is in its occasional air of fuzzy, drunken joy; there is an exuberant mushiness to the music, as if Gane and Sadier had recorded the album between fourth and fifth drinks on their third date, when they knew things were starting to go well. In this, *Peng!* feels unlike almost anything else in the Stereolab catalogue. Too Pure's Richard Roberts says it is his favourite Stereolab album. 'The record just flowed from start to finish,' he says. 'And it wasn't what I was expecting it to sound like, either, because it doesn't sound like *Super-Electric* or *Super 45*.'

Is *Peng!* a romantic record, I wonder? Roberts agrees, although not perhaps in the way that I mean it. 'I think that the romance is with music, the love of sound, the love of what you can create next,' he says. 'It is like that cup of hot chocolate in many ways. It's really comforting as a record, and you don't get that without being in love with what you're doing. For me, that's the romance of Stereolab: the love of what they were doing and where they *were* at that point.'

Personally, I think 'K-Stars', the fourth track on *Peng!*, is the most romantic song Stereolab ever wrote. Over a gentle drum machine patter and a warming blanket of sonic effects, Sadier sings of young people wandering around Paris, high on love and idealism, in what is ostensibly a reference to the Situationists.

The Situationists, with their love of Marxism and avant-garde art and their roots in the Parisian Left Bank, were a match made in heaven for Stereolab. Broadly speaking, the Situationist International was an organisation of artists, intellectuals, and political theorists formed in July 1957 whose views were based on Marxism, Dada, and surrealism and who were critical of twentieth-century capitalism.

Guy Debord's 1967 book *La Société Du Spectacle* (*The Society Of The Spectacle*) is the key text of the Situationist International, its central thrust being that, in the modern world, image and representation take precedence over direct experience, and this leads to alienation and passivity among the general public.

The word 'Situationist' refers to the construction of 'situations', which is one of the group's central concepts. It means, essentially, subverting the tools of capitalism as a way of mocking capitalism and liberating yourself from the stifling demands of everyday living. The Situationists liked to alter billboard adverts to undermine the messages on them, for example, and while I am far from an expert on the subject, you could argue that Stereolab's marriage of sweet pop melodies and political messaging was itself a Situationist act.

'I think Tim turned me onto the Situationist movement,' Sadier explained at the Red Bull Music Academy in 2015. 'I think he quite liked the aspect of things that are a bit nebulous. It's true, reality is hard to seize and to put in a box, and I think he didn't like that.'

On one level, 'K-Stars' is undoubtedly about the Situationists. Charles Long, the New York artist who would later work with the band for his exhibition *The Amorphous Body Study Center*, discussed the song with them when they first met in London. 'I talked about that song, about how important that was to me,' he explains. 'I said that song is what I'm trying to do with the project. It starts off with the click track, and then the warm synth and then the voices come in, and they say they were young, in their teens, you know, doing nothing.

'And I imagine that's probably when they explained it to me that that song was about the Situationists and how the Situationists would do this kind of weird art activity without making art, just go and stand on a street corner and let the world go by as an art experience.'

For Long, 'K-Stars' is also about the idea of the band as family. 'There are so many key songs that were for me about how one individuates, to borrow that word from Carl Jung, in a way, where you say goodbye to your family of origin—and for at least half of the people you run into, their family of origin was a tough story. And so, when you meet those people, that is your tribe. You are obsessed with T. Rex and you're smoking cigarettes and you're into what you're into—and you find other people, they're into it too. That, for me, is the magic where you build this new family.'

This in itself sounds romantic to me, albeit in a literary kind of way. But it is hard to escape the feeling that 'K-Stars' is *also* a song about Gane and Sadier's own love affair, which was itself forged in a day's wander around Paris. Sure, the Situationists bobbled around the French capital in a daze of ideas in the late 1950s, but who *else* had been wandering around Paris in the first vestiges of love, a lot more recently? Gane and Sadier, of course, after they met at that pivotal McCarthy gig.

Given that Gane also introduced Sadier to the Situationists, I find it hard to believe that 'K-Stars' isn't, on some, perhaps unconscious level, a meditation on their nascent romance, reflecting that beautiful first flush of adventure. And even if the lyrical connection between the Paris adventures of Gane/Sadier and the Situationists is unintentional, is there any way that Sadier could have sung lyrics about young people in Paris, in love, without thinking of her own recent history? She might seem slightly austere at times, but she's not made of metal.

'K-Stars', for me, is one of Stereolab's most intimate songs, the sound of a mask briefly slipping, over a rhythm that sounds like the beating of a heart, as warm layers of guitar and Farfisa organ (a key ingredient of the early Stereolab sound) welcome the listener into their waiting arms, the Situationist International and romance locked in their own political/personal snuggle.

When I was a teenager and just getting into Stereolab, with barely a two-week kissing spree of a relationship to call my own, I saw Laetitia Sadier and Tim Gane as the perfect example of how an adult couple should be. Lots of slightly older indie-rock fans had this feeling with Sonic Youth's Kim Gordon and Thurston Moore. But for me, it was always Sadier and Gane, joined in their perfect Anglo-French exploration of the avant-garde, who were the model to aspire to. (They later penned a song called 'The Emergency Kisses', which is one of the most romantic song titles I can imagine.)

•

I would have liked Gane and Sadier to stay together forever, but sadly, this was not to be. And if 'K-Stars' calls back to the first days of Gane and Sadier's love affair, 'Hillbilly Motobike'—released initially in 2003 on the *Instant 0 In The Universe* EP, then again in 2004 on *Margerine Eclipse*—is the song that may speak to their break-up.

Margerine Eclipse was recorded in extremely difficult circumstances. Mary Hansen, who had joined the band in 1992, died in a cycling accident in December 2002, while Gane and Sadier separated just before the band started to record what would become their eighth studio album. (The exact date of their split is hard to pin down, for fairly obvious reasons.)

'We decided to change and had change forced upon us,' Gane told the *Georgia Straight* in 2004 of the run-up to *Margerine Eclipse*. He appears to be talking about the impact of Mary's death on the group, rather than his split from Laetitia, although the way the article is constructed leaves some ambiguity. 'It wouldn't have been right to carry on as if nothing has happened. At the same time, we love doing music and we want to continue. We're not going to throw away all of our ideas and aspirations.'

Hansen's death inspired many of the lyrics on *Margerine Eclipse*. But it was inevitable, perhaps, that Sadier would also turn her eye to her recent romantic troubles. The most prominent example of this is 'Hillbilly Motobike'—the only song whose lyrics aren't printed on the album's sleeve—an iridescent Yé-yé jewel in which Sadier sings of love and endings.

What is amazing is that 'K-Stars' and 'Hillbilly Motobike', although a decade and a broken relationship apart, are very much spun from the same cloth. 'Hillbilly Motobike' is jubilant, bubbly even, as if Laetitia is kissing a troubled love life goodbye with the same vibrant spirit she welcomed it in—an 'I Will Survive' for the Marxist set. Such perversity is typical of Stereolab, a band who can marry the heaviest political ideas to the lightest musical touches, as if daring themselves to go further from cliché.

'K-Stars'' focus on Paris is also typical of the group's deep Gallic roots and cultural preoccupations, from the Situationists to Greek/French philosopher Cornelius Castoriadis and electronic music pioneer Georges Jenny. As a Francophile teen, this delighted me, and I was very happy when Debbie Ball, a founder member of Stereolab-influenced guitar band Electrelane, said she found the same foreign pull in Stereolab's music.

'I really loved the European-ness of Stereolab,' Ball says. 'I suppose that tied into how I saw myself. During my teens, both me and Verity [Susman] and Emma [Gaze] from Electrelane, we all went to the same secondary school, Hove Park. I got to know Verity really well through playing music together. And then we also had another thing that bonded us, that we were really good at languages, so we were both doing French A-level.'

Does she find Stereolab's music romantic, I ask? 'There *is* a romanticism about their music,' Ball agrees, citing the 'wide-eyed wonder' of 'Cybele's Reverie' as an example. 'I think that is entirely romantic. Do you equate romanticism with escapism as well? I felt like you could fully immerse yourself in their music and sort of *disappear* into their world.'

Ball's point is an important one. Romance can mean romantic love, of the kind you associate with amorous couples. But there are *many* different types of romance, the term being almost as wide open as love itself. This may explain why people find romance in so many different ways in Stereolab's music. For example, Kath Gifford, who joined Stereolab in 1993, locates romance in the band's hopefulness. 'There's something very sweet about Stereolab,' Gifford says when I ask about this. 'It's definitely sort of idealistic and also, I don't know, quite optimistic.'

Like many Francophiles, I have always found the idea of France itself romantic, a view that has endured two sometimes difficult years living in the French capital. Rampant Francophiles like me got their due on another *Peng!* track, 'Enivrez-vous', which takes its lyrics from a poem by the famed French writer Charles Baudelaire. (The band had in fact already raided 'Enivrez-vous' for inspiration on the *Super-Electric* EP, using the poem's opening line, 'Il faut toujours être ivre', or 'You should always be drunk', in the record's run-out groove.)

Stereolab never felt like a drinking band, and 'Enivrez-vous' isn't really a drinking song. Baudelaire, probably best known for his book of lyric poetry, *Les Fleurs Du Mal*, first published 'Enivrez-vous' (usually translated as 'Get Drunk') in February 1864 in the French newspaper *Le Figaro*.

Baudelaire was a dedicated drinker as well as drug taker: one of his most celebrated works is the prose poem 'Du Vin Et Du Haschisch' ('Wine And Hashish'), and he makes frequent references to wine in his works. But 'Enivrez-vous' is not so straightforward as a simple ode to booze. Yes, the poem is *superficially* about drunkenness, but Baudelaire soon clarifies that inebriation doesn't have to come about through alcohol. Instead, the effect can be achieved through 'wine, poetry or virtue—the choice is yours'. Like love, drunkenness is not so simple in Baudelaire's world.

What's more, Baudelaire explains that drunkenness is not in itself the end goal. Rather, we should drink to escape the dreadful burden of time crushing down on us, which seems like a very Stereolab thing to think.

Stereolab are not the only musicians to take inspiration from Baudelaire; among the many other admirers of his work are The Cure, Serge Gainsbourg, and noted Stereolab fan Tyler, The Creator. They are also not the only musical artists to have used 'Enivrez-vous' in their work. But it *does* feel like Stereolab make the poem their own on *Peng!*: Sadier recites it in insistent, excited French over a guitar/bass/drum line that seems to fizz with excitement, like champagne bubbles bursting on the palate, before a bizarre sonic effect wanders drunkenly in with the organ, its boozy squelch like the slurred-tongue speech of an excitable drunk. 'Enivrez-vous', in other words, feels a little like being drunk—with wine, poetry, excitement or possibly a combination of all three—in its gurgling, fuzzy excitement.

This is typical of *Peng!* at its best. Compared with something like *Dots And Loops*, the band's fifth studio LP, *Peng!* is shambling and slightly unformed. But you can hear the band's excitement filter through the cracks of its imperfections in a way that rarely happened later on in the group's life. On *Peng!*, the band could be drunk on wine or drunk on love or perhaps simply drunk on the possibility of what Stereolab could be, as the group gained in confidence and adventure.

It frequently sounds like Stereolab are having a hoot on *Peng!*—

see, for example, the jazzy glam swing of 'Stomach Worm', or the Roadrunner-esque race on 'The Seeming And The Meaning'. As such, the record is perfectly named: the album's title comes from the German onomatopoeia for a loud bang or pop, with the title and cover art taken from a comic strip originally published in the Swiss underground newspaper *HOTCHA!* The word seems to sum up the album perfectly. This is Stereolab's slightly juvenile explosion—their own loud pop, if you like.

Public response to *Peng!* was warm if not ecstatic, but Stereolab were an ever-moving beast. In July 1992, just two months after the album hit the shelves, they released the 'Harmoniun' / 'Farfisa' seven-inch single on their Duophonic Super 45s label, limited to 1,306 copies on translucent amber vinyl.

'Harmoniun', a scratchy, drone-y, pulsating beast that circles on and on, would become a live favourite in the group's post-reunion tours. The song's opening sample—in which a slick-sounding American radio voice introduces a stereophonic master tape, taken from San Francisco experimentalists Negativland's spoof radio track 'James Gabbert's Delight, Pat Boone's Cow, Evening Magazine, Etc.'—is *very* Stereolab too, mixing art, humour, sonic experimentation, and a general air of mischief.

'Farfisa', a double-step electric lullaby that is simultaneously punky and soothing, is notable for bringing one of Stereolab's key sonic ingredients to the foreground. The Farfisa organ was a popular instrument with both 60s garage bands and the new wave acts of the 1980s—think Blondie and the B-52's—for its slightly reedy sound that could cut through all kinds of amateur noise.

Speaking to *Tape Op*, Gane said that the Farfisa 'was the creator of the basic Stereolab sound', in part because it obliged them to keep the chord changes simple. 'It's got this natural distortion that covers up a lot of things! That's probably why it sounded so good [*laughs*]. It added a colour and dimension to the band that we were looking for,' he said. 'We had bought a Farfisa Bravo at a charity shop, which was the cheapest. It's so primitive that if you played anything more than a major chord, the harmonics would begin to break up. For me, what sounded good were two-note chords. Guitar and Farfisa chords were basically the sound of all those early Stereolab records.' So much so, in fact, that Gane said the group eventually stopped using the Farfisa for fear of chasing their own tails.

In the USA, Stereolab released 'The Light That Will Cease To Fail' and 'Au Grand Jour' as a pink seven-inch on defunct American label Big Money Inc in 1992—signs of flickering American interest in the band. More importantly, the group added two key parts of the Stereolab engine before the release of the *Low Fi* EP in September 1992: drummer Andy Ramsay and backing vocalist/keyboard player/guitarist Mary Hansen.

Ramsay would stay with Stereolab until they split in 2009 and came back on board in 2019, making him the group's longest-serving member apart from Sadier and Gane. He was also a member of various Stereolab spin-off bands, including Alternative 3, Europa 51, Splitting The Atom, and Turn On.

Mick Conroy, who played keyboards for Stereolab early on in their career, was in the band when Ramsay replaced Joe Dilworth. 'Andy hit the drums harder than Joe,' he says. 'Andy is a really solid drummer. With Stereolab, you need someone who can completely and utterly play in time . . . he sounds like the kind of person that could play to a click track.'

People don't talk as much about Ramsay as they should, although that, perhaps, is the point. Joe Dilworth is a fantastic musician—Paul Cox, in fact, calls Dilworth a 'genius drummer'—with an incredible feel to what he plays. But on those early Stereolab records, he is occasionally a bit overly fussy. Ramsay, on the other hand, is an absolute master of the classic Motorik beat that would prove so important to many of Stereolab's best early songs. (To be fair, Conroy says that Dilworth could also play the Motorik beat 'until the cows came home'.)

The Motorik (or 'Apache') beat was pioneered by German drummers Jaki Liebezeit (of Can) and Klaus Dinger (of Neu!) in the 1970s. 'It is funny because Jaki Liebezeit is always the example for the Motorik beat,' says Wolfgang Seidel, the former drummer in Krautrock group Eruption and author of *Krautrock Eruption—An Introduction To German Electronic Music 1970–1980*. 'But when you listen to him, there are no two bars alike! He plays very musically, reacting to every change in the musical texture that is produced. He has this very strict timing, but he feels it . . . with such big ears.'

Motorik is a fascinating contradiction—and that makes it very Stereolab, too. The beat is at the same time driving (hence the name), propulsive, and powerful, but also designed to be anonymous, a shrinking violet of hulking proportions. It is also simple—a no-thrills pulse of energy that does away with most rhythmical fripperies in favour of sheer human vigour—but playing it requires a certain repression of the drummer's ego, which is why many musicians can't do it.

John McEntire, the drummer and multi-instrumentalist in Tortoise, who later produced several Stereolab albums, says that playing a Motorik beat requires 'stamina and discipline', adding that Ramsay is 'very precise' as a drummer. 'He's amazing,' McEntire says. 'I can't imagine anybody else being in that band.'

To the listener, it felt as if Ramsay could play the same beat for hours, and this would be crucial in moving Stereolab forward. On the very well-named *Low Fi* song '(Varoom!)', for example, he brings an incredible clarity of rhythm. Dinger once said that the 'Apache' beat—he considered the name 'Motorik' to be too mechanistic—was 'essentially about life, how you have to keep moving, get on and stay in motion' and this is precisely the impression given by the heart-racing opening minutes of '(Varoom!)': the aching importance of forward motion.

Moe Tucker, drummer in The Velvet Underground, is sometimes considered another architect of the Motorik beat, and *Low Fi*'s title track is Stereolab at their most VU-friendly, its 'Sister Ray'-esque chug a perfect example of Gane's vision for Stereolab's sound as naïve pop melodies meeting rock minimalism.

Hansen's vocals would prove even more important to the band than Ramsay's steady hand. She was born in Maryborough, Australia, in 1966, making her two years younger than Gane and two years older than Sadier. After moving to London in 1988, she joined Essex indie band The Wolfhounds on backing vocals. And it was with The Wolfhounds that she met Tim Gane, then in McCarthy.

Sadier has said that she initially found it difficult to adjust to having Hansen in the group—'Two girls in a band. You can imagine,' she told *The Independent* in 2004—but their vocals clicked right from the off.

The two women share similarly cool, melodic voices, dripped through with a stand-offish charm that suggests 1960s bohemia. On *Low-Fi*'s 'Laisser-faire', Hansen's voice sounds removed, more Sadier's shadow than a flesh-and-blood backing. On the record's title track, however, Hansen provides the answer to Sadier's coolly posed question. And even if that answer is only 'ba da dum' or 'la la la'—as it would be on so many Stereolab songs—the band's new vocalist seemed to have the key to the song's success on her lips.

Stereolab weren't done with 1992. October saw the release of *Switched On*, the first in a series of compilation albums that were vital for listeners who had missed out on the band's limited releases. *Volume One* compiles tracks from the band's *Super 45* and *Super-Electric* EPs, as well as the two songs from the *Stunning Debut Album* seven-inch.

Stereolab are often considered to be a record collector's band for the embarrassment of limited editions, exclusive tour seven inches, and flexi-discs they released over their first two decades. In 1992, for example, they released two split flexi-discs: *Stereolab / Guitare Boy*, which came with the sixth issue of French fanzine *Tea Time*, and *Stêréölåb* / Submårinér* [sic], which was released with *Spacewatch*. That's a pretty impressive devotion to a format that sounds, at best, like music played through a windsock on a busy high street.

And yet collections like *Switched On* proved that the band were never elitist in their approach. Yes, you could collect the coloured vinyl and limited editions, but if you simply wanted to enjoy the band's music, Stereolab were there for that, too. This tradition has continued to the present day: almost all of the band's work can be found on streaming platforms, ready for the world to discover.

This openness makes sense. Stereolab are artistic, intellectual, and weird, but they are also a pop band with an idealistic edge; underground artists who wants to be heard; and hopeless romantics who say they don't write about love. And if that sounds contradictory, strap yourself in, because there is plenty more wilful incongruity to come.

03

'JOHN CAGE BUBBLEGUM'

COLLAGE

Issued just two years into their existence, 1992's* Low Fi *EP was a pivotal release for Stereolab. As well as being the first record to feature Andy Ramsay and Mary Hansen, it is also the one that made the technique of musical collage explicit in the Stereolab world for the first time.

I sometimes wonder if 'collage' is the right word for what I mean. Technically, a collage is a work that incorporates different materials or elements; this seems about right, but it isn't large or confounding enough for what Stereolab do. 'Bricolage'—essentially creating work from a diverse range of material—would perhaps also work, with the added bonus of coming from the French language.

Perhaps 'contradiction' would work, too: in an interview with the *Leeds Student* magazine in 1999, Gane told journalist (and later author) Anna Doble, 'People like to know exactly what you are, so that the music is easily digestible . . . easily consumable. But I think music is all about contradictions.'

You could argue that Stereolab's whole sound—at this time essentially a mixture of Krautrock drive and the sweetest pop melodies—is a work of collage, bringing together radically different musical ideas. But the technique the band debuted on the *Low Fi* songs '(Varoom!)' and 'Elektro (He Held The World In His Iron Grip)' is something else, resulting in songs with distinct and even contradictory musical phases. In evidence of the group's ever-increasing ambition, they are also the longest songs Stereolab had released to date, at nine minutes twenty seconds and a steady eight minutes, respectively.

'(Varoom!)' has two distinct parts. For the first three minutes of the song, Stereolab snap into a galvanic Krautrock groove, together with the interlocking vocal harmonies of Sadier and Hansen. It is a fairly typical work of early Stereolab, between pop and experiment, simplicity and noise. And then, three minutes and twenty seconds in, the song pivots: the drums stop, the guitar chords fade, and in their place comes what sounds like an echoing drum machine and a detuned guitar glide close to the dinosaur surf sound that My Bloody Valentine perfected on *Loveless*, released just ten months previously.

Not just a different song, this new section could be the work of a different *band*. The guitars wobble and haze for six thrilling minutes, expanding and contracting like water in a rock pool. Nowadays, in the digital era, '(Varoom!)' simply cuts off at nine minutes twenty, but on vinyl, the song ends in a locked groove—a very Stereolab move that allows the guitars to drone on forever.

'Elektro (He Held The World In His Iron Grip)' reverses the trend. The song starts fuzzy and experimental, Moog burbles flying around over a dirty two-chord sequence as the song gradually builds in intensity. (It actually sounds quite a lot like the closing section of '(Varoom!)'.) At the three-minute mark, this fades, to be replaced by the unexpected sound of piano and dreamy acoustic guitar, the two phases seemingly only linked by Stereolab's volition.

Stereolab would continue with the idea of putting different—and sometimes thematically distinct—musical sections together throughout their career, with the technique becoming a hallmark of the band. Was there, in fact, a better indication that Stereolab were *back* on their 2025 comeback album, *Instant Holograms On Metal Film*, than the appearance of sonic collages in several songs?

Stereolab really hit their bricolage stride on 'Jenny Ondioline', the eighteen-minute, multi-part epic on the band's second album, *Transient Random-Noise Bursts With Announcements*, released in August 1993. Its closing section resembles The Beatles' 'A Day In The Life', as re-assembled by Neu!.

Before that, though, there came 'John Cage Bubblegum', recorded in the spring of 1992 and released as a limited-edition seven-inch by US label Slumberland Records in February 1993, some copies coming with a stick of actual bubblegum.

Mike Schulman, who founded Slumberland, was the first person to distribute Stereolab's records in the USA, buying a small number of the band's early releases to sell via mail order and in the record store where he worked in Maryland. He initially made contact with Tim Gane in the late 1980s, when McCarthy were splitting, which led to his relationship with the nascent Stereolab; this in turn led to Slumberland releasing *Switched On* in the USA, and then 'John Cage Bubblegum'.

'When they sent me the DAT for that record ['John Cage Bubblegum'], I was just over the moon,' Schulman says. 'I was like, Oh my God, I can't believe we're putting this out. It's *so* good. It was called "Le plus beau" [a lyric from the song] at that time. I don't think they called it "John Cage Bubblegum" until I got the artwork for it, maybe. . . . It's a much better title.'

A *much* better title. And one that speaks to Stereolab's love of putting together two seemingly contradictory ideas that work in perfect harmony. Talking about 'John Cage Bubblegum' to *The Guardian* in September 2019, Gane spoke explicitly of the band's affinity for collage. 'We were trying to make what I called juxtaposition: a montage, or collage, to see how one thing influenced another,' he explained.

What is interesting here—and this, perhaps, is the reason I was unsure about the word 'collage' in the first place—is that 'John Cage Bubblegum' isn't a sonic collage in the mould of '(Varoom!)'. Quite the opposite, in fact: the song locks on hard to a propulsive guitar/bass/drum groove and stays there for three wonderful minutes that prove you *can* exercise to Stereolab music. (Martin Kean, who would leave shortly after the release of 'John Cage Bubblegum' to return to New Zealand, is on wonderful form here, his bass providing brilliantly exciting melodic counterpoint.)

In this case, the collage—or perhaps 'juxtaposition' is a better term—comes in the song's title, which combines John Cage, the pioneering American composer and musical theorist best known for 4'33", with the genre of bubblegum music, a light-hearted style of 1960s/70s pop that was aimed at children—think The Archies' 'Sugar Sugar', or perhaps The Monkees, depending on whose argument you listen to.

Laetitia Sadier is a particular champion of Yé-yé music, the European (but *particularly* French) style of pop that emerged in the early 60s and is often linked to bubblegum. Sadier's 2017 album as Laetitia Sadier Source Ensemble, *Finding Me Finding You*, bears the breezy hallmark of Yé-yé on tracks like 'Undying Love For Humanity'.

Yé-yé is sometimes considered a Francophone take on bubblegum, although the relation between the two genres is more complex: Yé-yé actually emerged *before* bubblegum, drawing inspiration from a diverse range of influences, including early rock'n'roll, baroque, exotica, jazz, and French chanson.

On *Low Fi*, Stereolab bring together wildly different musical phases within individual songs; on 'John Cage Bubblegum', the band use the song's title to juxtapose highbrow and lowbrow music. But this is just the tip of the antithetical iceberg. Stereolab *themselves* are inherently non-binary: experimental and poppy; British and French; masculine and feminine; sweet and sour; warm and steely; retro and futuristic; a guitar band with synths; and so on.

Thomas Golubić, the owner of music sync company SuperMusicVision and the man responsible for putting Stereolab's 'Tempter' into *Better Call Saul*, speaks of the band's combination of joy and anxiety. 'There's a sense of bliss to them,' he says. 'It's an immersive bliss, a bliss that takes a little bit of entanglement to get to, but once you do, you kind of ride it. I think anxiety is probably something [they express] as well, which is ironic: it's the two opposite feelings.'

'I've always been very much in love with Laetitia Sadier's vocals,' he adds, 'because there seems to be a kind person underneath all that. I don't know her personally; I don't know whether she is a kind person, but something about the music feels like there's a kindness in it. And the angular production sometimes works really beautifully as a counterpoint to that. They do play with opposites a lot. What's exciting about them as a band is that it's very different things coming together in a unique way.'

In the case of 'John Cage Bubblegum', the juxtaposition inherent in the song's title is clear: the experimental titan that is John Cage versus the sunny and essentially throwaway nature of bubblegum pop. And, of course, Stereolab can do both of these registers, often within the same song. This may have been clear sonically before the release of 'John Cage Bubblegum'—what is 'Laisser-faire' if not a perfect pop melody? What is the second half of '(Varoom!)' if not art rock at its finest?—but the song's perfectly judged name explicitly set out the Stereolab modus operandi. One year later, Stereolab would release a song called 'Avant Garde M.O.R.', whose title was similarly expository.

Simon Reynolds, the rock critic and author who championed Stereolab early on in their career, was among the listeners hooked by the apparent contradictions in the band's song titles. 'As a rock critic like me, who is very interested in avant-garde music, I thought, *That's interesting, that's funny and clever*,' he says. 'That's when I started really paying attention to them. And I started reading their interviews. Sometimes people have become attractive to write about because you realise you can have a good conversation with them. I think that's a weakness of journalists: sometimes they will write about groups that don't have the music. But Stereolab did.'

Reynolds sees the same kind of theoretical contrasts within Tim and Laetitia themselves. 'That's an interesting pairing, of him as the record nerd and her as the impassioned political thinker,' he says. 'Tim has political opinions too, obviously. But the obsessive knowledge of musical history and unusual taste, I think that was Tim's department.'

Laetitia, Reynolds says, 'is very serious. She simmers with a quiet intensity . . . you can imagine her on the barricades in 1968, or giving an impassioned speech at the Sorbonne.' When the two combine, the result lends 'a knowing, playful, self-conscious air to the way the music's put together,' Reynolds says, which meets 'this very penetrating intellect/political passion, which is completely devoid of irony'.

The ideas of collage and juxtaposition also connect to the band's love of the Dada art movement, for whom collage was an important creative technique. 'We were quite informed by Dada,' Sadier explained in the same 2019 *Guardian* interview mentioned above. 'They were about putting one thing against another and seeing what happens, and maybe you find a deeper truth in that collision.'

There is a contrast, too, in the lyrics to 'John Cage Bubblegum', in which Sadier contemplates a landscape that is simultaneously the most beautiful and the saddest in the world, echoing a passage from Antoine de Saint-Exupery's classically melancholic children's book *Le Petit Prince*, which explores themes like loneliness, loss, friendship, and love. These notions—of beauty and sadness—are not necessarily *contrasting*, but they are ideas that don't always go together.

Do we find a deeper truth in this kind of collision? Stereolab show that the world is not black and white and that contrasting thoughts can exist within the same work of art, with the differences serving to amplify their impact. Does a landscape appear more beautiful because it is also so sad? Do Sadier's gorgeous vocal melodies sound all the sweeter for the proximity of Gane's scratchy guitar rush? I think so. Call it what you will, but these collages/contrasts/juxtapositions/collisions give Stereolab's music a rare depth and an unusual profundity.

The B-side to 'John Cage Bubblegum', 'Eloge D'Eros', also toys with the idea of beauty, with the song's protagonist singing about their own physical charms and the attention it inspires. Eros is the Greek god of love, and it is possible that Sadier is voicing Eros himself, in all his head-turning splendour. German philosopher Herbert Marcuse's 1955 book *Eros And Civilisation: A Philosophical Inquiry Into Freud*, in which he proposes a non-repressive society, may well have also been on Sadier's mind.

I prefer to think, however, that Sadier is exploring the sensations *she* feels as someone—and it has to be Gane—contemplates *her own* youthful beauty in the song. I think of 'Eloge D'Eros' as one of Stereolab's songs of hidden romance, with Sadier's ecstatic 'yeah's like the explosion of love itself.

The fact that the song is written in French makes me wonder, slightly mischievously, whether Sadier snuck this ode to love under the linguistic radar, knowing that Gane, who tended not to listen to Stereolab's records after they were recorded, would not pick up on its detail, leaving a token of love to be discovered, or not, in a possible future, like a love letter smuggled across time. Because what could be more contradictory than a declaration of love that you know will probably go unread?

04

'SPACE AGE BATCHELOR PAD MUSIC'

RETRO-FUTURISM

'John Cage Bubblegum', 'Avant Garde M.O.R.', 'Super-Electric': Stereolab certainly have a way with song titles, often dreaming up names that perfectly sum up the music within while serving as a manifesto for the band's individualistic charms.

In March 1993, a new name was added to this list, one that would perhaps stick with the band more than any other and would later give a name to this book: *Space Age Batchelor Pad Music*, a record also known as *The Groop Played Space Age Batchelor Pad Music*, marking the first use of the 'Groop' epithet that the band later used for production credits on their records.*

'Those [uses] normally mean me, or sometimes me and Sean [O'Hagan],' Gane explained to *Tape Op*. 'It could also reference Laetitia and myself. It could also refer to Andy [Ramsay] and me. It's not necessarily all the band. Especially when we were working in Chicago, we couldn't afford for everybody to be there all the time. So

* We are using the word 'Batchelor', as it appears on the front cover of the record in question. We do know how to spell. At times.

they generally came over, did their parts and then went back. We called whoever was there The Groop. Oftentimes, it would just mean me.'

Space Age Batchelor Pad Music is a key record for Stereolab in many different ways. The mini-album was released in March 1993, just one month after 'John Cage Bubblegum', and comprised eight songs, including the perfectly named 'Avant Garde M.O.R.' and 'Ronco Symphony', which had previously been released as a flexi-disc demo.

Space Age Batchelor Pad Music was also the first Stereolab record to feature two important members of the band: bass player Duncan Brown, previously of art-metal group Milk, who would stay with Stereolab until *Emperor Tomato Ketchup*, and—crucially—Sean O'Hagan.

O'Hagan, an affable Irish musician, was only officially in Stereolab until 1994. And yet he worked with the band in the studio for many years, right up until 2010's *Not Music* (released after Stereolab went on hiatus).

There are a few people who you could consider as the third pillar of Stereolab after Gane and Sadier. Mary Hansen for her defining vocals, or Andy Ramsay for his longevity, certainly, but O'Hagan would undoubtedly be in with a shout for his multi-instrumental contributions, together with songwriting, production, and arrangements. On *Space Age Batchelor Pad Music*, O'Hagan is credited with 'Organ [Farfisa], Organ [Chord Organ Moog], Marimba [Marimbas] and Performer [Air Freshener Lid]'—more instruments than even Tim Gane on the same record.

'My friend Brian O'Neill introduced me to Stereolab at a show in Camberwell,' O'Hagan told Clayton M Davis in 2016 on his *Clay The Scribe* blog. 'I loved the energy and fresh sounds that rolled off this little South London stage. I was extremely excited, as this band were answering questions that I had been asking, namely, where do we go from here? I'd had enough of all guitars, no melody and no real variety. Stereolab were demonstrating a new set of tools.'

O'Hagan was invited to join Stereolab as a touring keyboard player, but as he later told *Popshifter*, 'I was allowed to make suggestions and the fun started.' You can see why this would happen. Not only is O'Hagan an incredibly talented musician but he was also very much on the same wavelength as Stereolab. Like Gane, O'Hagan initially made his name with a politically charged post-punk band—in this case, the fantastically scathing Microdisney, whose 1984 compilation album was called *We Hate You South African Bastards!* in reaction to the country's apartheid regime—and he had also recently formed a band that took influence from the more esoteric side of pop: The High Llamas, whose first album, *Santa Barbara*, was released in 1992.

O'Hagan and Gane got on well on a personal level, too. 'We are mates because we both think that the behaviour of much of the industry is distant from us, and we like humour and we both love football,' O'Hagan told Davis. 'We discuss a lot besides music.'

Gane and O'Hagan also clicked musically, sharing a lot of the same influences. In an interview with *Billboard* in 1996, O'Hagan mentioned 'The Beach Boys . . . The Left Banke, Van Dyke Parks . . . a lot of soundtrack music like John Barry and electronic experimental music like Kraftwerk and Neu!' as influences, which seems a very simpatico mix with Gane's esoteric tastes.

O'Hagan said that Gane influenced The High Llamas' music, which went from borderline conventional indie pop on their first record to something much more expansive on 1994's *Gideon Gaye*, a record heavily influenced by bossa nova, film soundtracks, and the ultra-smooth lounge music/easy listening of the 1950s and 60s (think Mexican band leader Juan García Esquivel). 'The Llamas' change from *Santa Barbara* to *Gideon Gaye* was largely down to Tim's influence on me and the way I worked,' O'Hagan told *Popshifter*. 'I wanted to loosen up.'

Clearly, though, the sphere of influence went both ways, with *Space Age Batchelor Pad Music* also drawing heavily on The Beach Boys and lounge music, as Stereolab eased up and chilled out.

Or at least they did on side one of the record. *SABPM* is a curious release in many ways, not least in that it divides into two specific parts that are musically distinct. The band's original plan was to record a seven-inch single, with 'We're Not Adult Orientated' on side A and 'U.H.F.—MFP' on side B. Both are fairly traditional Stereolab songs. But Sadier was ill on the first day of recording, which led Gane, Ramsay, and O'Hagan to improvise around some 'sketchy demo chords' that Gane found on a cassette when he returned home that night. These improvisations became the five songs that feature on side one of *SABPM*, a side titled 'Easy Listening'—a name that, while probably tongue-in-cheek, also has the ring of truth to it.

Calling one side of their record 'easy listening' was a bold move for Stereolab back in 1993, when *SABPM* was released. Easy listening as a genre is both easily explained—the title says it all, really—and strangely slippery to define. It is, essentially, music to relax to—a radio format that is designed to dissolve into the background, typically featuring instrumental covers of popular songs from the pre-rock'n'roll era. You can file it somewhere alongside elevator music, muzak, beautiful music, light music, and, perhaps, lounge music, although lounge tends to be more exotic and actually designed to be listened to. Batchelor pad music, in other words.

For Laetitia Sadier, easy listening was a family affair. 'My mum loved opera and my dad loved musique concrète and easy listening,' she told me when I interviewed her for *Line Noise* in 2024. I had asked if her parents' love of music had inspired her in any way. 'They did love music, yes, and I must have inherited something, that aspect, from both of them. I mean, my mum wanted to be an opera singer. So there you go,' she replied.

Suffice to say that in 1993, when the big indie albums came from PJ Harvey, Nirvana, Suede, and Blur, easy listening was in no way fashionable, not even in the borderline odious, semi-ironic way it would become two years later, when Mike Flowers Pops hit the charts with his cover of 'Wonderwall'.

Too Pure's Richard Roberts goes so far as to say that Stereolab introduced lounge/easy listening music to a new audience, with *SABPM* being perhaps the most influential record the band ever made. 'No one was doing that,' he says. 'And then we're trying to license the Esquivel records, because they had been talking about this guy. No one knew anything about it. I remember someone going down to Mexico on our behalf, to go and license the records . . . we trusted what they [Stereolab] were saying enough to want to go and do it.'

Side one of *SABPM* isn't *really* easy listening, though, and you suspect that Stereolab knew it. There's too much going on, for a start, for the record to slink into the background; and the music has moments of lightly spiked edges, which wouldn't work in a slippers-on context.

And yet the first side of the record *is* very different for Stereolab, with the group pulling into newly mellow avenues. The five tracks—three full songs, two sketches—amble along at relaxed BPMs, their drum lines built around lazy tom hits rather than the racing bass drum/snare combinations of the Motorik beat. The guitars are strummed nonchalantly rather than thrashed to within an inch of their lives; the bass wanders around a bit, melodically, as if on the second hour of a museum visit; and two songs, 'Avant Garde M.O.R.' and 'Ronco Symphony', feature the gentle sound of the marimba, a classic instrument of lounge music.

O'Hagan had clearly exerted a big influence on side one of the record. Track two, 'Space Age Batchelor Pad Music (Mellow)', featuring just under two minutes of squelchy and ever-so-slightly scratchy Farfisa chords, was composed by him alone—a first for Stereolab—and could have easily fitted onto a bootleg of Beach Boys studio outtakes, or, more relevantly, The High Llamas' *Gideon Gaye*. The same could be said of 'Ronco Symphony', which calls for rebellion over a blissed-out 1960s West Coast lounge glide—another fascinating example of Stereolab's love of juxtaposition.

Side two of *SABPM* feels, in a curious way, like a conscious rejection of side one, whether Stereolab meant it or not. This side of the record is called 'New Wave', a possible reference to French New Wave cinema, new wave music, bossa nova (which translates as 'new wave'), or perhaps all three. What side two *isn't*, though, is anything new in the Stereolab world, marking a return to the guitar chug of previous releases.

The differences are clear from the start. Whereas side one of *SABPM* kicked off with 'Avant Garde M.O.R.', side two immediately rejects the middle-of-the-road embrace of what has gone before with a track pointedly titled 'We're Not Adult Orientated', a three-chord Farfisa romp that jets along at a heart-racing speed. (Not for nothing is Andy Ramsay credited on the record with 'persuasive percussion'.) 'We're Not Adult Orientated' is 'classic' Stereolab in many ways, another song in the propulsive lineage of 'Super-Electric', 'John Cage Bubblegum', et al.

'U.H.F.—MFP', which follows, is more adventurous, marrying fuzz guitars to a bossa-nova-ish drum machine patter and various Moog squiggles, over which Sadier and Hansen weave a vocal mantra. The album closes with a live version of 'We're Not Adult Orientated', which is perhaps best remembered for the arched-brow 'Neu Wave Live' subtitle it wears.

The eight songs on *SABPM* are fascinating enough in themselves. But the record is equally notable for its aesthetic, from title to sleeve, with which Stereolab came closer than ever before to nailing their colours to the mast of retro-futurism.

Retro-futurism, as the name suggests, is an artistic movement or aesthetic that centres on how people in the past saw the future. Think of the pneumatic tubes in Terry Gilliam's 1985 film *Brazil*, a work that apparently inspired one of the first uses of the term 'retro-futurist' in a review. 'Retro-futurism is kind of a nostalgia for a future that hasn't materialised,' says author Wolfgang Seidel. 'These ideas that all the problems the world faces can be solved by technology.'

Retro-futurism—itself an example of the kind of juxtaposition that Stereolab inhabit—is baked into the very heart of Gane and Sadier's band, with the Stereolab name borrowed from a record produced by US record label Vanguard in 1960 to help users test out their fancy new stereophonic sound systems. (The first mass-produced stereophonic disc had been released three years previously, in 1957.)

The Vanguard Stereolab Test Record features blips and bleeps, cycles and tones—a typical song title: '150 Cycles In Phase, Out Of Phase, In Phase'—designed 'for use in aligning, calibrating and balancing stereo disc playback systems', which doubtlessly sounded very futuristic back in 1960. But in the CD-era 1990s, when Stereolab formed, this idea—and therefore the Stereolab name, too—felt like a throwback to the future of the past. Stereolab would also reference the Vanguard Test Record on the cover of *SABPM*, lifting its gridded atom and sound wave design and employing a variation of Vanguard's flag-bearer-on-horseback logo.

Stereolab's Duophonic Ultra High Frequency Disks label would use another 1950s/60s-style depiction of the atom as its logo, as well as the slogan 'The In Sound From Way Out', borrowed from the debut album by early electronic music duo Perrey & Kingsley (aka French composer Jean-Jacques Perrey and German-American composer Gershon Kingsley). Perry and Kingsley were among the first artists to use Moog synthesizers, and they also recorded for Vanguard Records. Later on, in another hint at retro-futuristic design, Stereolab would use a typeface on their 2000 EP *The First Of The Microbe Hunters* that looks to have been inspired by early digital characters.

On a musical level, Kraftwerk skirted around the edges of retro-futurism in the 1970s, offering not so much a view of what the future used to look like as a combination of futurism and nostalgia. Their hit song 'Autobahn', for example, combines cutting-edge electronic music technology with a musical throwback to the early Beach Boys, while their *Radio-Activity* album features a 1930s radio on the cover.

Tim Gane is a Kraftwerk fan. In a 2023 interview with *Synth History*, he mentions their classic 1978 album *The Man Machine* as a record he listened to in his youth. And the band appear to have looked to Kraftwerk as a source of inspiration several times. 'The Long Hair Of Death', from Stereolab's 1995 split single with Yo La Tengo, has a melody that sounds like it was inspired by 'Autobahn'; the group return to a similar synth riff on 'OLV 26', from *Emperor Tomato Ketchup*.

Stereolab also use instruments from the same family of synths as Kraftwerk, if not necessarily the exact same tools. Both groups make heavy use of Moog synths, and both use Farfisa instruments: Stereolab, the Farfisa Compact Duo; Kraftwerk, a customised Rhythm Unit 10. Klaus Dinger also played drums in early Kraftwerk, bringing his Motorik style to the group's eponymous debut album of 1970, before he left to form Neu!. There is, then, something of Kraftwerk to Stereolab.

The Moog synthesizer, of course, is the most retro-futuristic instrument ever to produce sound. At various times, Stereolab have used the Moog Opus Three, which the company describes as 'a multi-keyboard with a single divide-down oscillator bank and three treatments to generate its strings, organ and brass timbres'; and the Moog Rogue, a basic analogue synthesizer produced in the early 1980s. On their most recent album, 2025's *Instant Holograms On Metal Film*, keyboard player Joe Watson uses a Moog Matriarch, while producer Cooper Crain adds Micromoog.

Moogs have a special place in the hearts of synth specialists and electronic music fans. The company's instruments sound warm and full of life; quirky, otherworldly, and yet somehow very human at their core, like discovering an alien life form that looks exactly like a teddy bear and comes bearing hugs. The Moog modular synthesizer, invented by Bob Moog in 1964, was the first commercial synth and—with all due respect to the Ondes Martenot, the Ondioline, and other early electronic-music tools—the first instrument that really brought electronic music into the public eye.

If you listen to *Switched On Bach*, the Moog-heavy Wendy Carlos album from 1968, you can understand why it was this instrument that captured the public's heart. The music on *Switched On Bach* sounds strange and yet naggingly familiar; welcoming, in a way, and surprisingly well adjusted to Bach's baroque melodies. It feels like a warm 'hello' from the future, the very opposite of a dystopian view.

Stereolab would reference *Switched On Bach* in the name of their *Switched On* compilation album series, the first of which was released in 1992. And while Gane doesn't specifically mention her in interviews, it seems likely that he was a fan of Carlos's music.

'I'd started using modular synths when I was at school,' he told *Musician Magazine* in 1997. 'When I was fifteen, I heard two records from the seventies which had these sounds on them, and I couldn't figure out where they were coming from or what sort of people would make them. I had to find out what it [was]. Obviously, the Moogs were number one and the easiest to obtain. That sounds gets in your blood. Now I can't really write music without knowing that they're going to be used.'

Many musicians use Moogs today, and it would be wrong to say that they belong uniquely to an outmoded vision of the past. And yet the success of the Moog in the late 1960s and 70s meant that they were the introduction to electronic music for many listeners—The Beatles used a Moog on *Abbey Road*, for example—and this inevitably lends itself to the idea of the Moog as a retro-futurist device. For many people, the Moog was the sound of the future half a decade ago. And this is something that can't be easily erased from the popular imagination.

The other thing that makes Moogs solidly retro-futuristic is that, for all their popularity, Moogs aren't the sound of the present, let alone the future. Like the pneumatic tubes in *Brazil*, the Moog never became a genuine household technology, in the same way that, say, the digital audio workstation has become ever-present in music production, or Autotune has become a standard studio tool. That's a shame, perhaps. But it means that records like *Switched On Bach* and even Stereolab's own work keep a certain esoteric charm.

Stereolab have used Moogs throughout their career, finding new ways to wring innovation out of their equipment. 'When we first started using Moogs, they were mainly for siren sounds,' Gane explained to *Musician* in 1997. 'But then we began to use the Moogs as the basis of chords. With that approach, you can take a semi-original song and put it in a whole different atmosphere. So usually, now, that's the first thing to go on, because it gives the direction for everything else.'

David Callahan, who occasionally played live Moog with Stereolab in the early days of the band, explains the group's rather casual approach to the instrument. 'When I did the live shows with them, I wouldn't say I was more adept at the synths, but I knew how to make a few more noises that would go with them,' he says. 'Tim used to mark the Moog up with a felt-tip pen and say, Don't lift the oscillator above this point.'

Stereolab use their Moogs a lot. In the *Musician Magazine* interview, Gane explained that they filtered almost all of the instruments they use live through the Moog Rogue: 'guitars, vocals, organs, everything . . . our sound man has a Rogue at the desk, and he puts the whole band through it at the same time.'

Bob Moog, who participated in the *Musician* interview alongside Gane, Weezer's Matt Sharp, and Roger Manning of Imperial Drag, seemed shocked, questioning whether the sound distorts. 'It does,' Gane responded, 'but ours is the kind of music that works with that. It's like listening to music that someone else is creating.'

This creative use of the Moog underlines the argument that Gane wants to make—namely that Stereolab don't use the instrument in a purely nostalgic way. 'Synthesizers that were made up to the late seventies were doing something completely different from digital synthesizers,' he said. 'I don't think the Moogs or any of those others tried to emulate exactly the sounds of violins or basses. There were approximations of basses, but they were different. But that's exactly what makes them more interesting. It's a misnomer to state that we're using this equipment because we're nostalgic for something.'

There are numerous beautiful examples of Moog use within the Stereolab catalogue. The Moog version of 'Super Falling Star', originally released in 1992 on the *Volume* compilation series, is a gorgeous example of the Moog's open-hearted, bass-y hum, like slowly falling into honey. 'Les Yper-Sound', from *Emperor Tomato Ketchup*, uses the Moog Opus Three's capacity for both well-rounded bottom end and spluttering exoticism, and there is a fabulous video of Laetitia playing a Moog live on the BBC's *Later . . . With Jools Holland* programme. 'Moogie Wonderland', a B-side to the 1994 single 'Ping Pong', has both maximal Moog splatter and a wonderful title. And so on.

But *Space Age Batchelor Pad Music*, by virtue of its title alone, is the key record in Stereolab's embrace of retro-futurism. The record's name is perfect—so perfect, in fact, that US indie label Bar/None Records would later borrow it for a compilation of tracks by Juan García Esquivel in 1994. In the *SABPM* sleeve notes, Gane says that the album's song titles—and by extension, the album's title—refer both to 'genres of music I would have liked to have found in record shops and a description of the music we make'.

'Batchelor Pad' places the listener firmly in the 1950s, where a well-to-do young man is playing the latest lounge disc on his new hi-fi stereo system. To this we add the retro-futuristic promise of the 'Space Age', a term that conjures up images of *The Jetsons*, Sputnik, and the first moon landing, when it seemed like we would soon all be living in a charming lunar crater with friendly robots for company.

And what is the first song we would play in our lunar pads, when we have unpacked our bleeding-edge atomic hi-fis? I'd nominate 'Space Age Batchelor Pad Music (Foamy)', track four on *SABPM*, two well-named minutes of synth squiggles and blurred ambient melody that sounds like a benevolent alien missive from the dark side of the moon.

'(Foamy)', small but perfectly formed, is one of the most unique pieces of music in the Stereolab canon: simultaneously throwaway and profound, an afterthought that I never get bored of listening to; and a reminder that Stereolab could, when they wanted, create excellent electronic music. '(Foamy)' makes me think of how Aphex Twin's *Selected Ambient Works 2*, which was released a year after *SABPM* to enormous acclaim, could have sounded if Richard James had lightened up considerably.

SABPM is a self-referential record in many ways—perhaps the most in all of Stereolab's catalogue. The title—*Space Age Batchelor Pad Music*—isn't just the perfect gloss to the band's retro-futuristic charms; it is also preceded (in some cases) by *The Groop Played* (as in, *The Groop Played Space Age Batchelor Pad Music*), leaving absolutely no doubt about who the record's title is referring to.

'The Groop Play Chord X', the third song on the record, is another self-reflexive title, as is 'We're Not Adult Orientated', which reads like a direct—if probably tongue-in-cheek—message. 'Avant Garde M.O.R.', in this context, feels like a similar nod, while the U.H.F. of 'U.H.F.—MFP' would soon become part of the name of Stereolab's record label, when Duophonic became Duophonic Ultra High Frequency Disks.

This may all be coincidence. But *SABPM* feels to me like the work of a band who have decided to assert exactly *who* they are and *what* they care about, as they grow in confidence—which is pretty remarkable for a group barely into their third year of life. Some bands never find themselves; Stereolab did so early on. And they would soon leap further off into the musical ether.

SABPM was Stereolab's last record for Too Pure, a rather painful departure that I will explore later on in this book. In the USA, the band signed to Elektra; in the UK, they and their manager Martin Pike created Duophonic Ultra High Frequency Disks out of their existing Duophonic label to release their singles and EPs, and Duophonic Super 45s as a home for the group's more esoteric music, as well as releases by other bands.

The first fruits of the Elektra deal would be the *Jenny Ondioline* EP, which was released in August 1993. But before that, Stereolab had more arty business to attend to, with the release in April 1993 of the *Shimmies In Super 8* compilation on Duophonic Super 45s. *Shimmies* is one of Stereolab's most collectable records. This is not so much for Stereolab themselves, however, as for another band who appear on the double seven-inch compilation.

I mean nothing against Stereolab's contribution to Shimmies. 'Revox!', which appears on side C, is a gallivanting piece of space rock, with an intriguing lyrical conceit in which Sadier recites a list of verbs, first in French and then in English. But the appearance on the record of two tracks from Darlin', aka Thomas Bangalter and Guy-Manuel de Homem-Christo, later to become Daft Punk, and Laurent Brancowitz, who would later join Phoenix, explains the record's heavy resale price.

Those two Darlin' tracks, 'Cindy So Loud' and a cover of The Beach Boys' 'Darlin'', were not just the first Darlin' tracks to see the light of day; they remain the band's only official release on vinyl. (Two further Darlin' tracks, 'Untitled 18' and 'Untitled 33', would later be released on a compilation cassette from the *Banana Split* fanzine.)

'Guy-Manuel and Thomas Bangalter, they were friends of ours,' Sadier told the Red Bull Music Academy in 2015. 'A common friend had given us a tape by these two kids that were very young, they were seventeen, eighteen, maybe and they were called Darlin'. Darlin' with an apostrophe. We thought, *That's a nice track, fun pop track*.'

You can see why Darlin''s music would appeal: their Beach Boys cover on *Shimmies In Super 8* sounds indebted to Stereolab themselves, with its motoring beat and fuzz guitars, while you could imagine 'Cindy So Loud', with its cyclical pop vocal, as perhaps the first, basic demo for a Stereolab track. A *Melody Maker* review of *Shimmies* by Dave Jennings would famously describe Darlin's contribution as 'daft punky thrash', this tepid response hastening Darlin' toward their end and giving Guy-Man and Thomas a new nomenclature to play with.

Also on *Shimmies* were Paris band Colm, whose Daniel Dauxerre managed Darlin', and Huggy Bear, one of the leading lights of the Riot Grrrl movement in the UK. (It is telling that the *Melody Maker* review of *Shimmies* is far more concentrated on Huggy Bear than Stereolab.)

Stereolab releasing two songs by a pre-Daft Punk Darlin' isn't exactly Sonic Youth urging Geffen to sign Nirvana. But it is, nonetheless, an interesting example of Sadier and Gane supporting other bands, while giving an insight into their musical tastes. In the 2020s, you might even consider it an example of Stereolab as curators, although no one really talked like that back then.

There are several examples of this curation *avant la lettre* in the Duophonic Super 45s catalogue. The label released music by Minneapolis punk trio Arcwelder; Herzfeld, Malcolm Eden's post-McCarthy band; post-rockers Tortoise, with whom they would go on to have a long working relationship; Pram; Labradford; and—perhaps most notably—Broadcast, who became one of the UK's most revered indie bands.

Duophonic Super 45s was also home to many of Stereolab's split seven-inch releases, another indication of the bands that they saw as their peers. These include the 1995 split seven-inch with Yo La Tengo, 'The Long Hair Of Death' / 'Evanescent Psychic Pez Drop'; and 1998's 'Caliméro' / 'Cache Cache', which features Stereolab and cult French singer Brigitte Fontaine on one side and Sadier's Monade on the other. Stereolab are born collaborators, generous with their time and resources.

It feels like fine company, a real family of the avant-garde. Duophonic is weird, wonderful and gleefully abstruse: about as far from your typical indie label as Stereolab's retro-futuristic appeal is from your typical indie band. And it continues to be so today.

05

'JENNY ONDIOLINE'
REPETITION

With Duncan Brown, Sean O'Hagan, and Mary Hansen joining Laetitia Sadier and Tim Gane in what many people would consider the band's first classic line-up, and a new major label home, Stereolab were in a period of apparent tranquillity in the summer of 1993.

In the USA, the band had signed to Elektra, in a major label deal that their A&R man, the late Terry Tolkin, later described as 'VERY generous for our little Groop' in a post on Discogs.com. This covered all the world outside the UK and Ireland, where the band launched Duophonic Ultra High Frequency Disks as a more professional update of their old Duophonic label. Martin Pike had also been joined by co-manager Sheri Hood of Forever Changes Management, who would help to oversee the band in the USA.

Internally, though, Tim Gane was struggling with what would become the band's second LP, *Transient Random-Noise Bursts With Announcements*. In his sleeve notes for the 2019 reissue of the album, Gane mentions that the album's recording process was 'totally exhausting and seemed so chaotic at times', thanks to long recording sessions that were followed by 'intense deliberations late into the night' with producer/engineer Phil Wright, who shared a flat with Gane at the time, resulting in the 'rather lean and edgy' sound of the original record.

Certainly, *TRNBWA* is the noisiest, angriest, and most distorted of all Stereolab's albums. It has a very unconventional sound to it that some people find flat. 'We got the most bizarre drum sound,' Gane told *Uncut* in 2020, in a piece on the album's centrepiece, 'Jenny Ondioline'. 'I'd like to say it was intentional, but we'd taken this fairly expensive, high-end studio and made it sound like a basement. When we were remastering it, the mastering guy said it was the most bizarre mix of frequencies that he'd ever worked with. It's all middle—middle on top of middle!'

Perhaps because of this, *TRNBWA* is a controversial work: some people don't like it; many consider it to be a step backwards; and others—like myself—put it close to the top of the Stereolab pile. (It was the first Stereolab record I bought, so this is perhaps inevitable.)

The band recorded the album at Blackwing Studios, a deconsecrated church in Borough, South London, that would go on to become a regular spot. 'It was a church that was bombed during the Second World War, but one half of the church was never restored, and that became a secret garden with a wall around it, which was pretty amazing,' Sean O'Hagan told *Uncut*.

Stereolab had six weeks to record their new album, as well as associated B-sides and various extra tracks—a concentrated approach that Gane said gave the record 'a singular sound . . . all done in the same place with the same engineer. That does give it a completeness, whereas some of the other albums are a bit all over the shop because they were done in different locations with different people,' he told *Uncut*.

TRNBWA is sometimes lumped in with the shoegazing bands. Sadier has called shoegazing 'a very derogatory term', albeit one that makes some kind of sense, given that the album was released in 1993 and has a heavy focus on guitars. It's not *really* a shoegazing record, but it does make a virtue out of repetition and intensity, in a way that would resonate with the louder shoegaze acts.

There is a lot to love on *TRNBWA*. 'Tone Burst' is one of the most electric album openers from a band who are renowned for them,

Ramsay's snare trill ushering in guitars that burst with the energy of Tigger; 'Pack Yr Romantic Mind' is one of the band's most beautifully romantic-sounding songs, all Left Bank cool and gentle eroticism, even if the lyrics are closer to transgressive French philosopher Georges Bataille than a late-night nuzzler.

'Our Trinitone Blast' is one of Stereolab's great bursts of fury, with its unusually distorted vocals, while 'I'm Going Out Of My Way' sounds like The Beatles' 'It's All Too Much' rewritten by The Velvet Underground. Curiously, that's not the album's only Beatles link: 'Pack Yr Romantic Mind' originally included a sample of George Harrison's *Wonderwall Music* that the group were denied permission to use, forcing them to re-record the song, although not before promo copies of the album had already been sent out. *TRNBWA* is also the first Stereolab album on which they make extensive use of the Vox Continental organ, an instrument notably heard on ? & The Mysterians' garage classic '96 Tears'.

In addition, *TRNBWA* includes three illuminating examples of the sonic collage technique that Stereolab had experimented with on the *Low Fi* EP. 'Pause' starts with a scratchy recording of a voice speaking apparently random German numbers, taken from Swedish Rhapsody, a Polish 'numbers station' that sent coded messages to intelligence agents in the Western Bloc during the Cold War. It then pivots into a brooding, humming Stereolab song, adds the insistent patter of a drum machine and ends with a seemingly unconnected section of guitar feedback, fuzz and murky vocals. 'Golden Ball', meanwhile, has two sections that are linked by what sounds like a fault on the master tape or a skip of the listener's needle, in what feels like a reminder of the record as a physical object.

But the album's undeniable centrepiece—both literally and figuratively—is the eighteen-minute 'Jenny Ondioline'. On the double vinyl release, the song occupies the entirety of side three, its physical presence like the Monolith in *2001: A Space Odyssey*, resplendent in a moon crater.

'Jenny Ondioline' is a brilliant illustration of what makes Stereolab *Stereolab*, perfectly encapsulating the highbrow swagger of their early work. There's the name, for a start, a retro-futuristic reference to French musician Georges Jenny and his pioneering electronic synthesizer, the Ondioline, which went on sale in 1947 and found an early fan in Jean-Jacques Perrey. 'Jenny Ondioline' also makes potent use of collage, its runtime divided into three distinct sections (plus intro), with breaks between all three. These three musical phases are not so distinct as the different parts of 'Pause' or '(Varoom!)', but they have a heavy cumulative force.

Throughout their career, Stereolab have made dazzling use of repetition, but they are not *repetitive* as such. 'Repetitive' suggests something boring, lifeless, humdrum; Stereolab are precisely the opposite, teeming with life, vim and vigour, unable to make a boring record if they tried.

And yet simple patterns often repeat in Stereolab songs: the drums align to a particular rhythm; the bass and guitar fashion a two-chord vamp. This has been the case right from the start of the Stereolab adventure, from 'The Light That Will Cease To Fail', song one on side A of *Super 45*. Within this, though, Stereolab know how to tease out minor changes in tone, harmony, or texture, the combination of repetition (solidity) and deviation teasing out the music's textural rush.

In a 2009 interview with *Fact* magazine, Gane explained that his interest in repetition as a musical force emerged around 1993. 'There was kind of a change in the way I wrote from about '93 on,' he said. 'I got really tired of doing things the same old way. It was then that my interest in repetition, in repetition itself and in revealing something through layering, took hold.'

'Jenny Ondioline' is an early high point of this technique. 'We always wanted to do a side-long track,' Gane told *Uncut*. 'I suppose it goes back to my youth and those Can records where you've got some poppy songs on side one and then a really long track on side two. I loved that, it seemed exciting.'

Length by itself is all very well, of course, but on 'Jenny Ondioline', Stereolab's powers of invention through repetition are pushed to the limit. The recording starts with a brief, wall-of-sound guitar intro, using chords that will later reappear in the body of the song. It then switches into the main section, dropping the listener into an extreme two-chord push, Andy Ramsay on drums and Duncan Brown on bass exhibiting a beautiful economy and concentration to lock into their groove as the combination of guitars and synth fizzes and grinds.

Sadier then comes in with a vocal melody that, as if in sympathy with the instruments, repeats again and again. The chords do eventually change, but the song always comes back to the same two-note chug, as if tired of any such ostentation. Seven minutes in, it pauses, and you're expecting another of those great Stereolab collage shifts, but no: the same two-chord pattern returns, only pitched slightly higher.

The song's third phase, which occupies the last four and a half minutes, is yet another variation on a theme: the same pop pulse with added distortion and freak-out, like the closing moments in The Velvet Underground's 'Sister Ray,' as 'Jenny Ondioline' weirds out and takes wing. Rather than the Velvets' filthy boogie, though, 'Jenny Ondioline' sounds incredibly clean, a rush of toothpaste over a shot of dirty amphetamine.

'There was lots of noise, throwing things down, putting things backwards, stuff we taped off an audio test record, they were all added on randomly,' Gane told *Uncut*. The final composition of the song, he added, was done at the mastering stage—a fine example of the band's expanded composition process. 'The long version is really six or seven separate parts that we edited together.'

'Jenny Ondioline' may be made up of different musical parts, cleverly stitched together, but it is also an exemplar of the virtues of repetition in a catalogue that is full of similar tricks. The band's sound would relentlessly evolve over the course of the next two decades, taking in influences like jazz and electronic music; the signature two-chord guitar chug would fade away, but *repetition* would always remain. On *Emperor Tomato Ketchup*, the band's fourth album, Stereolab use the repetition of what Gane called 'small melodic cells' that flow in and around each other in a mass of activity. It creates a very different effect to 'Jenny Ondioline', but the power of repetition is still there.

The repetition of sound in 'Jenny Ondioline' is mirrored by the song's simple use of melody and words. Like Kurt Cobain—or many great songwriters—Sadier tends to lock in on one outstanding vocal melody that she repeats over the course of a song's verse, with another melody for the chorus. (This isn't the case all the time, of course, and it certainly isn't a criticism.) Often, this melody is met by simple yet effective lyrics that repeat key words over and over, like a mantra or prayer to the underground. This might explain why Stereolab's music can sound so oddly relaxing, even as it crackles with energy; the lyrical repetition calms the mind as the music boils the spirit.

There is an element of this in 'Jenny Ondioline', whose chorus includes a list of things that the protagonist claims not to care about, from fascism to democracy, in a lyric inspired by the German Dada painter George Grosz. 'I was reading a book of paintings by George Grosz at the time. He was German, and he painted a lot between the two World Wars. Like a lot of artists, he was utterly disgusted with what was going on, with the social climate and the social deprivation that was going on around him, and that he was maybe a part of as well,' Sadier explained to *Uncut*. 'In the book, they interviewed someone at the time, or maybe it was even Grosz himself, who said that they didn't care if all this went on, you know, the rise of fascism and socialism going down the drain. For him, what was really important was to remain creative and to use whatever's going on around you in the most creative ways. I found that take fascinating.'

There are more extreme examples of this lyrical repetition to come on *TRNBWA* and elsewhere. 'Crest' repeats two lines about the power to do and undo change, time and time again, like a speeding Luddite anthem or an extremely peaceful protest, Sadier's gentle voice advancing a political slogan with the utmost serenity. 'Brakhage', from *Dots And Loops*, uses just thirteen words, in subtly shifting patterns, in the first and third verses; 'Laserblast', from 2010's *Not Music*, builds up and out from the simple repetition of one line; and so on.

'Jenny Ondioline' is clearly influenced by the Krautrock bands of the 1970s, a freewheeling rodeo of radical German rock groups who also sought power through repetition. Inspired by the student protests of 1968 and repulsed by Germany's history in the Second World War, these musicians aimed to create rock music that had nothing of either traditional German music or contemporary American pop.

Krautrock, a name coined by British journalists that seems, regrettably, to have stuck, could be very varied. (Nowadays, the genre is more politely known as kosmische). But certain characteristics emerged, including repetition, the use of early synthesizers, and a penchant for improvisation, diverging away from the structure and melodic patterns of the traditional rock song.

'In the early 80s, I was a big fan of Krautrock music—like Faust, Neu!, and Can,' Gane told *Tape-Op* in 2013. This in itself was unusual. In the early 80s, Krautrock was often dismissed as outmoded, hippie music in the UK and Germany, even if the Sex Pistols/PiL's Johnny Rotten was a fan of Can. 'I'd been in two bands and I didn't want to do just another band,' Gane continued. 'I was looking for a way of combining the experimental with the commercial.'

Gane's first Krautrock record was Faust's eponymous 1971 debut album, which he bought after reading a review in the British music press. It was quickly followed into his collection by the group's follow-up, *Faust So Far*. 'I was struck by how different these records sounded to the relentlessness of some of the industrial-type music that was about at the time,' Gane told *Electronic Sound* in 2014. 'With their strange sounds coupled with those superb rhythms, they informed my musical development from there.

'I can't think of a single German band who deviated from that willingness to explore the further reaches of experimentation with heavy and industrial sounding compositions, along with some often extremely melodic tracks, and all of it generally on the same record. Faust typified that to me—very heavy, but with the light and the shade.'

This description could, of course, easily apply to Stereolab, who shared a lot with the Krautrock bands, including their love of repetition, the Motorik beat and their use of early synthesizer technology. At times, the link was even more explicit: Stereolab are said to have sampled songs by Faust, Neu!, and Kraftwerk over their recorded career and, if little definitive evidence exists of this (sampling being an infinitely twisted web), I can say that Stereolab's most Neu! song is 'Exploding Head Movie'; their most Can track is 'Outer Bongolia'; and their most Kraftwerk effort is 'OLV 26'. To my ears, anyway.

Reviews of *TRNBWA* were mixed, but the album sold well, providing the band with their first entry into the UK Top 75, where the record placed at #62 for one week in September 1993. It also broke the Top 100 in the USA. As it enjoyed its week of glory in the UK charts, I experienced my first Stereolab gig. I'd like to be able to say that I vividly remember when I first heard the band, but I can't. I imagine I first came upon them in the British weekly music magazines, *NME* and *Melody Maker*, which I read religiously from 1990 onward, and I may have first heard them on John Peel's BBC Radio 1 show.

Peel was a big supporter of Stereolab. The band recorded their first (of six) radio sessions for him in July 1991, on the back of their debut single, and it was broadcast in September of the same year. (You can find the band's Radio 1 sessions on the compilation album *ABC Music*, which was released in 2002.) The band also had the support of Radio 1's considerably more mainstream show *The Evening Session*, which aired from 1990 to 2002, playing the indie hits of the day, and of DJ Mark Radcliffe, who hosted the cult Monday evening programme *Out On Blue Six*. Between them, the three shows aired the band's music to an audience of millions.

It would be an exaggeration to say that Stereolab couldn't have become a success outside of the UK. But the power of the BBC—a centralised national broadcaster, with a remit that goes beyond commercial music—certainly helped. It also helped—for me, as well as the band—that the UK is a relatively small country geographically, with a strong local live scene.

At the time Stereolab emerged, I was living in Norwich, a city of just under 150,000 people, about two hours east of London. A lot of new bands played there, including Stereolab, who arrived at Norwich Arts Centre, a three-hundred-capacity converted church near the city centre, on Monday, September 13, 1993.

The Arts Centre was the venue where most bands played their first Norwich gig. I saw Curve and Oasis there, as well as hundreds of bands whose reputations have crumbled into history. The same tour saw Stereolab play venues on what is affectionately known as the UK's 'toilet' circuit—the name coming either from the venues' less-than-sparkling cleanliness or the fact that bands had to get ready in the toilets—including the Duchess Of York in Leeds, Esquires in Bedford, and the Joiners Arms in Southampton. These names provide a powerful Proustian rush for British music fans of a certain age.

For all their minor chart success and major label contract, Stereolab were still a DIY-type band for whom the toilet circuit seemed their natural environment. I remember talking to Laetitia briefly after the gig, as she helped the band pack up their equipment, which is hardly the behaviour of a superstar diva. I remember being terrified, that Laetitia was charming, and that we talked briefly about John Peel sessions. I don't remember why.

In fact, I don't remember much of the Norwich gig. The setlist for the band's concert at Bedford Esquires, four days previously, suggests they played a handful of songs from *Transient Random-Noise Bursts With Announcements*, including 'Crest', 'Jenny Ondioline', 'Lock-Groove Lullaby', and 'Our Trinitone Blast', as well as a spattering of *Space Age Batchelor Pad Music* ('Avant Garde M.O.R.', 'We're Not Adult Orientated'), and older songs like 'John Cage Bubblegum', 'Peng! 33', and 'The Light That Will Cease To Fail'—a mouthwatering setlist that, frankly, I feel like I should have remembered.

Most intriguingly, though, Stereolab kicked off that Bedford gig with 'French Disko', a song that was about to take them into some very strange places indeed.

INTERSTITIAL ONE
OUR FAVOURITE STEREOLAB SONGS

MICK CONROY (Stereolab, Modern English) I really loved playing 'Changer'. Only because it had two chords. And there was a lot of drinking going on in those days [*laughs*]. The power of the *argh-argh* [*imitates two-chord drone*]. Everything was really easy to play.

TOM ROWLANDS (The Chemical Brothers) I love their second album, *Transient Random-Noise Bursts With Announcements*. That is a great album. I listened to that a lot.

Tim Gane was really quite visionary. Such a cool collection of ideas going on with that band. He was very early on the whole Moog worship, and the way their records sounded was always really interesting. And Laetitia's voice.

Mars Audiac Quintet, that's a good one, too. I bought all these records because they felt interesting and they felt different. They felt like they had people who were really interested in how things sounded.

They are a band who really existed in their world . . . it's hard to have a vision for your band, a totally self-contained idea. And that band definitely felt like that, which is cool—standalone.

But I will go for 'Jenny Ondioline', also because I have an Ondioline now, even though at the time I probably didn't know what one was—a beautiful French instrument.

MORGANE LHOTE (Stereolab, Hologram Teen) I would say 'Ping Pong'. I didn't play on that one [in the studio], but I played it hundreds of times live. I think it's a perfect pop song. It was always something to look forward to, and every time I played it, I felt happy. I think it's one of the first tracks we played when I joined the band and during our first rehearsals. And I was like, *Yeah, it is my favourite song of the band, and I get to play it.*

MARK ROBINSON (Unrest) 'John Cage Bubblegum' is the one. Mike Schulman, who started the label Slumberland [in Washington, DC, where Robinson is also from], was such a big fan. 'John Cage Bubblegum' was probably the first record Stereolab put out in the United States, and it wasn't on their own label—it was on Slumberland. So, for people in DC, it felt like Stereolab was *ours* for the United States.

MIKE SCHULMAN (Slumberland) It's got to be 'John Cage Bubblegum'. It seems ridiculous because it's such an early one and not super-thoughtful . . . 'French Disko' is pretty great, but it always comes back to 'John Cage Bubblegum' and 'Super-Electric' for me. That song ['John Cage Bubblegum'] absolutely blew my mind. It's so powerful. You could dance to it. You could lie around and listen to it after a couple of drinks. It kind of did everything.

IAN POOLEY (artist and DJ) I prefer from Stereolab the more . . . like, not necessarily going so much in the *clubby* thing, you know? I like the classic ones, like 'Cybele's Reverie'; 'Fluorescences', I like; 'Miss Modular' . . . so classic Stereolab, for me.

ANNA DOBLE (author) I'm going to say 'Cybele's Reverie' . . . just takes me to a happy, sunny place, probably in the back of a beat-up Citroen, every time!

KATH GIFFORD (Stereolab, Snowpony) I think it's going to have to be 'French Disko'. Because it's a really brilliant song. It was really exciting [to play live]. Tim's groove—he's got a great groove.

06

'FRENCH DISKO' POPULISM

In November 1993, something outlandish happened on British television.* One Friday night, the continent's foremost art-rocking Anglo-French indie band appeared on Channel 4's* The Word *to play their latest song.

Stereolab—who else?—appeared nervous. As well they might be. *The Word* was big: hundreds of thousands of viewers big, conversations around the water cooler big, still only four channels on British TV big. And here were Stereolab, a band better suited to Friday night at the Camden Underworld, in front of the TV cameras.

'A band we saw a couple of weeks ago at the Whisky A Go-Go club in Los Angeles,' the host, the frenetically besuited Mancunian Terry Christian, announces, a none-more-90s Mr Blobby toy clearly visible in the foreground. 'This is Stereolab, "French Disko".'

The band had played the Whisky on October 28, 1993, on their second visit to the States. But still, the introduction sounded jarring.

* I have seen it said, many times, that Stereolab appeared on *The Word* in 1994. But that must be wrong, considering the timing of the LA gig that Terry Christian saw.

The venue, on LA's Sunset Strip, was once known as a home for Love and The Doors and later as a bastion of hard rock music and the hair metal bands of the 1980s. The very name speaks of lingering decadence, of uncut hair stuck together with the dregs of Jack Daniel's and unapologetic cigarette smoke. Not the kind of place you'd expect to find Stereolab.

And that wasn't the only thing that would prove jarring that Friday night. *The Word*, it is true, did have a reputation for showcasing new bands: Nirvana played 'Smells Like Teen Spirit' on the show, in what was one of their first international TV appearances; L7's Donita Sparks dropped her trousers live on TV when her band played 'Pretend We're Dead' in 1992. I remember seeing everyone from The Sugarcubes to Blur on *The Word* in the early 90s; Jo Whiley, later a renowned British radio DJ, booked the bands for the show's second and third seasons.

Outside of that, though, *The Word* was weird—a mixture of cheap shock tactics and supposed youth appeal. One of the most celebrated sections of the programme was 'The Hopefuls', in which random punters, desperate to appear on TV, would pull off stomach-churning tasks like licking a stranger's armpit or French kissing an old woman. It was designed as television for when the pubs closed—then still at 11pm in the UK—for people to stagger home to and fall asleep in front of. I was far too young to visit pubs at the time, so watching *The Word* would be the last thing I did on a Friday night before heading off to bed.

David Callahan, who played keyboards with Stereolab on *The Word*, compares the programme to a cross between *Eurotrash*, a late-night Channel 4 show that took a sardonic look at what was happening in Continental Europe, and classic British music TV programme *The Tube*.

'I watched *The Word* because there'd sometimes be good music on it, but otherwise it seemed to be full of this kind of titbits-type nonsense, kind of soft porn, kind of rubbish, going on,' he says. 'When we actually did it, it was interesting, but also it was *a lot*... the dancers were all kind of fake. They were all there arguing most of the afternoon about who was on the podium this time, *because you were on camera last week, and it's my turn this week*.'

This is where Stereolab found themselves, like arty fish out of beer-slop water, one Friday night in November 1993. Introduction done,

Andy Ramsay clicks his drumsticks together four times, and the band kick into a rather wobbly performance of 'French Disko', with Tim bouncing around like an overactive child and Laetitia looking resolutely nervous, as if she has only just concluded that the Situationists probably wouldn't have approved of this fluoro-set jollity.

Callahan says *The Word* helped to break Stereolab in the UK. 'In the end, you suddenly realised that you've got ten seconds to get it right, so you just launch into it,' he says. 'Listening to it now, with a critical ear and eye, the band is playing quite fast, and it's quite nervous.'

'It was quite a silly show, actually, where they had competitions of who would eat the most maggots or something, that kind of stuff,' Sadier explained at the Red Bull Music Academy in 2015. 'The presenter, whose name I forget, he saw us at the Whisky A Go-Go, as he said in his Mancunian accent, when we played in LA. He was supposed to go and see some other band, [but] he was not on the guest list, so he ended up getting a ticket to see us—we were playing down the road. He loved us, and he invited us to play on his show. I think that's one of the only two times we ever appeared on British television live.'

This explains the *practicalities* of the band's invitation to *The Word*. But on a more fundamental level, you have to wonder how Stereolab got themselves into a situation where Terry Christian would be checking out—and even enjoying—their LA gig. And what does it tell us that Stereolab accepted his invitation to late-night televisual heaven?

The key to this is 'French Disko'. If Stereolab have a greatest hit, it is this: the Stereolab song with the most plays on Spotify—north of eighteen million at the time of writing. A lot of the people I spoke to for this book named it as their favourite Stereolab song, even when I tried to encourage them not to.

'French Disko' is typical of early Stereolab in many ways: it's a sweeping guitar number with racing beat and entwined harmonies. What sets it apart is the utterly unforgettable melody and the ecstatic take-off in the song's chorus, as Sadier calls listeners to resistance. That this was enough, in the Stereolab world, to make the song into something approaching a hit says a lot about how close Stereolab sail to pop respectability at times.

What is fascinating is that Stereolab didn't realise what they had in their armoury, with the song only being released on a hair's breadth decision. The group first demoed 'French Disko' around the recording of *Transient Random-Noise Bursts With Announcements*, with this demo eventually released as a bonus track on the 2019 reissue of the album.

The song—then known as 'French Disco'—was basically all there, even at this stage: the relentless chug, winning riff, strident vocals, and a melody that sits somewhere between panic and celebration, as Stereolab so often did. There are no drums on the demo, but you can intuit the percussive dash that will one day drive the song along.

Writing in the *TRNBWA* sleeve notes, Gane says that the group's demos around this time were 'just working material' to play to the other band members, as a way of showing them the structure of the song. Tim and Laetitia (and sometimes Mary Hansen) laid them down quickly and roughly; you can hear this on the 'French Disco' demo, which is wobbly, inexact, and home to a number of errors that would doubtless have been corrected on any version intended for public release.

Later on in the band's life, their demos would often differ significantly from the final recorded versions of the songs, but at this stage, they tended to sail pretty close to the versions we hear on the records. Listening to the demo of 'French Disco', you can understand this approach: you could, potentially, add *anything* to the song, but why bother? Some listeners—including Gane himself—actually prefer the demo version to the final song, thanks to the relaxed sound of the vocals.

It's an interesting point. I've always been swept along by the fizzing energy of 'French Disc/ko'. But what *makes* the song is the contrast between its mad instrumental scramble and the laidback vocals in the verses, which in turn reflects the song's idea of struggle in the face of the absurd—another very Stereolab concept.

Absurdism is most commonly connected with the French writer and philosopher Albert Camus. The idea, essentially, is that, in the absence of a god, the universe is irrational and meaningless. Meursault, the protagonist of Camus' *L'etranger*, kills an unnamed man for reasons that are never adequately explained and may not even *have* a real explanation, in what is a key absurdist text.

Later on, Camus's thinking evolved. His 1947 masterpiece, *La Peste*, explores characters in the Algerian town of Oran who find some kind of meaning in life by fighting against the plague that is sweeping their town, in an allegory for the French resistance to the Nazi occupation during the Second World War.

'French Disc/ko' is nowhere near this specific, but it speaks to similar ideas. The lyrics initially reference the absurdity and pointlessness of existence, before Sadier points out the power of resistance, in a switch worthy of Camus. It is this contrast—between meek acceptance of the absurdity of life and the fight against it—that drives the song.

Gane says the band mixed the song three times and didn't get it right. Version two of these mixes appears on the reissued album as 'French Disco (Early Version Mix)', a slightly rough-around-the-edges take on the much-loved song. 'French Disco' didn't make it onto *TRNBWA*, however, because Gane thought the initial demo had a poignancy that the band had failed to capture on any of the polished studio versions.

Mix three of 'French Disco' *did* get released, as the final track on the *Jenny Ondioline* EP. But the band did so without a great deal of enthusiasm. In his sleeve notes, Gane explains that he made the decision to include it on the record in the mastering studio at the very last minute because he wanted four songs on the EP and 'French Disco' was available—a fairly shocking revelation about what might be the band's most loved song.

It's not that Stereolab didn't *like* 'French Disco', exactly. Gane loved the demo, and the band would often kick off gigs with the song in 1993, including the fatal Whisky A Go-Go gig that Terry Christian attended. And they would, eventually, re-release it. The public, however, *loved* it. The song received (relatively) heavy airplay on British radio, ending up at #5 on John Peel's listener-voted 'Festive Fifty' chart of the greatest songs of the year. ('Jenny Ondioline' was #39.)

'We decided it ['Jenny Ondioline'] would be the lead single [from *TRNBWA*], but it got flipped soon afterwards, and [DJs] put on "French Disco" instead,' Martin Pike told *Uncut* in 2020. 'We didn't have any money to repress or re-sleeve anything, so we just stickered the remaining copies in the warehouse with a sticker that said *Includes "French Disco"* or something like that.'

And then *The Word* came calling. The band's appearance on the Channel Four show was a mark of the song's popularity—and populist appeal. If the band's wobbly performance was not exactly their best—and the incongruous sight of frantically raving, half-undressed dancers not exactly adding to the song's charm—it certainly boosted their fortunes in the UK.

'French Disc/ko' was also notable for introducing producer, recording engineer, and mix specialist Paul Tipler to the band's orbit, after he was brought in to remix the song. (Tipler is sometimes listed as the engineer on the *Super-Electric* EP, but he says this is incorrect.) 'What I think I heard was basically somebody said to them, if you get this guy to remix "French Disco", you make it an A-side, it'll get airplay. I think it was their plugger, maybe,' Tipler explains. 'I remixed "French Disco", and it kicked off. And so then I kept working with them for the next three or four years.'

Tipler's remixed version of the song is the 'French Disko' that we all know and love. In all honesty, there's not a *great* deal of difference between the two versions, and if you weren't paying attention, you might not even notice: the new one is slightly shorter, dropping the song's intro and outro, and it sounds sharper overall.

'It basically just needed a mix,' says Tipler, who prior to this had worked with everyone from The House Of Love to Kingmaker. 'I think we might have re-recorded a little synth part or something, but just a different person mixing it can just make a massive difference, if they know a little bit more than the person that mixed it in the past.

'When someone says they were going to make it a single, you mixed it in a certain way,' he adds. 'Vocals louder and things like that, because it's going to hopefully get on the radio. It's not like a dark B-side or a dark album track or something.'

'French Disko', as it now was, was printed up as a seven-inch that the band sold on their European tour supporting Pavement in early 1994, backed with a new version of 'Jenny Ondioline'. It was also released on a two-track CD single—something new for the band—and duly charted in the UK at #75, for one week, in January 1994, right at the very limit of what you could consider a chart hit.

This was the start of Stereolab's brief dalliance with the UK singles chart. In July 1994, 'Ping Pong' made #45, and is still the band's biggest singles hit; 'Wow And Flutter' reached #70 in November 1994;

'Cybele's Reverie' charted at #62; 'Miss Modular' hit #60.

On the British albums chart, *Mars Audiac Quintet*, the band's third studio album, made #16 in August 1994, becoming their biggest UK hit of any kind; *Emperor Tomato Ketchup*, their fourth studio album, reached #27; *Dots And Loops*, their fifth, made #19; and 2025 comeback album *Instant Holograms On Metal Film* peaked at #29. A modest chart career.

I was going to call 'French Disko' an accidental chart hit, but I'm not sure that's right. Certainly, Stereolab didn't realise the power of the song they had on their hands, and it doesn't seem like their label did either. But Stereolab *did* play the commercial game to some extent by re-releasing the song, stickering the *Jenny Ondioline* EP, and even appearing on *The Word*. (All good things, in my book.) So, they weren't a band running away from commercial success.

Tipler says that 'French Disko' is probably the most important song in the band's career. 'Because that was the one that they did on *The Word*,' he explains. 'Andy [Ramsay] always says to me that, basically, before *The Word*, they were playing in front of a hundred people; after *The Word*, they were playing in front of a thousand people.'

Stereolab had also recently signed a major-label deal with Elektra in the United States. The label, which was founded in 1950 by Jac Holzman and Paul Rickolt in the former's college dorm room, grew in importance in the 1960s as the home to Love, The Doors, Stooges, and MC5, balancing a love for the counterculture with business sense. In 1970, the founders sold Elektra to Kinney National Company, later to become Warner Communications, putting it firmly in major-label land. All the same, in the 90s—under the leadership of Bob Krasnow, whose early career included a stint working as a promotions man for James Brown—Elektra still had some of its original left-field spirit, signing the likes of Ween and Luna.

Of all the US major labels, then, Elektra probably made most sense as a home for Stereolab, particularly given the extraordinary leeway their deal afforded them. Terry Tolkin, the former music journalist who signed the band to Elektra, explained the deal in a lengthy post on Discogs in July 2019.

According to Tolkin, the terms of the deal were very generous for Stereolab, 'Mainly because I was intimately involved in granting them whatever they and I could think up in conference calls from my office. . . . The Groop's barristers would then phone our crazy proposals to Elektra's lawyers on the floor below me, who would then call me in my office to ask if I was willing to accept our own demands or not. Well, guess what happened there?'

Under the terms of their Elektra deal, Stereolab had 'complete autonomy in the world outside of North America.* They could record and release 45[s] and EP-length material on their own Free Will. They could do it on any Independent label and in collaboration with any Indie artist that they so desired to do so with. Usually, we, EE [Elektra], would even pay for it, directly or indirectly. Anything more elaborate than that required formal approval by EE, which was always gonna be ME, with a capital *ME*. I can't ever remember saying no to any of our schemes.'

So, yes, Stereolab had a major label deal. But it was far from the supposed big-time subjugation that many bands experienced after signing to majors. Stereolab were, in many ways, in debt to Nirvana's huge breakthrough with *Nevermind* in 1991. That album's unexpected success caused American major labels to throw money at all kinds of oddball indie/alternative acts they didn't really understand in a desperate bid to strike gold twice.

And they were certainly lucky to have Tolkin, who died in 2022, as their A&R man. In his Discogs post, he called himself the band's 'enabler in chief': 'I really believed in taking my Artists as far from the responsibilities and restrictions of straight Life as I possibly could. How can you be at your creative peak if you're worried about whether or not you can pay your rent that month? I concentrated on this aspect because I could do something about that. With money. In my job.'

Dean Wareham, whose band Luna were also signed to Elektra in the 90s, says that Tolkin 'was more rock'n'roll than any band he signed. He was a massive music fan. At major labels, you meet some people who love music and some people who love the music business. But he loved music.'

Wareham says that Luna might not have had quite the same

* The Elektra deal actually covered the world excluding the UK and Ireland.

freedom as Stereolab on Elektra. 'But they never interfered with us or told us what to do. I mean, they would always generally say, Hey, you know you need to write something for the radio or you're going to be dropped? And I think they told us that four albums in a row, and then on the fifth album, it finally came true. Terry protected us.

'I think maybe people are more uptight about the indie versus major thing in the UK, where the major labels really do kind of suck,' Wareham adds. 'But they were more varied in the States, and it was just kind of, if someone's going to offer you a bunch of money, I think most people are like, *Yeah, we'll take it. We'll take that money.*'

Krasnow, too, had a history in the avant-garde, having created the Blue Thumb label in 1968 to release the second album by bluesman extraordinaire Captain Beefheart—a decision Tolkin reminded him of when he showed some signs of baulking at the Stereolab signing.

'I brought up Krasnow's early, consummate, nearly career-suicidal support for Captain Beefheart,' Tolkin wrote of one early meeting with the Elektra executives. 'I reminded him to remember how even when one record label after another was dropping Beefheart as fast as they signed him, that Bob had mortgaged his own fukin [sic] house so he could start Blue Thumb Records and pay for the recording of the Magic Band's *Safe As Milk* album on his and Beefheart's own terms. And you had just become a first-time Father too, Bob.'

Beefheart or not, in the end, Krasnow was won around to the Stereolab cause by their music, in this case 'We're Not Adult Orientated' from the *Space Age Batchelor Pad Music* EP. But it could, in reality, have been any number of songs from the band's early career, such was the group's ear for a pop hook.

Stereolab love pop music, and Stereolab write pop songs; sometimes harsh, sometimes downright strange, but *pop* songs nonetheless. They are part of a great lineage of pop experimentalists. Some of the greatest, most successful pop music in history—from The Beatles' 'Tomorrow Never Knows' to Billie Eilish's 'Bad Guy'—allies the expected to the unforeseen, the familiar with the unknown. People who are unfamiliar with the glory of pop music, or who blindly dismiss it, often miss this. They think pop music is bland. And, okay, *sometimes* it is. But a lot of pop music is extremely clever and downright weird. And this is by design. Great pop artists, writers, and producers know that an unusual hook, tone, instrument, or timbre can reel the listener in; ally this to a sweetly familiar melody, to *keep* them there, and you're looking at a hit. Think of the mandolin lead in R.E.M.'s 'Losing My Religion', the sitar in The Beatles' 'Norwegian Wood', or Britney Spears adopting dubstep bass on her 2011 single 'Hold It Against Me': all strange choices, all hits.

This is precisely what Stereolab do, anchoring experimental sounds with the sweetest pop melodies and undercutting vast vocal hooks with instrumental outlandishness. Think 'Ping Pong', 'Crest', 'Cybele's Reverie', 'Fluorescences', 'John Cage Bubblegum', 'French Disko', and so on. Gane defined the band as a 'high-concept pop group' in a 2009 interview with *Fact* magazine, and that sounds about right.

So, yes, Stereolab weren't trying for a chart hit with 'French Disko'. But they weren't NOT trying for one either. This is a band in love with the sweet sound of Yé-yé and bubblegum pop, who signed a major label deal and ploughed Elektra's money into obscure seven-inch singles and peculiar collaborations but still stayed with the label until their eighth studio album, *Margerine Eclipse*. This is a band with some of the sweetest pop melodies of their generation, who understand the power of pop as a genuinely subversive force.

•

If you wanted an illustration of the art/populism duality at the heart of Stereolab, you could find few better examples than the final months of 1993, as 'Disco' became 'Disko' and *The Word* came calling. The band released three singles during that period, and they vary wildly in sound, commercial potential, and ambition. (One of them, the *Crumb Duck* EP with Nurse With Wound, we will come to later.)

'Lo Boob Oscillator' / 'Tempter' was a limited seven-inch release on the US label Sub Pop, then still very much in vogue thanks to its success with Nirvana. I like to imagine that Stereolab were thinking of Sub Pop's reputation as a monster of grey-scale grunge when they delivered 'Lo Boob Oscillator', one of their most exquisite pop numbers, its guitar sound as clean as a whistle. (At least in the first four minutes: the song's second half is notably more spiky.)

Ostensibly an ode to the moon—in French—the words of 'Lo

Boob Oscillator' delve into the nature of freedom, appearance, and reality, over a gorgeous Mellotron groove played by Kath Gifford, their first appearance on record with the band.

Gifford, who replaced Sean O'Hagan on keyboards, already knew Stereolab socially before they joined at the suggestion of bass player Duncan Brown. 'I learned piano when I was a kid,' Gifford says. 'I was a singer in the previous band [Zero]. But you don't really need to be a keyboard player to be able to play Stereolab keyboards.'

Gifford's first appearance with the band was in the video for 'French Disko'; their first recording session together was in July 1993 at Bang Bang Studios in Crouch End, London. 'I managed to take a microdot [a fearsomely strong form of LSD] the night before and had a really bad trip and then turned up at the studio really early,' Gifford says. 'I was scared of falling asleep and not turning up, and I thought it was really important. I was feeling a bit shaky at the start of it, but then it turned out to be a really good day.' After recording 'Tempter', Gifford says, the band basically made up 'Lo Boob Oscillator' on the spot. 'Tim had a structure for the other one ['Tempter']. Then we just messed around to do "Lo Boob Oscillator".'

Gifford wouldn't stay long in Stereolab—appearing only on one studio album, 1994's *Mars Audiac Quintet*, before being replaced on keyboards by Morgan Lhote—but played an important role in the band. As well as looking *supremely* bored on *The Word*—'I think I probably was quite nervous, but I had also had time to get quite bored during the day'—Gifford contributed keyboards as well as occasional backing vocals, both of which are evident on 'Lo Boob Oscillator'. There is something animalistic about the song's backing vocals, which are reminiscent of the hooting of an owl, that I have always loved. The presence of three vocal layers suggests Stereolab's growing pop nous, which would come into vibrant flower on *Mars Audiac Quintet*.

'The big thing for me about being in Stereolab was that they opened my ears up to listening in a way I'd not done before—particularly the texture of sounds (as well as a whole world of music I hadn't come across before either),' Gifford says. 'The mellotron [on 'Lo Boob Oscillator'] had a unique melancholic sound.'

Gifford's entry into Stereolab also offers a telling insight into the rather incestuous London indie-rock scene in which Stereolab still operated. As well as playing with Stereolab, Gifford was part of Moonshake, a band formed in 1991 by David Callahan, once of The Wolfhounds, for whom Mary Hansen had sung backing vocals. Both Hansen and Gifford sang on Moonshake's final album, 1996's *Dirty & Divine*, which was stickered to alert users to Hansen's presence—an indication of Stereolab's growing indie star-power.

Despite its low-key release, 'Lo Boob Oscillator' became one of Stereolab's most commercially successful songs. It appears on the 1995 compilation *Refried Ectoplasm* (*Switched On Volume 2*) alongside the aforementioned 'Tempter', a metronomic, drum-machine groove that is heavy on the Farfisa. 'Lo Boob Oscillator' also featured in the 2000 Hollywood adaptation of Nick Hornby's *High Fidelity*, which grossed $47.1 million worldwide, and has also appeared in an advert for Hotels.com in which a father books a room in an arty hotel in an attempts to convince his daughter that he isn't just some sofa-dwelling bore.

Stereolab's music has featured only rarely in commercials. As well as the Hotels.com clip, 'Parsec', from the 1997 album *Dots And Loops*, was used in an advert for the VW Beetle. But the band's work has appeared semi-regularly in films and TV. Some of my favourite examples include 'Lo Boob Oscillator' (again!) appearing in the eighth episode of Netflix's sparkling romcom adaptation of *One Day*; 'The Flower Called Nowhere' being used in the appropriately psychedelic *Atlanta* episode 'New Jazz'; and the band covering Akira Ifukube's *Godzilla* theme tune for the 2004 film *Godzilla Final Wars*.

Best of all—and almost certainly most iconic—is Kim Wexler listening to 'Tempter' in headphones as she reviews various documents in 'Coushatta', series four, episode eight of *Better Call Saul*, which first aired in September 2018. Thomas Golubić of SuperMusicVision says that the idea of using Stereolab was essentially to establish the difference between Kim Wexler—who would *definitely* listen to Stereolab—and the series' lead character (and Kim's romantic interest) Jimmy McGill, who wouldn't.

'A big part of the story is Jimmy McGill's love for Kim and his sort of *battle* to be worthy of her,' he says. 'Kim is a very straightforward and loving person, and she's very committed to Jimmy, but he doesn't know that. I don't think he ever fully feels worthy of her love and that weird self-loathing—which is part of the story of how he becomes Saul Goodman—it was important for us to establish how that relationship works. There are moments when they're very close and moments when they are very far apart; music sometimes plays a role in that.

'In the sequence in particular that we featured Stereolab, we knew we had a scene where Kim was focused on working,' Golubić adds. 'She's frustrated with Jimmy. She's been dragged into a rather elaborate ruse because he's trying to essentially liberate his colleague, who he got in trouble. And in short, she's now been dragged, once again, into something that is complicated and exhausting, and it's created a fissure between the two of them.'

Golubić first got into Stereolab in college, and he used to work to the band's music—just as Kim is trying to do in this scene. 'We wanted to have Kim having headphones, we thought a lot about the visceral experience of having headphones on and when you're in your own headspace and how you can use that to separate yourself from other people,' Golubić explains. 'So, a lot of it was: What would she be listening to that could be fully immersive and would help the audience to understand that she is deep into something else and she's kind of screening Jimmy out?'

Stereolab, Golubić says, were the perfect band for Kim Wexler: experimental but not *too* strange; far out but always rooted in pop. 'We thought about, *Who is Kim Wexler? What would she respond to?* And in many ways, Stereolab seemed like a perfect example for her. They're an experimental band; they're a pop band, but they're not an overtly commercial pop band. They have this wonderful mixture of French and English. . . . And I felt like that really captured Kim's personality. I believe that Kim Wexler would have Stereolab as one of her favourite bands. And in the same sense that I used them for studying, I think she would as well.'

The particular sonics of Stereolab were important, too. 'If we had said that Kim is a Liz Phair fan, which is certainly possible, that would not have translated as well, because Liz Phair is more melodically oriented. There isn't a wall of sound around her [Kim]. It doesn't feel like you're underwater. And I think, with Stereolab, you really feel like you're in a submersible submarine and all around you is water. And I think that that was a key part of that,' Golubić says. 'I don't view Kim as being an experimental music listener. I view her as being somebody who will be a little bit left of centre but not radically left of centre. And I feel like Stereolab fits in that really beautiful sweet spot.'

Interestingly, the choice of band was far more important than the choice of song. Golubić says that he chose 'Tempter' because its release in 1993 would roughly correspond to Kim's college years. But he also thought it would be easy to license—perhaps someone had pitched it in the past, although he doesn't exactly remember.

All this was, of course, many years in the future in October 1993, when Stereolab embarked on their first full US tour, after playing four dates there in 1992. The tour—on which Terry Christian would get his introduction to the band—saw them play with Washington DC indie-rock band Unrest, whose co-founder, Mark Robinson, says that Stereolab were 'incredible' on those dates.

'It was such a sound that you kind of get lost in, really, you kind of forgot where you were and the sound would just envelop you,' he says. 'They're kind of like a jam band—they're jamming on that stuff. That's a terrible term to use. It's improvisation but also almost psychedelic, like you were seeing, I don't know, the Grateful Dead or something like that. Not that kind of music, but the fact that they're experimenting with their own songs and *within* their own songs.'

To mark the occasion, Stereolab released a split seven-inch single with Unrest on the latter band's Teen Beat label. Stereolab's contribution was 'Mountain', a song that, in a way, feels like the end of Stereolab mark one, the last call of the slightly scratchy act that emerged from the London indie scene. The song's make-up—rasping beat, drone guitars, et cetera—feels typical of early Stereolab, in a way that the band would soon be moving away from—an impression enhanced by the song's lo-fi recording.

'Lo Boob Oscillator', with its big, bright pop melodies and gentle Mellotron sound, 'Mountain' is not. And you certainly can't imagine 'Mountain' on *The Word* with Terry Christian and his gyrating dancers. And so, with a final, rasping finale, the band moved on.

07

'PING PONG' POLITICS

The year 1994 was a big one for indie music in the UK. Oasis released their debut album,* Definitely Maybe, *and Blur unleashed their defining statement,* Parklife, *the two albums sitting at #1 and #2 on the* NME*'s 'Albums Of The Year' list that December.

The spectre of Britpop may have been unleashed the previous year, with *Select* magazine's notorious 'Yanks go home'/Suede/Union Jack cover. But it was in 1994 that it started to flower.

This is not the place for a debate as to the merits of Britpop, although, for the record, I am largely in favour. (I turned seventeen in 1994: what do you want?) Stereolab were half British, and they certainly played pop music, but they were absolutely not a Britpop band, even if Laetitia Sadier does feature on one of *Parklife*'s most-loved songs, contributing a gorgeous spoken-word vocal, in French, to 'To The End'.

I'm never quite sure if Stereolab benefited from, or were harmed by, the rise of Britpop. On the one hand, excitement around guitar music in the UK helped all kinds of indie bands into the charts, and Stereolab were close to their commercial peak at the time; on the other, Britpop temporarily swept away a lot of the art and politics on which Stereolab thrived from the indie charts, leaving the group to stick out like a sore thumb.

Obviously, this isn't entirely black-and-white. Pulp, one of the leading Britpop bands, had deep political leanings and called their fifth studio album *Different Class* in recognition of its examination of the British class system. The revolutionary socialist newspaper *Socialist Worker*, no less, praised *Different Class* for its radicalism, and the message on the back of the album—'We don't want no trouble, we just want the right to be different. That's all.'—is clearly a politically charged statement.

On the whole, though, Britpop wasn't political. Oasis, its leading lights, were more concerned with fags and booze and having a good time, while Blur were more observational than activist. At the same time, however, the previous trends in indie music—shoegazing, grunge, Madchester—were *even less* political than Britpop.

Despite all this, there undoubtedly *was* (and perhaps still is) a tradition of indie music being allied to left-leaning politics, particularly in the 1980s. The whole idea of being 'independent' indicated a desire to live outside the capitalist major-label system, with bands creating their own, alternative ways of releasing and promoting their music.

Several of the leading indie bands of the 1980s went significantly further in their political engagement. Leeds post-punk band Gang Of Four, for example, were a product of the UK's left-leaning university culture, taking their name from a counterrevolutionary collective in post-Maoist China, while The Redskins were active members of the Socialist Workers Party. Even well-known bands like The Smiths were engaged with left-wing politics, taking part in the Red Wedge tours of 1986 that were designed to boost support for the Labour Party.

Among the most radical left-leaning indie bands of the 1980s were McCarthy, the group formed by Tim Gane, Malcolm Eden, and John Williamson in the mid-1980s. (The name—a reference to US anti-communist zealot Joe McCarthy—is something of a giveaway.) While Gane was arguably the band's musical engine, Eden was its political heart. After Margaret Thatcher came to power in the UK in 1979, he found himself drawn to Marxism, as he explained in a 2007 interview with *Lacewings*. 'She had a very forceful way of putting her arguments. Nobody in the opposition really had an answer to her. That's why she kept winning elections, in fact. To find a good answer to the Tories, you had to go to the root of the matter. That's what got me interested in Marxism.'

Eden, the band's lyricist, made sure these views came across loud and clear in McCarthy's songs. Their debut album, 1987's *I Am A Wallet,* includes songs like 'The Wicked Palace Revolution', 'The International Narcotics Traffic', 'Charles Windsor', and 'God Made The Virus', prompting Manic Street Preachers' Nicky Wire to call it 'the most perfect record, a Communist manifesto with tunes'.

'A lot of bands in post-punk were extremely politicised, bands like Magazine, Gang Of Four, and Wire,' Laetitia Sadier told *Westword* in 2012. 'They were very political—and McCarthy, of course. At that time, I think there were more political bands than apolitical bands. It was a way of fighting.'

Given Gane (and, briefly, Sadier's) history in McCarthy, it was perhaps inevitable that Stereolab would themselves be considered Marxists, though the band have never agreed with the description. 'A long time ago, someone decided to call us Marxist pop, and that's kind of stuck, even though none of us are Marxists,' Gane told the *Washington Post* in 1999. 'I've never even read Marx. Basically, Laetitia writes lyrics which touch upon topics that could be called political. We never do it in a sloganeering way. I prefer to adopt a critical perspective, to always question things.'

Sadier has spoken of the influence of Cornelius Castoriadis, who became a critic of Marxism later on in his life, on her thinking, while the group's love of releasing collectable records in all kinds of wonderful limited editions hardly speaks to an outright rejection of capitalism.

For all this, you can understand why people would read Marxism into Stereolab's lyrics. And 'Ping Pong'—the band's first release of 1994, and the first taste of their forthcoming third studio album, *Mars Audiac Quintet*—is central to this.

'Ping Pong' was initially released on the four-track *Ping Pong* EP in July 1994, as a precursor to the album. It is ridiculously evident from the song's first note that the band have hit on something very special. 'Ping Pong' sounds ultra-bright, *sparkling* even, with an irresistible vocal melody wrapped in layers of backing vocals and soaring brass arrangements by Sean O'Hagan.*

The band returned to Blackwing Studios in South London, where they had recorded *Transient Random-Noise Bursts With Announcements*, to work on *MAQ*, with Paul Tipler, who had remixed 'French Disko', tasked with engineering and mixing the record. Kath Gifford, who replaced O'Hagan on keyboards, remembers the recording sessions as a very relaxed time.

'It was quite chilled,' Gifford says. 'It just seemed to be like, *This is what we're going to do*. And so we did it.' So there was no big plan? 'Well, because Tim and Laetitia wrote the songs, it was *their* plan. And we were . . . I was, you know, facilitating their plan.'

Tipler says that Tim and Laetitia 'ran the show' in the studio. 'Back then, it was pretty much Tim and Laetitia, and everybody else maybe had a little input,' he says. 'Tim had a vision of where things should be.'

For the mixing of *Mars Audiac Quintet*, Tipler says that the band would largely leave him alone to work. 'I'd be left to do all the boring stuff and get it into shape, and then they come in and go, Yeah, could that be brighter? Or, Could that be slightly further out?' he explains.

Even more than 'French Disko', 'Ping Pong' is Stereolab at their most irresistibly pop, a diamantine clarity of focus provided by a rock-solid base of four chords that climb and retreat like a cat slinking up and down stairs. In the sleeve notes to the 2019 reissue of *Mars Audiac Quintet*, Gane says that, unusually, 'Ping Pong' was written to fill a specific gap in the album, which he felt needed 'an out-and-out pop song' to complete the circle of its sound and running order.

People don't tend to focus so much on the song's musical make-up, however, as on its lyrical conceit. In a voice of perfect nonchalance, Sadier uses the song to comment on the blithe, uncaring nature of the capitalist economic cycle, in which boom follows bust and war is a tool for growth, while the fate of the individual—who loses their job,

* O'Hagan actually left the band as a full-time member during the recording of *Mars Audiac Quintet* to concentrate on The High Llamas, but he continued to contribute extensively to their studio work.

home, and even life to the demands of capitalism—doesn't matter a fig.

'I had a discussion with a friend,' Sadier told *Melody Maker* about the song's genesis. 'He was saying, Capitalism is alright, because recovery is in-built: there's a slump, then a war, and then you have to rebuild everything, and that stimulates a recovery. And he thought that was all right! I thought that was perfectly shocking!'

When people call Stereolab 'Marxist pop', it is often 'Ping Pong' they are thinking of, although 'Wow And Flutter', the second single from *Mars Audiac Quintet*, also comes up. It's a similar song in many ways: another hypnotic chord base, another devastating pop melody, and another brilliant vocal arrangement. It also addresses the capitalist system, via symbols of economic hegemony such as IBM, the US flag, and capital itself, concluding that none of this is inevitable and change is therefore possible.

These are gloriously unusual themes for three-minute pop songs, and you can understand the temptation for commentators to jump to all sorts of radical conclusions. (I have been guilty of this myself in the past.) 'Marxist pop' has a way of rolling off the tongue, and it is a useful way of expressing, in just two words, how *different* Stereolab can be. There have probably been fewer than a handful of genuinely Marxist pop stars—*not* rock bands—in history, and, depending on your political leaning, it might be refreshing to think of Stereolab in this way.

Toby Manning, the author of *Mixing Pop And Politics: A Marxist History Of Popular Music*, says that he considers Stereolab to be part of 'a very small pantheon of Marxist popular music. … Bear in mind I also include The Clash, The Jam, and Public Enemy in this, who might also demur,' he adds. 'I don't take much account of an artist's testimony—PJ Harvey denies she's a feminist; Paul McCartney claims songs about his exes are about family pets, et cetera.' 'Ping Pong', Manning adds, 'is dialectical materialism set to music, as is, for example, [*Emperor Tomato Ketchup*'s] "Tomorrow Is Already Here".'*

* Asked about 'Tomorrow Is Already Here' in a rare interview in 1996, Mary Hansen told *Pitchfork*, 'Laetitia [Sadier] always wants to make people think about things and she always wanders and contemplates life and what it means and how people can change their situations and how situations can change people. That's what it's about, how society changes people but people can also change society.'

Manning undoubtedly knows what he is talking about, and I am *very* far from an expert on the subject. For me, though, calling these songs 'Marxist' is going a step too far. The key tenets of Marxism (for dummies) are that capitalism is flawed and that the struggles between social classes will lead to a Communist revolution. Capitalism is unsustainable, according to Marxian economics, which means that socialism—the shared ownership of the means of production by workers—is an economic necessity.

'Ping Pong' and 'Wow And Flutter' are clearly not pro-capitalist. But I don't *necessarily* think they are *anti*-capitalist. Rather, they are songs that question the status quo; that wonder if things have to be this way, or if another way is possible. This, I think, is the key to Stereolab's politics: they are a band who *question* everything. In the capitalist West, this means questioning capitalism. But I like to think that, had they grown up in the USSR, Stereolab would be equally interested in questioning the tenets of communism.

'To me, music and politics go perfectly hand in hand—any form of art and politics,' Sadier told *Westword* in 2012. 'I'm just surprised there's not more politics in music these days. Maybe it's part of the same phenomenon of being brainwashed and absolutely wanting to make a career and therefore stay in the format of what is commercially acceptable. Of course, you take risks [in not doing so], though Rage Against The Machine had a great career.'

Rock critic Simon Reynolds also brings up Rage Against The Machine in discussing Stereolab, pointing out the very different ways in which these two politically charged groups of the early 90s went about their musical business. 'There was a wave of these groups in the early 90s bringing political content back to music: Manic Street Preachers, Rage Against The Machine, Senser,' he says. 'They tended to do the obvious thing of having angry-sounding music and angry lyrics.' Stereolab, on the other hand, brought 'dulcet music' that was 'angry but not overtly shouting . . . angry but cold, thoughtful anger, lyrics and delivery informed by political rage but given the clarity and penetration of having read books on Marxism.'

'Music was not just mere entertainment to us,' Sadier explained during her Red Bull Music Academy interview in 2015. 'I don't know if it's because I was born in May '68 or what, but I always felt quite, *Why are things the way they are?* Because there's big discrepancies. To me it feels . . . I don't know, it's just not right. Things are not right, and when I see something that's not right, I want to put it right.'

The reference to May 1968 is telling. This was the month in which student protests in France against capitalism and American consumerism led to paralysing strikes across the country and eventually a snap election. It is considered one of the most important events in modern French history, a movement that succeeded 'as a social revolution, not as a political one', according to Alain Geismar, one of the student leaders at the time.

The Situationists also played a key role in May 1968. They too were critical of capitalism and were deeply involved in the occupation of French universities during the month of protests. Guy Debord, one of the founding members of Situationist International, was a Marxist, and his 1967 book *La Société Du Spectacle* explores Marxist theory.

Debord, Sadier explained in her Red Bull interview, 'was a very insightful guy into society. He was also very bitter, I think. But who would not be when you look at society and how it's run and how it's governed and the forces that govern our lives?'

Again, though, I think it is too much to call Stereolab Marxists, particularly when they themselves have rejected the term. I have a theory that some people want Stereolab to be Marxists so that they can agree with them, and others do so that they can find perceived inconsistencies in the band's thinking and accuse them of hypocrisy. (A Marxist band? Selling records?! How *dare* they.)

'I never really read Karl Marx in much depth,' Sadier told me when I interviewed her for *Line Noise*. 'But I understand that there is an analysis and there is a method to critical thinking that Marx has established at a particular point in time which is still relevant.'

I've always thought that there is something very *French* to Sadier's political engagement. 'Are you romanticising the French and their capacity to take the streets?' she asked, when I broached the subject. 'No, you're not. They do. People are a bit more politically aware, inclined. Certainly, they're more *râleur*—they complain more, and they complain with less suppression, compared to the British, who will suppress their emotions, and those will include frustration at their bosses or their governments. In France, we are quite open and quite unstripped.'

At the root of Stereolab's politics runs a mixture of left-leaning idealism, rejection of society's norms, and a belief that a better life is possible, inspired by, but not in blind devotion to, the work of the Situationists. This belief is hard to sum up in one word—Sadier has called herself 'an idealist'—but it makes the band's views far more interesting.

People demand coherence and simplicity: that's why we want to call Stereolab Marxists and be done with it. But life isn't like that: it's complicated, and it doesn't move in the straight lines we want it to follow. And this is rarely more evident than in political beliefs.

This has, on occasion, led Stereolab into some tricky political places. In 2018, Sadier expressed her support for the controversial conservative professor Jordan Peterson, although she swiftly rowed this back, claiming that her tweet was about 'his right to hold his ideas rather than support for them per se'. On the whole, however, it feels like Stereolab's lyrics come from a place of warmth, belief, and empathy.

'I think that my way of politics is trying, first of all, to know myself: know what are my impulses, what I'm made of, what are my conditionings? What my unconscious is driving me to do; trying to understand that and come to grips with that,' Sadier told me in 2024. 'We are creators of our society. So, depending on what we inherit and how much we're going to repeat the patterns, then we're going to create a different society.

'And there are a lot of traumatic things that, unfortunately, we tend to repeat and not question. So, as you say, it's about observing and questioning certain behaviours that we have, that totally escape our awareness most of the time. And it is a case of trying to be aware.'

On *Mars Audiac Quintet*, there are several compelling examples of Stereolab's questioning tone and rejection of accepted thinking, which you can, if you like, take as political. The doomy 'Three Longers Later' talks about a person who is called up by the state to join the army; 'Nihilist Assault Group'—what a title!—questions where morals come from, while calling out censorship; and 'Three-Dee Melodie', the gorgeous, tightly-wound opening song, questions the role of religion in providing meaning for society.

'I was brought up a Catholic, and it was horrible,' Sadier told me in 2024. 'So, I also have issues with the idea of God, Jesus, the Virgin Mary. And so much hypocrisy. Priests who tell me that I'm dirty because I'm a woman, I'm a girl, from a young age. So, I really had my very bad experiences with this world.

'But I realised that they basically perverted the idea of the sacred and the idea of the life force. And then they gave it a bad name. And it was all to control, it was all for control's sake. It was not to serve humanity and make us emancipated and rejoice in the fact that we are alive. It was all about making us sinners, therefore bad, therefore punishable, et cetera, et cetera.'

MAQ's 'L'enfer Des Formes', meanwhile, is about political apathy, as Sadier told *The Guardian* in 2019. '[It's about] walking away from our responsibilities, and I'm the worst one,' she said. 'We're governed by a system that had its time, it worked for a while, but now it's not working for the majority of people on this planet. And we know this, but how do you unlock this thing in humans as a community? It's this massive interrogation for me.'

Stereolab would continue to question and prod throughout their career. Some of my favourite of their 'political' songs—for want of a better word—include 'Motoroller Scalatron', from 1996's *Emperor Tomato Ketchup*, which uses clever word play and extreme repetition to question the nature of society; 'Gus The Mynah Bird', from 2001's *Sound-Dust*, which calls for self-determination in the face of widespread corruption; 'Bop Scotch', from *Margerine Eclipse*, which marries a rinky-dink musical backing to a strident reclamation of justice, freedom, and equality; and 'Nous Vous Demandons Pardon', from 2008's *Chemical Chords*, which asks for forgiveness for France's colonialist past. (There are many, *many* more examples.)

On a musical level, *Mars Audiac Quintet* is a fascinating, fabulous beast that is in my top three Stereolab albums most days of the week. It feels like the band's most perfectly *pop* long player, a conscious step away from the gritty sound of *Transient Random-Noise Bursts With Announcements* and also, perhaps, a rejection of what has gone before.

'Nihilist Assault Group' was originally intended to be a side-long song suite, à la 'Jenny Ondioline', only for the group to pare it back to its seven-minute run time. Gane told *Uncut* in 2020 that the song 'sounded too much like "Jenny Ondioline", but not as good'. This seems like a very harsh judgment to make, but I wonder, too, if the decision was made so as not to establish a pattern. Obviously, having a side-long song suite on every Stereolab album would be a wonderful thing. But I also like the idea of the group not being tied down by tradition and expectation.*

The other big change on the album lies in the drums. *Mars Audiac Quintet* isn't immune to the delights of the Motorik beat, but there are a number of songs where they appear to make a strategic shift away from it. Such a beat would fit perfectly on 'Three Longers Later', for example, but Ramsay instead uses a shuffling, powerful, and more complicated drum pattern, agitating the song rather than smoothing out its rush.

'Transona Five', meanwhile, is a winning example of Stereolab glam-rock boogie, its shuffling beat and bluesy sound suggesting Slade in space, weirded out on heavy repetition. (See also 'Heavy Denim' on the *Wow And Flutter* EP). In the album's sleeve notes, Gane says that the idea was to take 'those old blues rock riffs' and extend them into 'numbing trance states to lose the blues rock aspect of it and have it build up and up, taking on a ritualistic intensity'.

Gane goes on to call the idea 'rather silly', but it is not that far from the modus operandi of the Krautrock groups he so admires, who also used repetition to take rock'n'roll beyond its blues roots. What's amazing is that Gane also says he was 'scrabbling around for ideas' at the time, which seems almost totally contrary to the boundless creative feeling of *Mars Audiac Quintet*.

After 'Ping Pong' made #45 in the UK singles chart, *Mars Audiac Quintet* became Stereolab's highest-charting album, reaching #16 in August 1994. In his book *Fried And Justified*, Mick Houghton, the band's former publicist in the UK, says that 'Ping Pong' 'could well

* You can hear the rest of the suite as 'Nihilist Assault Group (Parts 3, 4, 5)' on the *Wow And Flutter* twelve-inch, which was released in October 1994, and 'Nihilist Assault Group—Part 6' on the 2019 reissue of *Mars Audiac Quintet*.

have made the Top 40 but for their independent distribution'. 'Wow And Flutter' also had a brief chart dalliance, making #70 in November 1994.

This chart success seems fitting for what was Stereolab's most pop-friendly record to date. The band's appearance on the 1994 Lollapalooza tour seems oddly appropriate, too. The headliners that year were the Beastie Boys, Smashing Pumpkins, and A Tribe Called Quest, although Stereolab played the side stage alongside The Boo Radleys, Flaming Lips, and The Verve.

Nirvana were originally set to headline Lollapalooza in 1994, only for Kurt Cobain to turn it down, apparently because he was worried about being seen as a sell-out. Gane largely enjoyed the tour: 'That was a good experience,' he explained to *The Guardian* in 2019. 'Got to see Beastie Boys every night.' He grimaces. 'And the Smashing Pumpkins.'

Playing Lollapalooza—forty-five shows from July to September 1994—also gave Gane the opportunity to stop worrying about the group's next album. 'After finishing the LP, I entered a troubling time personally, in regards to what to do next,' he writes in the reissued *MAQ*'s sleeve notes. 'It was obvious to me that *MAQ* was an end stage, and we couldn't just carry on knocking this kind of stuff out, but the question was, what to do next?'

It seems Stereolab's 'pop' phase—for want of a better word—was coming apart almost as they made it. Gane & co would eventually find a way forward with their music, alighting on the gloriously metronomic grooves of 1996's *Emperor Tomato Ketchup*. But before then, it was time for some art.

08

'POP QUIZ' ART

When I first heard* Transient Random-Noise Bursts With Announcements, *Stereolab's second studio album, back in 1993—and for many years after—I was convinced that the sampled voice that runs through 'Pause' was saying 'sex, art'.

This seemed to me like the perfect introduction to Stereolab. It was only years later, when the internet went mainstream, that I discovered the words were, in fact, 'sechs' and 'acht', the German words for 'six' and 'eight', used as part of an elaborate Cold War code. The knowledge was disappointing, because sex and art lie at the core of Stereolab's sound.

By sex, I don't mean anything erotic. Stereolab are sexy in a more general kind of way: exciting, fresh, sometimes French, and full of life. Art is more complicated. On the one hand, you have Stereolab's own art—their music. Musical taste is a very personal thing, but Stereolab, more than most bands, feel like the kind of group for whom the word 'art' applies to their work, in its variety, care, and imagination.

Art can also refer to the band's brilliantly curated record sleeves. As befits a band who care greatly about records as objects, Stereolab put a great deal of effort into their sleeves, which feature eye-catching yet often simple designs, recurring motifs, strong blocks of colours, and impactful use of text.

'We always set out to make records that we would want to own,' manager Martin Pike told *The Vinyl Factory* in 2019. 'We always thought in terms of vinyl because, as record collectors, that was the format we all loved dearly. We would design everything around how the LP would look, no matter what.' As evidence of this, the band have also produced a large number of elegantly coloured, limited-edition records, like the numbered gold edition of *Transient Random-Noise Bursts With Announcements* that has pride of place on my shelves.

Much as Stereolab's individual sound was there from the start, so too was the band's aesthetic sense. Richard Roberts, whose Too Pure label put out several of the band's early records, says that Stereolab took their record sleeves very seriously. 'In some of those first records, we had no artwork budget,' he says. 'It had to come from the bands. I'm looking at *Peng!* right now, and it doesn't say Stereolab on the front cover . . . it's this bright yellow thing, with the orange Day-Glo colours on it. And for me, it didn't matter; it was an outstanding look.'

'They did it deliberately—they definitely went for a brand, and they kept it all the way along,' says Sean Forbes from Rough Trade, the British independent record retailer that sold the first Stereolab record. 'You can pick up a Stereolab record now, and it still looks like a Stereolab record.'

For an indie band who can't rely on huge marketing budgets, a distinctive look is important. Mike Schulman, who founded Slumberland Records in the USA, says that the look of Stereolab's early records helped audiences to grasp where they were coming from, in the pre-internet days. 'It was so striking and so distinctive,' he says. 'There was that consistency across releases and the pop art aspect of it, it was kind of Warholian, in a way. There was so much that seemed to fill out the picture of what they were about, in a way that was really inspiring.'

Stereolab took their artwork *so* seriously that it almost caused a falling out with Too Pure, when the label wanted to release a series of records in bespoke Too Pure packaging—à la Warp Records' classic purple sleeves—including a Stereolab single. 'That's one of the things that they really hated,' says Roberts. 'They were so pissed with this idea.' So pissed, in fact, that it never came to pass: there would be no Stereolab record in custom-made Too Pure packaging, and Stereolab continued with their own distinctive artwork.

The band's first few record sleeves, up to *Space Age Batchelor Pad Music*, featured a character the band called 'Cliff', who looks out at the world with a toothsome and slightly troubling smile, lambchop sideburns, and overgrown side parting, suggesting his late 1960s origins. His finger, which is pointing right at you, is either a regular finger or a gun, depending on the record.

Cliff was taken from a cartoon strip called 'Der Tödliche Finger' ('The Deadly Finger') by the artist Antonholz Portmann, which ran in *HOTCHA!*, an underground magazine published by Swiss artist and writer Urban Gwerder, in 1970. As Gane explained in an interview with the *Chickfactor* fanzine in 1993, 'He's a figure of the establishment who is eventually shot by the forces of the revolution (peng!).'

Over the cartoon's six panels, we see Cliff's finger mutate into a gun, which then shoots—'Peng!'—in a puff of smoke, as the text addresses an anonymous person who loves peace and quiet and law and order but is also a lieutenant in the army and therefore deserves to be shot. It is an arresting series of images, and the text is fascinatingly ambiguous: I can't decide whether the person addressed in the cartoon actually *deserves* to be shot, in the artist's view. In any case, the cartoon made for a brilliant series of record covers.

After ditching Cliff, Stereolab's next series of covers made overt reference to the obscure 'hi-fi/stereo-effect records' that Gane, in particular, was attracted to, in a brilliantly retro-futuristic run of art. 'It's a juvenile thing, Gane told *Chickfactor*. 'I like themes running through the records, things that connect them together so that we can have our own Blue period and Op Art phase.'

The cover of *Space Age Batchelor Pad Music* copies the cover image of the Vanguard *Stereolab Test Record* from which the band took their name, while *Transient Random-Noise Bursts With Announcements* is based on the cover of *Hi-Fi Sound Stereo Test Record*, a record issued by the Hi-FI Sound label in 1969, its image of a needle hitting a groove rendered in glorious purple and yellow.

This wasn't the only way that the band plundered the *Hi-Fi Sound Stereo Test Record*, either. In what is a particularly satisfying package of 360 use, where art reflects music reflects inspiration, the band took their album title and several song names from the *Sound Stereo* record—its first track is called 'Test 1 (Channel Recognition, Phasing And Balance. Transient Random-Noise Bursts With Announcements.)'—and also sampled it on 'Jenny Ondioline'.

After signing with Elektra, Stereolab had more money to use on their record covers, calling on graphic design company Trouble for *Mars Audiac Quintet*. It also meant they had a budget to employ a photographer and hire the vintage synth that appears on the covers of *MAQ* as well as the *Ping Pong* and *Wow And Flutter* EPs in fish-eye vision.

From 1997's *Dots And Loops* until 2008's *Chemical Chords*, Stereolab worked with Julian House, a musician, graphic designer, and co-owner of the Ghost Box label, who also collaborated with Broadcast on their sleeve designs. House's love of collage and old record sleeves, together with his wide-ranging artistic influences, clearly dovetailed with the band's own interests.

'The bands always have an input,' House told *Soul Riot* in 2008 of designing the Stereolab sleeves. 'The process begins with talking to the band about what they like visually, where the record is coming from. Quite free discussions that will involve film, politics, pop culture . . . not just design. . . . Then I make some things and we talk about what's working, and it progresses from there.' In the same interview, he describes his inspiration as 'the pulp end of things, which still informs me today, as much as classic design . . . strange old vinyl LPs, paperback books, found ephemera.'

The result was the most striking artwork in Stereolab's history, marrying bold graphic images with unusual typography and impactful colour design, its retro-futuristic look in keeping with the band's musical aesthetic. House's designs never repeated themselves, but you would know a Stereolab record sleeve when you saw it, a stylishly consistent variety that was much like the band's music itself.

Stereolab's connection to the world of art also came in direct inspiration. Yoko Ono was a reference for the band, and they played with her at the Bell Atlantic Jazz Festival in New York in 2000. The band's 1999 album *Cobra And Phases Group Play Voltage In The Milky Night*, meanwhile, is apparently an allusion to the COBRA avant-garde art group, who were active in Europe from 1948 to 1951.

Dadaism, the European art movement of the early twentieth century that emerged as a response to the horrors of the First World War, was a particularly prominent influence on Stereolab, with Gane naming Dada artist Hannah Höch, a pioneer of photomontage, as an influence in a 2023 interview with *The Arts Desk*.

But the band's most direct link with the art world came in February 1995, with the opening of *The Amorphous Body Study Center*, a show by sculptor Charles Long at the Tanya Bonakdar Gallery in New York, which was soundtracked by Stereolab's music.

The exhibit was a captivating meeting of minds. Long had moved to New York from Philadelphia in 1981 and became involved in an art scene with close links to the musical world. 'We're living in a five-floor walk-up with four people in what's called a railroad apartment, and we're listening to the Gang of Four,' he explains. 'And we're all into Marxism and reading [French philosophers] Deleuze and Guattari, and people are getting shot and people are dead on your doorstep.

'We're going to these clubs, especially the Tunnel over on the West side. And we're seeing art bands like Glenn Branca up onstage with eighteen guitarists, and then the next is Blondie, and then the next is Grandmaster Flash.' Long is in full flow, and I don't want to interrupt, but this seems like a very *Stereolab* amalgam of influences, with politics meeting philosophy meeting the musical avant-garde and pure pop.

Long first came across Stereolab in the early 90s, when his art career was on the rise but he was still working odd jobs to make ends meet. 'There was one room in the studio that was just for making cassette tapes, and I had tons of early electronica,' he says. 'I was making these really bizarre tapes, and I was doing construction work. I would bring them to the site, and my crew was all artists, and they were like, Charles, your tapes are fucking us up in the studio. Keep making these fucked-up tapes.'

One fateful day in 1993, Long paid a visit to his favourite New York record store, where they recommended him *Peng!* on CD and the 'John Cage Bubblegum' seven-inch. It was meant to be: Cage is a hugely important artist for Long, and he would later work with the idea of gum on *Bubble Gum Station*, the lurid pink centrepiece of *The Amorphous Body Study Center*.

It didn't take long for the artist to see the connections between his work and Stereolab's music. 'I listened to *Peng!* [while] making some crazy piece in plaster. I was using crack vials that I was picking up off the street; I was extending them through clay and casting their path and then making this *forest* of crack vials,' he says. 'I'm listening to *Peng!*, and I'm like, *Okay, shit's lining up here. It's really making sense.*'

Long went to see the band play live at Maxwell's in Hoboken, New Jersey, in November 1993. 'I brought with me a cassette of my weird electronic noise, bad records, and I came up to the stage afterwards and I gave it to Laetitia,' he says. 'It was a great show. They had a tiny LED strip that had words running about capitalism during the show. And I was just in heaven. I was just like, *Okay, everything's gonna work out now. Now I know my family.*'

Long's love of—and connection to—Stereolab grew. He saw the band play live again in New York in 1994, and this time he came prepared. 'I talked to the band more, and I was fawning over them, saying, Everything's making sense: the utopia, the dystopia, the Marxism, we're forming our own family,' he says.

The artist was especially taken with the band's use of analogue synths—a photo of which features prominently on the cover of *Mars Audiac Quintet*. 'As a sculptor, with this new thing coming out called the CD, which I hated, I was like, What's going to happen to music?' he says. 'It's going to get turned into digits, when we have this wonderful history of forcing electrical energy through these gates that create this warm buzz. That's the body; it's like we're heading into dematerialisation. But there's a way in which the Moog is a body and that the transistor is a body.'

When Tanya Bonakdar offered Long an exhibition in late 1994, his mind immediately gravitated toward Stereolab. 'When I was at the last Stereolab concert, when I was watching it, standing there in this dirty, stinky, beer-soaked room, I'm thinking, *There's got to be a better way*,' he says. 'I love this band so much; I would love to make a place where you're sitting down and you're with people and you're connecting with people. You're not just facing the stage, and it's not this endless endurance experience of super-loud music coming at you while you just stare at people playing music. How do we honour the love that I have for this band?'

While he was pondering this, one sleepless night, Long picked up a piece of blue modelling clay and added a keychain and RCA jack to it. 'I look at this thing and I go, That's it. That's fucking *it*. I'm going to fucking make a show where you have to bring your analogue blob body and plug into amorphous blobs to hear music that Stereolab makes,' he says.

Inspired, Long immediately started hammering out the *Amorphous Body Study Center* manifesto and making sketches. English novelist J.G. Ballard and Canadian director David Cronenberg were both influences, as, of course, was Stereolab's music and the concert environment. 'There are going to be these blobs with consciousness that is beamed into it from some other location that gives you the sense that you're a self,' Long says of his inspiration for the show. 'And then you'll plug the blob in, and you'll be connecting to these other blobs. That's what was really driving this. And the idea that, *Why would you go to an art gallery to see art? Why would you go to see a band? Why would you do anything?* You would just have your blob plug in and go.'

Long explains that he was also focused on the band's retro-futurism and 'the way that they were pushing analogue into the foreground. So you would have this incredibly dumb, bloppy sound, you know, *bloop, bloop, bloop*. All kinds of crazy sounds of transistors and boxes that are being connected with chords.'

He describes retro-futurism as 'the feeling of making art and music for a future that's probably not going to come. That's why [they're] borrowing from the 50s and 60s and 70s to make that music. Because that is a utopian idea: how things are going to be great. But we can see that they're not going to be because capital, which they [Stereolab] constantly bring up, is a pile of shit, and it's destroying the future that's never going to come. So, we got to have our future now in a fantasy.'

Bonakdar—a British woman who Long calls 'super fascinating and beautiful'—loved his Stereolab idea, which meant the artist now had to get the band on board. Their US A&R man was dismissive of the idea, but Long managed to contact Martin Pike, who loved it.

Long travelled to London in November 1994, only a few months before the exhibition was due to open, to meet Stereolab in a London café. 'I'm so nervous because it dawns on me that this idea is possibly the dumbest idea I've ever come up with, and that the art world will hate it,' he says. 'I saw the critics that I knew, and I saw them turning their noses up at it—that I had done this cool, fun thing with a band—and that they would not see it as critical and serious, like regular art.

'And I said, I'm bringing my favourite band into this shitty, stupid art world. And I still think it's a shitty, stupid art world. I love the community. I think all the people in it tend to be wonderful. But the way that we operate is brutal.'

Long showed the band some preparatory drawings he had made on the plane and explained his idea for the show. 'And they were so sweet, you know?' he says, still audibly delighted by the memory, three decades on. 'Laetitia is just like, Charles, this is really beautiful. And Tim's like, Yeah, it's great, what do you want us to do? Because they didn't quite get it yet. And I said, Listen, you just do what you do. Because I am your carrier. I am your delivery device. I am your format. I've already internalised you.'

I ask Long if he considers Stereolab to be an 'arty' band, with their love of the Situationist International and Dada. It's a wildly open question, of course, but he agrees vigorously.

'What I saw in the band, personally, was at the moment that music was going to disappear into digits, I saw music by the band being made material,' he replies. 'It was made warm and fuzzy by having to force that electricity through those transistors, that bodies were necessary, that this wasn't code. And that they were doing it at a time when we knew that this was probably going to be the end of it, and we were all running around—the smart ones of us—we were all running around buying vinyl and buying tube amps.

'I think the band evoked, certainly in this artist, in a huge way, visual and physical form,' he elaborates. 'Their music sounded like that, that they were a bit of a supergroup themselves, with Tim and Laetitia and Mary being all so different and Andy banging it out on those drums like a motherfucker.'

Long also mentions the band's propensity for borrowing from

other styles of music. 'They were stealing like crazy,' he says, making a comparison with David Bowie. 'Laetitia gave me a cassette at the opening of our show. And it's French Yé-yé music. I had never really heard it. I mean, I knew some of the more famous people, but that cassette was so eye-opening for me.

'I think, in a way, that is also what makes a great art band—that you go around and you rescue the failures. You don't necessarily [have to] be like Elvis borrowing from Little Richard and stuff like that . . . you go around and you borrow from people that are never going to be heard from again. And artists become attracted to that. They recognise that. They go, Wait, this is like music my parents listen to, but it's more fucked up.'

Long returned to New York to work frantically on the exhibition, and Stereolab headed into the studio to record the seven songs that would soundtrack it.* 'I know for a fact that they had two drawings up in the room [when they were recording],' he says. 'They had the drawing for the *Bubble Gum Station*, and they had the drawing for *Good Separation And Soft Blue*. And so they made it based on those two, for sure.'

Long says that when he received a tape in the post with the songs Stereolab had recorded, he was too scared to play it. 'I just stood there looking at it,' he says. 'I didn't play it for probably ten hours. I was so, so afraid. I thought, *What have I done? I brought my favourite band into this thing. What have they done? It could be terrible. It could be amazing.* I was scared to play it, and I did finally play it, and I was like, *Wow. I can't believe I'm one of the first people hearing my band.*'

The purpose of *The Amorphous Body Study Center*, according to the exhibition's official website, was 'to promote a better understanding between the body and the mind, to emphasise the new role of the body as prescribed by the rapid developments in communication'. To do so, Long created a number of 'amorphous bodies' in rubber and plastic that are described as 'distributors for the audio works created by the band'.

There are six pieces in total. *Bubble Gum Station*, the exhibition's centrepiece, was described by journalist Simon Reynolds in *Artforum* as

* On the *Aluminum Tunes* compilation, which came out in 1998, *Amorphous*'s track six, 'Space Moment', and track seven, an instrumental reprise of 'The Extension Trip', are combined into one track.

'an enormous mound of plasticine that the viewer is invited to mould and mark', inspired by the tacky globs of bubblegum that children sometimes stick under their school desks.

Long calls *Bubble Gum Station* 'the mother, I guess? . . . I don't know whether I'm the mother or Stereolab's the mother, but we have a giant breastfeeding these children. And they're nursing at the breasts, massaging it with their hands, making this thing and looking kind of funny, too.'

Buloop Buloop is a water cooler with a vast glob of plastic on top of it; *Changing Our Mind* is like a cow's udder rendered in bright, purple-pigmented rubber; *3 To 1 In Groovy Green* contrasts a rather staid couch with a nebulous blob in the most artificial green colour; *Good Separation In Soft Blue* puts five white cushions around a seemingly misshapen blue globule; and *We Love You Big Dummy* is a black rubber work on top of a stereo component cabinet.*

'A visit to the centre will allow one to commune as a body amongst other bodies through plugging in with headsets to any one of the amorphous sculptures created by Charles Long,' the website explains. The band's music 'not only serves to establish a conducive mood for the mind to consider the public body but the headsets discourage the need to use the body to talk. This is a time to listen, observe and be.'

Perhaps this appears quite serious when written down on paper. In reality, though, *The Amorphous Body Study Center* sounds like a *riot* (to my infinite regret, I have never seen it in the flesh).

'It was really fun,' Simon Reynolds tells me of the show. 'It was very different to a normal exhibition. You were invited to touch some of the exhibits; not all of them, but some of them you were actually meant to palpate this plasticine.' It was, he explains, 'a different vibe to your usual grave, solemn exhibition, White Cube space, everyone shuffling around, staring reverently at the art and reading the artist's rationales on the white card boards. It was goofy and fun.'

I ask Long how he decided which song to pair with which sculpture,

* Appropriately, art critic Mark Van De Walle, in his review of the exhibition, focused on its retro-futurism: 'All of the works in the Amorphous Body Study Center are plastic-based, reminding us that, as in the fifties, sixties, and seventies, the future belongs to plastic. Plastic is the real stuff of Retrofuturism, the basic material for its base materialism.'

expecting a long and thorough explanation. But no. 'Martin shows up at the gallery first, and we've got the show installed. But we don't know what songs are going to go with what pieces yet—we hadn't even thought about it. And the show is going to open that night.

'It was a close call . . . we had all these boom boxes in the art office, and we popped one CD into each, and then we pick up a track and then it was just like, *boom, boom, boom, boom*. I think Tim and Laetitia were there, and we just assigned the tracks to the stations. And it went perfectly.'

This approach, Long says, was typical of the freewheeling collaborative methods that he has used ever since. He mentions John Cage's idea of indeterminacy—a way of composing music in which some aspects are left open to chance or to the interpreter's choice. 'This really goes to the core of what I wrote about in the *Amorphous Body Study Center* manifesto,' he says. 'And it comes out of the band. I was obsessed with this dualistic idea, autonomy and connection, and I still am to this day.'

The idea of the exhibition, he adds, 'was that we would be really acknowledging and distilling out autonomy and creating the connections between it. So you would bring your blob to the gallery, hook up to a blob, and someone else would bring their blob and connect. But now that we have three blobs connected, we're using Stereolab as the consciousness juice that is connecting it all.'

The Amorphous Body Study Center was a huge success for Long, who would later collaborate with the band on two further works: *Unity Purity Occasional* and *B.U.A. (Burnt Umber Assembly): An Entanglement Of Wholes.*

Long says that Stereolab's involvement brought artistically inclined bands like Sonic Youth and Yo La Tengo to see the New York show. 'I'm sure the show became part of how [Stereolab's music] ended up in all the art schools,' he adds. 'I would meet all these people over the years, slightly younger than me, typically, and they'd be like, Well, that's all we listen to.

'It's the music that fits,' he says. 'It's optimistic, it's political, it's romantic, it's fun. It's got a lot of weird sources. It's eclectic, and every album is just chock-a-block full of really new and very strong songs. So, it ended up being very important for a lot of people that I know that didn't get involved in music like I did; they make beautiful paintings, beautiful sculptures, but the music fit. It helped them make these kinds of pop surrealist artworks.'

For Stereolab, writing music for an exhibition was a chance to clear their minds, away from the stress of recording a new studio album. Gane has said he was having doubts about where to go with the band's music after the success of *Mars Audiac Quintet*, and his rather dismissive comments in the *MAQ* reissue sleeve notes about 'Melochord Seventy-Five (Original Pulse version)', a version of a song that would be released on *Music For The Amorphous Body Study Center*—he essentially says it's boring—don't suggest a band bursting with song ideas.

This seems harsh: 'Melochord Seventy-Five' is no 'Ping Pong', but it has a certain Kraftwerk-cruising-the-Autobahn charm. Elsewhere, the exquisite 'Pop Quiz' and 'The Brush Descends The Length' touch on jazz, an influence that would become much more important to the band later on; 'Space Moment' is admirably drifty; 'How To Play Your Internal Organs Overnight' has a gorgeous string arrangement; and the lyrics to 'The Extension Trip', which touch on plasticity and flexibility, suggest that Laetitia was paying close attention to Long's aesthetic.

It is, in short, an excellent Stereolab EP to listen to while lounging around drinking water, playing with plasticine, and idly contemplating 'the public body', with none of the vicious shrills and climaxes of some of the band's earlier music.

Recording *Music For The Amorphous Body Study Center* also helped to pave the way for Stereolab's monumental fourth studio album, *Emperor Tomato Ketchup*. Gane relates in the sleeve notes to the reissue of *Emperor* that the band had started working on it in London before recording *Amorphous Body Study Center*, but things hadn't really clicked. He felt deflated by the process and was unable to connect to the tracks that the band had recorded. Something was missing.

A couple of days later, the band returned to Blackwing Studios to work on *Amorphous Body Study Center*, and the atmosphere changed. 'It really put us back in the mood,' Gane writes in the sleeve notes, 'and four days after finishing the Charles Long record we finally arrived in the USA to work on the second half of *Emperor Tomato Ketchup*.'

The band's experience with Charles Long and *Music For The Amorphous Body Study Center* was positive, then, with this fun and slightly silly record serving as a palate cleanser for a band at the end of their collective tether.

•

Apart from soundtracking *The Amorphous Body Study Center*, 1995 was a quiet year for Stereolab in terms of new releases. The band appeared on a joint flexi-disc released by the Wurlitzer Jukebox label alongside Melbourne indie band The Cat's Miaow, their two contributions, 'The Eclipse' and 'Yes Sir! I Can Moogie', accounting for less than two minutes of music.

They also released a split seven-inch with Yo La Tengo, to be sold on their joint UK tour, pairing Yo La Tengo's 'Evanescent Psychic Pez Drop' with Stereolab's 'The Long Hair Of Death'. While the Stereolab song, with its vocal drone, is decent enough, it is perhaps more notable for later being torn apart by Nurse With Wound on the 1997 EP *Simple Headphone Mind*, where it is converted into two suitably epic tracks: 'Simple Headphone Mind' and the twenty-one-minute 'Trippin' With The Birds'.

July 1995 saw the release of *Refried Ectoplasm* (*Switched On Volume 2*), the band's second round-up of singles and rarities. It also included the previously unreleased song 'Sadistic', a raspy punk number whose lyrics are based on Marquis de Sade's *Dialogue Between A Priest And A Dying Man*, considered one of the most direct expressions of atheism in de Sade's work.

'These, my dear fellow, are the only principles which we should follow. There is no need of religion or God to appreciate and act upon them: the sole requirement is a good heart,' the dying man concludes toward the end of de Sade's piece.

Stereolab borrow the second part of this creed for 'Sadistic', and it seems an excellent summation of the band's humanistic beliefs, as reflected back through their art. It was timely, too: a good, sturdy heart would certainly be required over the next few months, as Stereolab prepared for one of the most pivotal moments of their first decade.

09

'METRONOMIC UNDERGROUND' GROOVE

Stereolab have released so much music over their lifetime that the idea of the band struggling for inspiration seems innately wrong. They are artists, magicians of the avant-garde, but they are also workers—a band who put in the hours.

And yet Stereolab *did* struggle when it came to following up *Mars Audiac Quintet*, a record that marked a commercial peak for the band and also, in a way, the end of their poppiest phase. *MAQ* was, in fact, the last album that Stereolab would record in a way that most indie bands would recognise.

Tim Gane explains in the sleeve notes of the *Mars Audiac Quintet* reissue that it was the final album the band rehearsed before recording. 'One of the things we realised around this time was that we had to make a leap into more unknown areas to progress,' he notes, 'using the old *studio as instrument* concept really became an important component to our realising that.'

'It was a difficult time,' Gane explained to *The Guardian* in 2019. 'There was bad feeling, a lot of relentless touring.' After the band had released studio albums in 1992, '93, and '94, 1995 passed without a new Stereolab LP hitting the shelves—a sign, perhaps, of their creative struggles.

Eventually, two different songs would offer Stereolab a way out of their morass. One was 'Young Lungs', which was eventually released on the 1996 EP *Cybele's Reverie*, a record that cued up the release of the band's fourth album, *Emperor Tomato Ketchup*.*

'Young Lungs' was perhaps the last Stereolab song to be played live in concert before it was recorded, as the band increasingly turned to using the studio as an instrument—a way of working that was pioneered by the BBC's (very Stereolab friendly) Radiophonic Workshop in the 1950s, then perfected by Joe Meek, Phil Spector, The Beatles, The Beach Boys, and other artists.

'Young Lungs' doesn't sound like an obvious leap into the unknown when viewed from a modern-day perspective, and you can certainly imagine 1995 Stereolab building the song to a triumphant peak on their joint tour with Yo La Tengo that summer. But what the song does have is a sense of space, influenced by the extraordinary jazz composer Sun Ra and his use of simple riffs among his far-out musical experimentations.

Gane also notes the influence of Tortoise—a Chicago band who would go on to become very important to Stereolab's development—in the sound of 'Young Lungs'. Tortoise drummer John McEntire would co-produce *Emperor Tomato Ketchup*, and Gane suggests the song may have been influenced by the prospect of working with him.

In 1995, Tortoise were in the ascendant. Their eponymous debut album was hailed with positive reviews on its release in 1994, and their career-defining second LP, *Millions Now Living Will Never Die*, blew minds when it came out in January 1996. It was around this time that Stereolab and Tortoise toured the UK and Ireland together, releasing a split seven-inch to mark the occasion. Tortoise contributed the enigmatically bubbling 'Vaus', while Stereolab took the cryptic option with 'Speedy Car', a racing jazz number in 5/4 time that sounds like Ronnie Scott's Jazz Club after too many Italian espressos and French cigarettes.

* There is also a version of the song called 'Old Lungs' that was released on an album from festival promoter All Tomorrows Parties in 2002, and which later turned up on the 2019 reissue of *Emperor Tomato Ketchup*.

McEntire's introduction to Stereolab was *Space Age Batchelor Pad Music*. 'I fell in love with it immediately,' he says. Given the tight connections that would later bind Tortoise and Stereolab, I wondered if he felt like he had encountered a kindred spirit. 'I didn't, really,' he says, after a long pause, 'because Tortoise wasn't super active yet at that time. I did come to feel that way later on, for sure, even though stylistically we were very different.'

McEntire first met the band in person at a US gig when Stereolab were supported by Gastr Del Sol (a Chicago band that featured future Stereolab producer Jim O'Rourke), which suggests their concert at Chicago's Metro in September 1994, 'and then we just sort of kept in touch'.

The love between the two bands was a two-way affair. 'Tortoise used to sleep on our floor when they first came over from Chicago,' says Moonshake's David Callahan. 'John McEntire said the roster of Too Pure was, to quote, *immaculate*. So, you can probably figure out from there why Chicago became a second home to Stereolab once they started playing in the States.'

McEntire says that there was 'obviously a commonality' between Stereolab and Tortoise, 'in terms of what the inspirations and the objectives were. We both were mining very deeply a lot of the other music that we really admired in the past, from all sorts of genres, seeing how that could be somehow transformed into a new palette.'

For their troubles, Tortoise were labelled 'post-rock'—a term notably employed by Simon Reynolds to describe bands like Seefeel and Disco Inferno, who were, in his words, 'using rock instrumentation for non-rock purposes, using guitars as facilitators of timbre and textures rather than riffs and power chords'. With the release of *Millions Now Living Will Never Die*, post-rock became an accepted descriptor for Tortoise's drifting, elegant ambient rockscapes.

Stereolab are sometimes also called post-rock, too, and while I don't necessarily agree with the description—they are just too *pop* for that—there is certainly some shared territory with the post-rock bands in their use of space, as well as the influence of Krautrock, jazz, and minimalism on their work.

'I was never really sure if Stereolab belonged in that category (admittedly a pretty diffuse and open-ended one),' Reynolds tells me. 'I suppose around *Emperor*, when they were working with John McEntire, they were quite closely aligned. But they never really got with the modern digital technology, which to me is a hallmark of what I thought post-rock was about. They are like an edge case or fellow traveller to post rock—a bit like Pram, maybe.'

'Young Lungs' is one of the best examples of Stereolab's proximity to post-rock styles. The song, in both its 'Young' and 'Old' recordings, is driven by a simple, fuzzed-up bass line, to which the band add interlocking layers of melody via guitar, brass, and keyboard, each tier complementing but never filling the mix, like an old-school cartoon animation where each new drawing adds new depth to the field. It is a notably spacious song, with the band feeling no obligation to fill every last nook and cranny.

'Young Lungs' is not a song in a rush. Motion comes from the introduction of new layers, and while the band would build the song to a frenzy live, this was a very different kind of frenzy to the supercharged rush of 'Super-Electric'. 'Young Lungs' is a thoughtful song—a ponder, rather than a brain rush—and if it never quite got the love it deserves, that might be down to the recording, which Gane says the band never got right.

This was a challenging time for Stereolab. 'I couldn't do it anymore,' Gane told *Wired* magazine in 2008. 'I just had a brain meltdown. It occurred around the end of an album called *Mars Audiac Quintet*. After we finished that album, there was about a year where there was nothing interesting that I could write. Because I just couldn't think any more in this style that I thought was interesting, it felt a total trap for me, it weakened me a lot.'

This period was, Gane explained, 'the worst period for me in the history of the band, in terms of writing the stuff and also in terms of, like, general sort of happiness. And I think that at that point,' he added, 'the band probably should have stopped, or would have stopped, normally.'

'Young Lungs' offered a new perspective for a stuttering Stereolab—Gane has called it a 'catalyst'—where they didn't have to rush around frantically and fill every available sonic space.

The other song that helped rescue Stereolab from the wilderness was 'ABC', a cover of a track by the New York avant-garde psychedelic rock band The Godz, released on the 1996 compilation album *Godz Is Not A Put-On* alongside covers by the likes of Royal Trux and Comet Gain.

'ABC' isn't a particularly well-known Stereolab track, even after its re-release on the 2022 compilation *Pulse Of The Early Brain*, and Laetitia barely appears on it (or at least she's not easily heard until the song's final moments). But recording it unlocked something in Gane's musical brain. 'Listening to their track and thinking about how to do a cover of a song that was pretty much a free improvisation, I heard four notes go by that stuck in my mind for some reason,' he explains in the *ETK* reissue's sleeve notes. 'Listening back to them again, I decided to loop them and keep on repeating them, building them up into a kind of hypnotic pulse that lurched every time it came back around.'

It was at this time that the lightbulb went off. Stereolab had always used repetition for artistic means, a two-chord sequence, for example, serving as a base for subtle changes in tone and intensity. But 'ABC' offered a new path: using repetition to create what Gane called 'small melodic cells, from bass riffs to melodies' that can co-exist within one song, 'flowing in and around each other until the track became a mass of activity and the final song could be sculpted out of it'.*

This pairing—the space of 'Young Lungs' and the free-flowing loops of 'ABC'—would combine into one of Stereolab's masterpieces: *Emperor Tomato Ketchup*, released in March 1996.

Gane has said *Emperor* was the album he most enjoyed writing. 'For me, it was totally new,' he told *Wired*. 'Now, listening to them, it actually seems like a natural process to go from the one before [*Mars Audiac Quintet*] to that one. It seemed radically different at the time, but now it seems smooth.'

I disagree. *Emperor* was a leap forward for Stereolab in many different ways. The album was recorded between London and Chicago in 1995, with Paul Tipler at the helm at Blackwing and John McEntire

* The idea of 'cells', incidentally, can be traced back to American composer Terry Riley. His pioneering 1964 composition 'In C' is made up of fifty-three short melodic phrases—or 'cells'.

producing the four Chicago tracks: 'Les Yper-Sound', 'Tomorrow Is Already Here', 'Monstre Sacre', and 'Anonymous Collective'.

Ray Dickaty, who played saxophone on *Emperor Tomato Ketchup*, remembers the London sessions as 'sort of ramshackle, but cosy . . . a good professional sound, especially with Paul at the controls.'

Gane invited Dickaty, who he knew from his work with Moonshake and the jazz-influenced band Skree, to add saxophone to a number of tracks. In the end, Dickaty's saxophone only appears on 'Percolator' and 'Freestyle Dumpling', which was recorded at the *Emperor* sessions and came out on a single released with the Japanese edition of the *Aluminum Tunes* compilation.

Dickaty remembers playing on 'Metronomic Underground' and 'Cybele's Reverie' as well, adding that he didn't receive instructions from Tim as to what to play in the studio. 'They would just play the track, and I would improvise and try out many different ideas quite quickly—because you had to be quite quick,' he says. 'And then we'd slowly start to hone down the idea that was coming through that seemed to work: like, *Yeah, that's it. That's the one.*'

Dickaty remembers being particularly impressed with Andy Ramsay on drums and Duncan Brown on bass—'just how tight they were together. They could just continue playing without seeming fatigued,' he says. 'It's like, *Here we go again*. Just continue. Twenty minutes of that, with precision, is amazing.'

He was also impressed by the idea of composing from musical cells. 'Now lots of composers use it, and to be honest, it's one of my compositional tools as well, the idea of cells and cells that then coalesce and produce something else. That's when the surprise happens, when you start layering cells on top of each other.

'Especially now, with the technology of computers, moving them slightly in and out of each other, until something happens—a harmony or a melody starts to emerge, something that you could not have actually sat down and written with pencil and paper. So, the cells idea opens up an awful lot of structural narratives that can go in different directions.'

It was, according to McEntire, a pretty relaxed arrangement that took him to *Emperor*'s producer chair. 'Tortoise played a show opening for Stereolab in St Louis, the university there,' he explains. 'Tim and

I got to talking afterwards, and I just put the invite out there: *If you all would ever be interested in having me produce, engineer, something for you. You know* . . . [come] on over to Chicago.'

McEntire wasn't aware at the time that Stereolab had been struggling to record in London. 'I found that out very much retrospectively,' he says. 'I think it's funny what he said in the liner notes for the reissue, about those tracks that I worked on. I kind of agree. I think Paul's amazing, and I think stuff that he did for them is absolutely spectacular. But I kind of see Tim's point, too, because I think that those songs that he brought to me required a bit of a push, beyond just a documentary sort of style.'

Working in a new environment, with new friends, proved exactly what Stereolab needed to kickstart their creative process. McEntire was the perfect foil in many ways: he not only played several instruments—on the record, he is credited with analogue synthesizer, electronics, maracas, tambourine, vibraphone, and guitar—he had also studied Technology In Music And Related Arts at the prestigious Oberlin Conservatory Of Music.

'[The sessions] were great,' says McEntire, his face lighting up at the memory. 'It went really quickly—in my memory, at least. Then we did a fair amount of experimentation, stuff like the drums on "Les Yper-Sound". And the synth programming on that, too—that was kind of a revelatory thing. Tim especially was just so willing to entertain any idea, the tracks with the marimbas and things like that, he was definitely happy to accommodate oddball ideas.'

Emperor was also the first Stereolab album to feature Morgane Lhote, who had joined on keyboards in 1995 to replace Kath Gifford, making her live debut in Nottingham in June.* Lhote, who would stay with Stereolab until 2001, has a similar story to Laetitia Sadier in many ways. She grew up in Paris but left the French capital for London, in search of musical adventure. 'I don't especially like Paris, which is way too conservative for my tastes, and I wanted to start a band in London, where the music scene was a million times better,' she told *Feminatronic* in 2016.

* Slint's David Pajo also played live bass with the band in 1995 but didn't record with them.

Lhote's introduction to the Stereolab world was effortlessly chic, starting with a party in her parents' flat. 'It must have been in 1993,' she tells me. 'I'm from Paris, from the 13th District. My parents had an apartment there, and every summer they would go to Brittany. I had their apartment to myself, and I was eighteen, so I had a party, of course. And it's quite a small music scene [in Paris], and everybody knew each other. So, I knew the guys from Daft Punk. And I think some people from that music scene invited Tim and Laetitia. I met quite a lot of new friends at that party. It was quite a *meaningful* party.'

A year and a half later, when Lhote was twenty, she moved to London. 'Uni wasn't working for me,' she explains. 'So, I was like, I'm going to go to London and start my own band. And then I bumped into Tim in the streets, and it was like, *Oh, you live here?*'

Initially, Lhote was going to join Laetitia in her side project, Monade, who made their recorded debut in 1996. 'I saw Laetitia at a concert—it was one of the small concerts in Camden—and she said, Oh, we should do some music together. Come round and we'll jam,' Lhote explains. 'I was going to play guitar with her. I don't even know if the project was called Monade at the time. But Laetitia said, Tim was asking me if you play keyboards. And I said, No, but I can learn.'

The band gave her three months to learn fifty songs. 'I would spend eight hours a day: it was like a full-time job learning the keyboards,' says Lhote, who was working in a pub in Camden at the time. 'Three months later, I went round to their place, and they [Tim and Laetitia] gave me an audition, which was pretty relaxed. I wasn't even really nervous because it was so chill.

'They had this portable keyboard, and it was not even a full-size keyboard, so it was kind of hard to play because the keys were so small. And whenever you would press on certain keys, they would stay stuck. They said, Okay, we're gonna test you on "Lo Boob Oscillator". And so I played that, and they were like, Yeah, you're fine. And that was it.'

Lhote joined Stereolab in the summer of 1995, after the band had already recorded several songs for *Emperor Tomato Ketchup* at Blackwing Studios in London. Among the Blackwing tracks was the epic album opener 'Metronomic Underground', the second song written for *Emperor Tomato Ketchup* after 'Young Lungs' and, for me, the most important song on the album, where loops, space, and time combine into an almighty groove.

What, exactly, do I mean by a groove? It is a term that seems both utterly banal and ruthlessly packed with meaning; a word long used by musicians that seems to disappear under the microscope of analysis, a bit like jazz's elusive 'swing'.

British musicologist Richard Middleton, in his book *Key Terms In Popular Music And Culture*, says that, although the concept of groove has 'long [been] familiar in musicians' own usage', academia has only recently tried to start to analyse it. And, perhaps, not entirely satisfactorily. He writes that a groove 'marks an understanding of rhythmic patterning that underlies its role in producing the characteristic rhythmic "feel" of a piece'. That makes some sense, but it seems to be kicking the problem further down the timeline, opening up questions about what, in turn, 'feel' means.

Perhaps the most important thing about groove is that you know it when you hear it. Stereolab certainly have it, on 'Metronomic Underground' in particular and on *Emperor Tomato Ketchup* in general. Neu!, Can, and Tortoise, too. But it's not often found in indie bands of the 1990s. Moose, fun though they are, don't really have groove. Nor, I would argue, does PJ Harvey, a contemporary of Stereolab, although fans of both may disagree.

A groove is something you can dance to—a subtle force of propulsion, where constancy meets change. It is a musical call to action, rhythm in motion. A lot of it has to do with the bass and its ability to keep a pulse that is constant, interesting, and yet maybe slightly off-piste. Think of the masterful bass lines on The Temptations' 'Papa Was A Rollin' Stone' or James Brown's 'Cold Sweat, Pt 1.'—both are entirely unflashy yet absolutely vital to the songs' success. James Brown, much like Stereolab, was fond of songs that did away with unnecessary chord changes, focusing instead on pushing one note to its extreme. Is *this* the groove? Perhaps. Or at least one idea of it.

'A big part of it [the groove] is the way the drummer and the bass player communicate, and how their feels hopefully complement each other,' says McEntire. 'That's the foundation for the groove.'

The ability of the bass player to *lock* into a groove and stay there might sound easy for someone who has never done it. But it requires discipline, commitment and concentration, the musician's personal ego taking a back seat to the good of the band. And Duncan Brown—on his last album with Stereolab—fulfils the role to perfection on *Emperor*.

Take 'Metronomic Underground'. After a brief drum and squelch synth intro—drummer Andy Ramsay is also in excellent form on this album—the bass comes in with a brilliantly inventive pattern that is simultaneously melodic, rhythmic, utterly solid, and tinged with a jazz-infused otherness.

When I think of 'Metronomic Underground', it is the bass line I think of first. It is perfect—an utterly fabulous hook in a song that is full of them. But it's very much used at the service of the song; twenty-two seconds in, the bass locks in and doesn't move an inch for the next seven and a half minutes, even as Ramsay is excused the odd drum fill.

The bass, even more than the drums, provides the rhythmic pulse of 'Metronomic Underground'. The bass line is there on the demo version of the song, which was released on the *Emperor Tomato Ketchup* reissue; McEntire says that Gane always included a bass line when he made a demo, which gives an idea of how important the instrument is to him.

Simon Johns, who played bass with Stereolab from the recording of *Cobra And Phases Group Play Voltage In The Milky Night* to the band's hiatus in 2009, explains how the bass would provide the foundation for the group's recording process.* 'Tim would write demos on his four-track, on his guitar,' he says. 'They'd take these demo cassettes, stick them in the computer and arrange the song [using Pro Tools], and then record the drum part. Then I would come in and play the bass over the top. Tim had written most of the bass parts, and some of them were more taxing than others.'

To record these, the group developed a method of building the bass line up in groups of individual notes, rather than recording the whole bass line live. 'It's just expediency,' Johns explains. 'I can sit there for hours learning how to play that one bass line, wasting vast amounts of

* This is, of course, *after Emperor Tomato Ketchup* and following the advent of Pro Tools. But it is instructive as to how the bass fits into the group's general feel.

money. Or we can just do it really quickly by recording it in chunks.'

'We weren't spending hours in the studio, coming up with wild and crazy bass lines,' Johns adds. 'I could tune into the way that Tim conceptualised the bass line and how it works. So, I take that material, make it a reality, record it, put it together in the computer, and then that would be it. And then on to the next layer: the guitars and the keyboards. And that's where the more involved recording and experimentation happened, with the more melodic instruments on the top.'

The band's rhythm tracks could be fast, complicated, and hard to play. But they were also rock solid, as the song demanded. 'There's no showmanship, there's no wanking in the rhythm section,' says Johns. 'The [songs'] chords are so dense. There are stacks of two or three chords going on at the same time, with different extensions.

'You can have a bass line that moves through those chords quite effectively. But you have to keep it under control. Otherwise, it just falls apart: it sounds messy; it sounds chaotic. And if you don't want the music to sound chaotic, the way that you keep it under control is to make sure the rhythm section is stable.'

'Of the albums or EPs I recorded with Stereolab, we never recorded live—as a band, I mean, we all recorded our parts separately,' Lhote adds. 'We would practice our parts, and then everybody would go in and record their parts for the day. Before the recordings, they would give me a tape with the songs, with Laetitia's vocals and Tim's guitar. I would say my parts mostly were an accompaniment to the guitar, playing similar chords to the guitar but being like a rhythmic reinforcement, having more syncopated parts. Tim's guitar would be the grounding chord. The keyboards on top would be sometimes the same chords but with more syncopated rhythmic aspects to it.'

'Metronomic Underground', originally called 'Chrome Tubby' in a nod to dub legend King Tubby, was built from the bottom up, bit by bit, and then pieced together at the mixing stage. And you can hear this in the song, which is a perfect illustration of Gane's idea of small melodic cells that build to a mass of activity. Every part of 'Metronomic Underground'—including the voice—is operating in its own perfect loop; every part has its own distinct space, but these coalesce into a perfect whole.

Gane says in the sleeve notes that 'Metronomic Underground' marks the beginning in earnest of the 'arranged in the studio/studio as instrument' approach that would become the band's norm from hereon in. But this quasi-scientific sounding approach shouldn't be confused with something cold or unfeeling. Yes, the song is metronomic—it is *insanely* regular—but it is also bustling with life and spontaneity.

'Metronomic Underground' is also one of the times that Stereolab came closest to out-and-out dance music. I remember a DJ—probably Rob Bright—play the song in the second room of famed Manchester club Bugged Out!, sometime in the summer of 1996, and people dancing along like it was the most natural thing in the world, as opposed to a new experiment in sound by a crazed Anglo-French political rock band.

The song was also remixed by Wagon Christ, aka English producer Luke Vibert, known for his eclectic productions, embarrassment of pseudonyms, and links to the Aphex Twin. Stereolab have only ever commissioned a handful of remixes, but Vibert's love of warped grooves and odd synth sounds made him a suitable fit.

Journalist Simon Reyolds says that there was a certain connection between Vibert and Stereolab in their musical methods. 'Vibert is a huge fan of library music and actually put out a couple of compilations of it,' he says. 'A lot of people making trip-hop or even jungle in the 90s, a lot of the practice of that music is being a record collector and digging in the crates and finding obscure loops and samples and things. And it's very similar to the way that someone like Tim would scavenge through the past.'

This is something you often hear about Tim Gane. He is known as a brilliant collector of sounds and manipulator of influences, not afraid to borrow a musical idea that he will then bend and collage into beautiful new shapes. Reynolds speaks of Gane 'processing pop history. One way to innovate is to do something completely new,' he says. 'Another way is to do these weird additive things, combining very unlikely things or finding a latent, secret potential in something in the past.'

Emperor Tomato Ketchup is home to several other mighty grooves. 'Percolator' is a brilliant example of the band's new theory of interconnecting cells—a wildly bubbling bass line that sounds about twice as fast as anything else on the album meeting insistent keyboard stabs, a jazzy drumbeat and an alto saxophone freak-out, courtesy of Ray Dickaty. 'Motoroller Scalatron' sits somewhere between mantra, call to action, and intellectual puzzle as a bewitching drum rhythm combines with a bass line off on its own logical course, anchored by simple, repeating synth chords and a nursery rhyme vocal that attempts to unite these disparate voices into collective action. 'OLV 26' sounds like a homage to Kraftwerk's *Autobahn* album, sitting somewhere between the driving grooves of the title track and the more astral sounds of side B. The bizarrely speedy, oddly pulsing 'Les Yper-Sound' is like a groove collapsing under the weight of its own dark momentum. And so on.

Overall, *Emperor Tomato Ketchup* is probably the Stereolab album on which the groove's rhythmical force runs strongest, but there would be many other examples of it raising its deviously funky head throughout the band's life. In November 1996, for example, they released the four-track *Fluorescences* EP, often seen as a bridge between *Emperor Tomato Ketchup* and 1997's *Dots And Loops*, which includes the monstrous 'Soop Groove #1', a rock-solid, thirteen-minute exercise into the force of two chords and a bass line, like James Brown meets Neu!. Similarly, 'Outer Bongolia', which opens the 2000 EP *The First Of The Microbe Hunters*, has always made me think of fusion-era Miles Davis meets *Space Age Batchelor Pad Music*, for the way its relentlessly tight rhythm underpins the musical chaos above.

Emperor Tomato Ketchup also includes some of Stereolab's most sublime pop songs. 'Cybele's Reverie', the single that preceded the album, is utterly gorgeous, its opulent string arrangement (courtesy of Sean O'Hagan), brilliant vocal interplay, and devastating chorus sending it to #62 in the British charts. 'Reverie' is the right word, too: this is one of Stereolab's most wistful, nostalgic songs, as Sadier looks back to a childhood where everything seemed more authentic, more *alive*, compared to the experience of adult life.

The album's title track has an outrageous mid-section two and a half minutes in, where a jazzy and unexpected chord sequence sends the song tumbling into a very efficient melancholy. 'The Noise Of Carpet' is a classic Stereolab two-chord rush that calls back to earlier songs like 'John Cage Bubblegum', albeit with a sophistication to the layers of vocal interaction that brings the song right up to Stereolab's masterful present. 'Monstre Sacre', meanwhile, is one of the saddest songs in all of Stereolab's work, the strings like an echo to classic Serge Gainsbourg in their swoop of emotion and the vocal melody swelled with the pop lip tremble of looking through the window on a rainy day.

Emperor also saw the band start experimenting with electronic treatments, with McEntire on hand to assist. Rather than merely playing electronic instruments, as Stereolab had done in the past, this involved using electronic effects to treat existing sounds in bold new ways, like the bizarrely tight guitar sound on 'Les Yper-Sound' (the song's name apparently a reference to a 'fake' band created by musique concrète pioneer Pierre Henry and French composer Michel Colombier in the 1960s). This kind of electronic treatment would become ever more prominent on *Dots And Loops*.

Given the combination of new sounds *and* a new recording process on *Emperor Tomato Ketchup*, it was inevitable that people would draw concrete yet erroneous conclusions, with Chicago inevitably linked to the new Stereolab sound and London associated with the old. But things were never that clear-cut. 'Metronomic Underground' and 'Percolator', perhaps the key songs in the band's transition toward interlocking loops and space, were both recorded in London.

I'd argue, in fact, that for the listener, there is no vast gap between the album's London and Chicago recordings, beyond a slight electronic tinge to the Chicago output. This the band would soon expand on with *Dots And Loops*, their fifth studio album and another key record from a group who had definitely found their groove.

10

'SPARK PLUG' AUTONOMY

Critical reaction to* Emperor Tomato Ketchup *was gushing, and the album charted at #27 in the UK and a relatively impressive #67 in the USA. I say 'relatively' because this gets to the question of who exactly Stereolab* were *at the time: were they a major-label act whose label had chart pretensions, or an indie band who were way out in the experimental ether?

The answer, of course, is both. Stereolab did have a major-label deal in the USA after signing with Elektra in 1993. And their US label had certain ideas of how commercial they could be, as Terry Tolkin, the late Elektra A&R who signed Stereolab, related in a lengthy Discogs post:

'When I got the final mix and sequence of *Mars Audiac Quintet* at Elektra in the spring of 1994, I walked a dub into CEO Bob Krasnow's corner office on the 17th floor of 75 Rock and officially hand delivered him a copy of it on a DAT. Just over an hour later, the exact amount of time it would take to listen to the entire album, Ruth Rosenberg (Bob's career-long assistant) buzzed me on the intercom and hurriedly told me to come into Bob's office . . . I didn't even get a moment to ask him what was up. He simply blurted out: Terry, this is a fukin HIT record!

Every song on this album has a place in Pop history! We're gonna shoot a Million Dollar Bullet on Promoting every groove on this record!'

Despite Krasnow's enthusiasm, *Mars Audiac Quintet* wasn't exactly the hit record that Elektra envisaged, peaking at #92 in the US charts. But the label stuck with Stereolab from *Transient Random-Noise Bursts With Announcements* to *Margerine Eclipse*, eleven years and seven studio albums, before cutting them free. By June 2004, when the axe fell among a significant Elektra cull, *Margerine Eclipse* had sold over forty thousand copies in the USA—a respectable amount, but nowhere near the alternative sales bonanza that Nirvana and Pearl Jam were bringing in when Stereolab signed on the dotted line.*

That's not to say that Stereolab's major-label deal was a failure or in any way a bad thing for the band. We're used to hearing tales of bands signed to horror-show deals, where the label in question tries to mould the group into something they aren't and the resulting album either stinks the place out or gets shelved.

But there are good major label deals, too. Loud Records' deal with the Wu-Tang Clan allowed the group's individual members to sign their own solo deals with other labels and take the Wu-Tang name with them, while Daft Punk's contract with Virgin gave the French duo outright creative control over all aspects of their music. Stereolab's deal with Elektra was very much in this category, with complete autonomy in the UK and Ireland, where the band remained independent. According to Tolkin, Stereolab were free to record and release 45s and EP-length material on any independent label and in collaboration with *any* indie artist, with Elektra footing the bill.†

Sadier expanded on this in a 2024 interview with Toby Amies for

* It's funny to read a *Billboard* news story from 2001 about the release of Stereolab's seventh studio album, *Sound-Dust*—a record that even fans tend to find underwhelming—in which Elektra claims that it 'has a more approachable and more upbeat sound that shifts back towards the warmer tones and more melodic textures of their earlier albums', as if Stereolab are about to unleash R.E.M.'s *Out Of Time* on the world, rather than an album influenced by Ligeti, Bernard Herrmann, and Jacques Lejeune.

† On that last point, Gane is not entirely in agreement. In an interview with Carsten Wohlfeld for *Luna Kafé* in 1999, he explained, 'When we record an album for Elektra, it is "the next album" and we use the advance that they give us. The other records that we make, we record with our own money, and Elektra doesn't have anything to do with them.'

Bomb Magazine. 'When we did sign to a major label, Elektra, in the United States, we had a contract that said that if they didn't like the album that we presented them with, they had ninety days to release it or we could take it to any other label,' she explained. 'Some labels have kept bands under their thumb, totally smothering them to death. We were untouchable, really.'

Sadier went on to compare her relationship with the music industry to the idea of 'détournement'. This was an artistic practice developed in the 1950s by Letterist International and then taken up by the Situationists, in which artworks, adverts, and other images could be transformed by creatively disfiguring them. 'I don't think one can exist completely outside of spectacle or capitalist forces, which are pervasive,' she told *Bomb*. 'But one can be aware of them and turn them around as the Situationists did with the *détournement*.

'Owning the final recordings, as we should say, is an important thing for one's freedom as an artist,' Sadier added. 'And owning your means of production affords you even more freedom! We need as much freedom as we can get in this capitalist world that robs people of their free will, time and wealth when it comes to labour.'

Autonomy—essentially the freedom for an individual, state or, in this case, a band to govern themselves and decide their own action—is one of the key tenets of Stereolab's belief system. They reject accepted thinking and question everything, in a desire to be free in their own decision-making.

Naturally, the idea of autonomy also comes into the band's art. Asked about her inspiration for lyrics in her 2015 appearance at the Red Bull Music Academy, Sadier explained that they come in reaction against society. 'It was not like, oh, scratching my head, *What shall I talk about?* No, it was like, *Well, this system is just appalling. We're having to serve it when it should be serving us, and the governments are serving the system when they should be serving us . . .*

'There were notions such as autonomy, which seemed very important to me, that we have to strive at being autonomous. That means we give ourselves our own law, and if everybody does that, then we're all empowered of [sic] our own law and we're more inclined to relate to each other in better ways.'

Sadier's love of autonomy has long been influenced by the work of the Greek/French philosopher Cornelius Castoriadis. Castoriadis was born in Istanbul, then known as Constantinople, in 1922, with his family moving to Greece later that year. He became interested in Marxism at the age of thirteen and had joined the Young Communist League of Greece by fifteen.

After moving to Paris to study in 1945, Castoriadis got involved with the Parti Communiste Internationaliste before growing disillusioned with Trotskyism and co-founding Socialisme Ou Barbarie, a group of socialist libertarians (including Guy Debord, later a founding member of Situationist International) who also published a journal of the same name. (Sadier would borrow the group's name for the debut album by her group Monade.)

Castoriadis had a very active intellectual life, as a philosopher, social critic, economist, psychoanalyst and author of *The Imaginary Institution Of Society*, in which he examines the impact of society on the human psyche. Fittingly, though, Castoriadis is best known for his ideas on autonomy. Essentially, these refer to a condition of 'self institution', whereby autonomous societies create their own laws and are aware of this fact, as opposed to heteronomous societies, which delegate this process to an authority outside the society, often a god figure or the idea of historical necessity.

Castoriadis's ideas on society are particularly important to Sadier. In a 2024 interview with *Jacobin*—which bills itself as 'a leading voice of the American left, offering socialist perspectives on politics, economics, and culture'—she explained that she has always been 'a bit of a butterfly' when it comes to her political views. 'I could say that I'm on the left, but even then, if you look at [then Labour Party leader] Keir Starmer, who's supposed to be left-wing—he does right-wing politics,' she said.

Sadier explained that she sees politics as 'a big bridge that goes to my family, my neighbours, London and society at large'. Castoriadis, she said, 'explained this very well, how we impact society. Society shapes us and we shape it in return, and there is this circular aspect. It's not all one way where you receive and you don't give back.'

When I interviewed Laetitia for *Line Noise* in 2024, she talked about humans as being the 'creators of our society'. Later, when we were talking about her Catholic upbringing, she came back to the idea in a roundabout way. 'We're leaving the Age of Pisces. Pisces was about a saviour coming from outside and it was going to save us, and it was probably a he,' she said. 'We're moving to the Age of Aquarius, and the Age of Aquarius is like, Well, your saviour is *within*: you're your own saviour, mate! You know, not someone out there who's going to come on their horse and sweep you off your feet. That I find really interesting, this kind of re-shifting of the perspective that now we are responsible for our reality.'

Society and freedom are ideas that return again and again in Stereolab's work. However, there are two songs that very explicitly deal with Castoriadis's idea of autonomy. The lyrics to 'Spark Plug', an entirely groovy pop song on *Emperor Tomato Ketchup*, lay out the idea that there is little point to *any* new form of society or way of living if it is not prepared for autonomy, including autonomous production and autonomous organisation. 'Mass Riff', originally released on the *Instant 0 In The Universe* EP in 2003, clearly explains that freedom can only be guaranteed by autonomy.

But Stereolab didn't just *sing* about autonomy—they practised it. The most obvious example of this is the band's Duophonic label, which Sadier and Gane created with manager Martin Pike to release their first record, the *Super 45* EP. 'Always from the beginning, the label was there,' Gane told *Chunklet* magazine. 'It wasn't like we sent off any demos or didn't get any replies. So, we borrowed £1,600 from Martin's dad in 1991, and with that we financed the first seven-inch.'

Well, *almost*. *Super 45* was actually released on ten-inch vinyl. And what a ten-inch it was. One of the things I love about Duophonic is that, right from the start, it encompassed art, collectability, and chaos. The band pressed 880 copies of *Super 45*, but they ran out of sleeves and had to make the last forty out of freezer bags with spray-painted covers. This is catnip to collectors—they go for upward of £350 these days—but was less ideal for the band.

'The sleeve to the first Stereolab single had a fax paper sleeve,' Gane told *Chunklet*. 'We didn't have any money to do it on anything else. But now it's like, *Oh, the original sleeve!* It's just a cheap piece of paper that looked like crap.' This, incidentally, is why Stereolab have resisted calls to reissue their early records in their original forms. The music is all out there, on various compilations, so why fetishise an object that may have been born out of necessity?

The band sold *Super 45* through the Rough Trade stores in London and via mail order. After John Peel played it on his Radio 1 show and Leeds indie stars The Wedding Present offered the band a gig, the EP quickly sold out.

Quite a lot of bands do this: rather than face the soul-destroying task of shipping demos around to sniffy record labels, they opt to go it alone. Often, though, that first record is seen as a calling card—something to get labels, managers, promoters, and the like interested in the band and offer them a deal. The band's own label then fades back into obscurity, its job done.

Stereolab *did* sign their first record deal after the success of *Super 45*, with London indie label Too Pure. And it would be Too Pure that released the band's next record, *Super-Electric*, in September 1991, and their debut album, *Peng!*, in May 1992.

Too Pure was never a massive label, but it was a big deal in the London indie world that Stereolab inhabited—a significant step up from releasing a record on Duophonic. Too Pure, which was founded in 1990 by Paul Cox and Richard Roberts, was home to Stereolab sister band Th' Faith Healers; and PJ Harvey, who (as a band) released their debut single, 'Dress', on the label in December 1991.

Too Pure grew out of the Sausage Machine, a North London club night promoted by Cox and Roberts that had a reputation for finding young talent, including shoegazers Ride. The label's first release was a compilation album of tracks recorded live at the Sausage Machine in 1990, called *Now Thats Disgusting Music—Live At The Sausage Machine*. Its second and third came from Th' Faith Healers, and its fourth release was *Super-Electric*, on ten-inch vinyl.

Richard Roberts says that Joe Dilworth introduced him to Stereolab, giving him the *Super 45* EP as a birthday present. He was blown away. 'I can remember various meetings with the band all over the place,' he says. 'And that would have been the important thing at that point: who are they and what are they about? That would have been far more important than, *Oh, we love you. We can see this selling half a million copies.*'

'Joe [Dilworth] brought us the first Stereolab EP, and we liked it,' Paul Cox adds. 'I don't know why they went from releasing their own EP to wanting someone else to do it, because if you talk to them at all, they're very DIY.'

Cox says that Tim Gane knew exactly what he wanted to do with Stereolab, both musically and in terms of releasing records. 'And anything that didn't quite fit was very quickly dismissed,' he says.

Too Pure encouraged this independence. 'Tim was very experienced in what he was doing anyway,' says Roberts. 'He had been in McCarthy prior to all of this; he had a very definite idea, and I didn't want to impinge on that. We let them go and do what they wanted to do. They had this definite identity, despite the cost. They wanted these ten-inch singles. They had ideas for artwork, which, for me, was critical. If a band didn't have an idea of what they wanted the record to look like, then I think they haven't really thought through who they are. That makes sense.'

Cox says that Too Pure didn't really have a particular sound. But he points out that the label's three key early signings—Th' Faith Healers, Stereolab, and PJ Harvey—were 'strongly female represented. So I think me and Richard had—how's the way to put it?—a sympathetic ear for women in indie rock, as it were.'

'There *was* an aesthetic, though, which was that every record [on Too Pure] should be different,' Roberts argues. 'We also encouraged our bands to recognise that they were all a team together, as in they worked together in many ways. You'll notice musicians crossing over, even to this day, working with other musicians from that era.'

Mark Clifford of post-rock/electronic act Seefeel, who were also signed to Too Pure in the early 90s, says that the label could be 'pretty haphazard. That is not disparaging, because I absolutely love them,' he adds. 'But I would say they were kind of ramshackle, which strangely works in a way that almost shouldn't. I think it worked because they just chose good music. They were very, very good at choosing music. They had very good taste.'

When I mention to Paul Cox that I had heard Too Pure called

'ramshackle'—albeit in a very affectionate way—he seems slightly taken aback. 'Indie labels that have only just started, I mean, what are they supposed to be?' he asks, entirely reasonably. 'You don't have an office, and you don't have any money. And it depends what you mean by ramshackle. If we came across like that, I think we'd have been a little bit proud about that and a little bit offended at the same time.'

Stereolab could have made Too Pure their permanent home and forgotten about the inevitable headaches of running their own label. But the band weren't finished with Duophonic, which released the *Stunning Debut Album* seven-inch, in November 1991. This dual dynamic continued over the next few years, with Duophonic releasing Stereolab's 'Harmonium' / 'Farfisa' in 1992 even as Too Pure prepped *Peng!* for release. (Minneapolis punk band Arcwelder became the first external band to release music on Duophonic the same year, when the 'Favor' / 'Plastic' seven-inch hit the shops.)

It has always taken a certain mentality to run an indie label. Britain in the early 1990s had a well-established structure of independent record distributors and local record shops, which meant that, with some headwind, selling a thousand seven-inches was an achievable goal. Even then, labels probably wouldn't make much money, and they ran the constant risk of major labels and bigger indies poaching their bands.

As Duophonic was very much Stereolab's label (even if it did release music by other people), it was insulated from these threats. Stereolab were successful, in a kind of indie way, right from the start. They could sell records and probably even make some money. And the only people to really poach from Duophonic were Stereolab themselves.

All the same, creating Duophonic and then sticking with it was a choice that I would argue was born out of the band's love for autonomy. In an interview with *The Wire* in 1996, Gane spoke of the 'do-it-yourself' aesthetic that lay behind the label, calling it 'empowering'.

Releasing a record can be a creative act. As well as recording the music, someone (be it label or band) has to decide on the way it is released, from format to sleeve colour, and this can lead to some imaginative decisions. In this way, Duophonic is another outlet for the band's ever-whirring minds: in *The Wire*, Gane said that, by releasing your own music, 'you learn' and this then 'creates more music, more ideas'.

Speaking to *Chunklet* about reissues, Gane also made an interesting point that could almost serve as a founding statement for Duophonic: 'We fancy doing what we fancy doing at that particular point.' In other words, no one is ever going to tell Stereolab what to do.

'I think for any band, doing their own label is really sensible, because you learn how it all works,' says Sean Forbes from London indie retailer Rough Trade. 'A lot of bands who just signed to majors, they don't have a clue how the process works. All they want to do is moan.'

If we go back to Castoriadis and his ideas on 'self institution', by being autonomous, Stereolab were able to remain self-aware—conscious of their own place in society—rather than delegating the processes of their career to a major-label god figure. Which is quite an elaborate way to say that sticking out Herzfeld seven-inches was a good way to keep the band grounded, even as unspeakable music 'biz' types were trying to blow smoke up all kinds of places. Duophonic was the great autonomy that lies at the heart of Stereolab, enabling other freedoms.

An alternative argument would be: so why did they sign to Elektra? But I see that as a move borne more out of opportunity than necessity. Signing to Elektra gave Stereolab the money to tour the USA, make videos, and spend more on recording than they could otherwise have afforded. But they didn't *need* the deal, and they could have existed without it. Besides, a deal that advantageous toward the band was hardly a sell-out.

Asked about his inspirations for Duophonic by *Chunklet*, Gane named two paragons of indie values: Bristol label Sarah Records, which operated from 1987 to 1995, and Olympia's famed K Records. While there was some musical crossover between the two labels—British cardigan troupers Heavenly were signed to Sarah, and their records were distributed by K in the USA, for example—Gane puts his admiration for the two down to the rather more prosaic (although not, perhaps, for a record collector) fact that both labels released ten-inch records, a format Stereolab also favoured.

That said, it is hard to overlook the *other* parallels between Sarah and K. For a start, both labels were fiercely DIY, standing proudly outside the major-label system. Sarah saw twelve-inch records as a rip-off for fans, while K valued the idea of lo-fi projects as an alternative to corporate culture. The two labels had strong political beliefs, too, as reflected in their rejection of the corporate world. It's not hard to see an echo of this in Duophonic.

For all that, Stereolab's split with Too Pure after the release of *Space Age Batchelor Pad Music* in 1993 seems to have been a painful one. Roberts says both sides *did* want to continue to work together, to help bring the band to a bigger audience. But it wasn't to be. 'This time was probably the most painful we ever experienced at the label. We had lost a band that we loved, and we had lost our friends,' he says.

In fact, Roberts says he couldn't listen to Stereolab's music after they left Too Pure. 'It really hurt,' he explains, the lingering pain evident in his voice. 'I'm not saying I didn't hear any of it. And I was happy for them when I'd see them on TV or see a video come along, and they'd be in the video. But I found it really difficult to listen to this band after that because it hurt. This band really hurt.'

Cox was also saddened by the decision. 'It was amicable because we're all nice people, I think, but for me and Richard, obviously, it was intensely disappointing and really sad, and I couldn't believe it,' he says. 'You're very involved when you're running an indie label, perhaps more so than when it's your job or at a major label. *This* is not your job. This is your *all*, putting your everything into it. You're putting your savings in, and you've got to get a bank loan to start the label and all this stuff. So, you're very involved.'

In the UK and Ireland, Stereolab remained on Duophonic, although it was at this point that the label split into Duophonic Ultra High Frequency Disks, which would shadow the Elektra releases, dealing with the band's more commercial music, and Duophonic Super 45s, which was intended for Stereolab's more esoteric singles, as well as music from other bands. *Simple Headphone Mind*, Stereolab's second work with Nurse With Wound, was released on Duophonic Super 45s, as was the group's 1998 collaboration with Brigitte Fontaine, 'Caliméro'.

Having their own label and a deal with Elektra didn't stop Stereolab recording for other labels, either. Their 1993 split single with Unrest came out on Teenbeat, while the 1996 single with US artist Füxa, to which Stereolab contributed the air-y waltz 'You Used To Call Me Sadness', was released on London's Lissy's Records. 'We license our recordings and just give them to people,' Gane told *Chunklet*, 'then we don't have to ask for permission if we want to use it. We just want to be in control of our own music.'

Duophonic Super 45s, meanwhile, has released music by bands who are in line with Stereolab's own musical and commercial values, including Tortoise, Sean O'Hagan's The High Llamas, Pram, and Broadcast. The latter band—a group of rather mystical psychedelic explorers who were grounded in the fact that they came from Birmingham—are often bundled in with Stereolab in the public imagination, even if the actual connections are fairly weak. Martin Pike managed Broadcast as well as Stereolab, and the band released two records on Duophonic Super 45s. Musically, too, there are traces of resemblance—both Stereolab and Broadcast have filmic elements and were influenced by psychedelic rock. But it doesn't go that much further.

Both Duophonic UHF and Duophonic Super 45s have also released music by Tim Gane's post-Stereolab band, Cavern Of Anti-Matter, while Stereolab's 2025 album *Instant Holograms On Metal Film* was a joint release between Duophonic UHF and Warp.

Commercially, *Emperor Tomato Ketchup* was one of Duophonic's most successful releases. More importantly, the record was an artistic triumph that helped to shock Stereolab's creative processes back into life and ease them out of their malaise.

The year 1996 was not done, however. August saw the release of *Überschall 1996*, a joint single with Foetus and Faust for the Überschall Festival in Germany, to which Stereolab contributed 'Percolations', a John McEntire remix of the *Emperor* track 'Percolator'. The song's treated electronic loops pointed to where the band would soon be going on *Dots And Loops*.

The *Fluorescences* EP, released in November, was also a kind of bridge to *Dots And Loops*, with 'Pinball'—which once bore the perfect name of 'Heavenly Van Halen'—and 'Soop Groove #1' leaning toward loops and electronics.

All this, and there was still time for Stereolab to contribute 'One

Note Samba / Surfboard' to the *Red Hot + Rio* compilation album, released in October 1996 to promote AIDS awareness. The record, part of a long-running *Red Hot* series, was intended as a contemporary tribute to the bossa nova sound and, in particular, the music of legendary Brazilian artist Antônio Carlos Jobim, whose 'One Note Samba' Stereolab had sampled on *Transient Random-Noise Bursts With Announcements* (albeit as covered by Perrey and Kingsley).

For *Red Hot + Rio*, Stereolab recorded versions of both 'One Note Samba' and another of Jobim's songs, 'Surfboard', alongside the American jazz flautist Herbie Mann, who spent much of his lengthy career, which took him from Latin music to funk and disco, in pursuit of the elusive concept of the groove. In a 2002 interview with Jim Newsom for *Port Folio*, Mann recalled, 'I realised that in order to play a specific music, you had to go where the sauce was. I'm not going to do an album where I want real, authentic Brazilian rhythms and record it in Jamaica. If I go to Brazil to make a Brazilian record, if I use Latin players to make a Latin record, why don't I go to the place where it's natural for those players to play that groove?'

'One Note Samba / Surfboard'—the two songs are joined together as one track on the album—was also Stereolab's first dedicated excursion into the bossa nova sound, which would flourish later in their work, particularly on *Dots And Loops*. This wasn't the first time that they had taken on the influence of bossa—there are hints of it to *Space Age Batchelor Pad Music*, for example—but 'One Note Samba / Surfboard' makes the connection explicit.*

'One Note Samba / Surfboard' is not so much bossa-nova *influenced*—as you could have said about *Space Age Batchelor Pad Music*'s 'U.H.F.—MFP'—as straight-up bossa nova, and Stereolab handle it with aplomb, driven along by some delightful flute lines from Mann, who plays like he is escorting butterflies to pasture.

When I interviewed Sean O'Hagan for Radio Primavera Sound in 2024 (before I had started work in earnest on this book), he mentioned 'One Note Samba / Surfboard', recalling how the idea of being in the

* Interestingly, SuperMusicVision founder Thomas Golubić says that Stereolab's combination of apparently opposing musical ideas reminds him of bossa nova's tendency to combine a relaxed musical feel with complex rhythms.

studio laying down guitars and keyboards to then send to Herbie Mann was 'crazy'. You can see what he means. But at the same time, the song includes enough of Stereolab's DNA—the synth squiggles, a slight air of guitar chug—that it feels very true to the band, while fulfilling the promise of *Red Hot + Rio* to deliver a contemporary take on the bossa nova sound.

Stereolab's flirtation with bossa nova came from a genuine love of the genre. 'Tim is a huge fan of Brazilian music and knew a lot about it,' says former Stereolab keyboard player Morgane Lhote. 'And for me, there was a really big introduction to that genre, learning about artists like Joyce and Os Mutantes and Jorge Ben and Marcos Valle and Gal Costa. We got the chance to play in Brazil [in 2000], which was amazing... it was really cool to be able to play in a country where there were the roots of the music that Stereolab was really influenced by.'

Brazil loved Stereolab right back. Luiza Sá, the guitarist in CSS, is a huge fan of the band. 'I love Stereolab. In fact, I saw a show in São Paulo in my late teens,' she says. 'It was such a special, intimate show at Sesc Pompeia's theatre, which is part of a great cultural centre designed by the renowned architect Lina Bo Bardi that offers cheap tickets and services to people.

'After the show, I went to a small bar and nightclub that was very important to me, called A Torre Do Dr. Zero, because it was the best place to be, with a crowd of artists, musicians, fashion designers, writers, everyone cool. When CSS started, we also started a party at this club. Somehow, everyone in Stereolab ended up there too, and we basically danced all night together. Just a fun night of lots of dancing is all I remember. I think they liked Brazil.'

I ask Sá how Brazilian she thinks Stereolab are, aware that it is a slightly awkward question. 'I hate putting actual numbers on things because Stereolab's sound is influenced by Brazilian music, but it's also so unique,' she says, 'so perhaps you don't have to know where its elements come from to enjoy it. But it's a pleasure to find Brazilian music in there.'

'You could say a little or a lot and for sure some songs more than others and probably a more specifically internationally known, 60s kind of Brazilian music,' Sá adds. 'I mean, they're not Brazilian people at all, and that's clear to me in their music. It's like us Brazilians exploring rock or doing our version of other genres that aren't Brazilian. I guess that's mostly what CSS has done. I'm not equating the two (God no!) because again, different from a lot of musicians (and us), they really created a unique sound.'

Stereolab are generally thought of as an indie band, but 'One Note Samba / Surfboard' shows how hard it is to pin them down to any one thing. How many other indie bands could cover Jobim in this way, let alone do it with such aplomb? On *Red Hot + Rio*, they sit alongside artists like Money Mark, Mad Professor, David Byrne, and George Michael, as well as Brazilian singers including Astrud Gilberto and Milton Nascimento, and it suits them entirely.

'One Note Samba / Surfboard' is an example of Stereolab's groove. But it is *also*, for me, a mark of their autonomy: a band who are their own bosses capping off a monumental year by doing something strange, new and wonderful just because they *can*. They continued to draw power from autonomy as they approached 1997, which would be another crackling year of change.

INTERSTITIAL TWO
OUR FAVOURITE STEREOLAB SONGS

MARK CLIFFORD (Seefeel) I love 'Turn On' [by Turn On, aka Tim Gane, Andy Ramsay, and Sean O'Hagan]. It's one of those records. I don't know why I like it . . . when I bought it, I listened to it all the time. I think, for me, it did Stereolab in a better way. At least for me—not in a better way for other people, that's just for my own tastes. I really like early Stereolab. I love their artwork. I love the continuity in their artwork as well.

LUIZA SÁ (CSS) This is probably not the coolest answer, but I really love 'Super Falling Star'. First song on first album? Sure! Of course, I'm charmed by their very 60s, very bossa nova meets (even Brazilian) rock sound that is so present in fuller, more rhythmic songs but when they do slow, perhaps more melancholic, songs, they break them down a little and you're able to see their voices and harmonies and the materials they use to build up their sound. It's very chic and moving, polished and raw at the same time. It's a 90s interpretation of the 60s and still something else, unique, electronic—I think they could be in conversation with the band Broadcast (which I love).

THOMAS GOLUBIĆ (SuperMusicVision) 'Percolator' is one of my favourite songs. It has such an odd melodic structure to it. It brings you in with this sense of curiosity. It never fully resolves. And there's the rhythm of it: it feels exciting and dynamic. And it always feels like it's building toward something, and it almost explodes, but never quite. It keeps you on edge. That's one thing I really like about Stereolab: they don't always resolve the feeling. And that combination of the songwriting and the vocals has this weird element of being both soothing and anxiety inducing, which is a lovely, weird, and very modern conception.

DAVE TAYLOR (Switch) I lived in the south of France for a year and fell in love with Ludovic Navarre and his St. Germain project. There's a track on *Cobra And*

Phases called 'Puncture In The Radax Permutation' that reminds me of Rose Rouge—I'm sampling that next!

Most of the contemporary music I listen to makes me feel one of two things. Either it makes me jealous and inspired because I wish I was that good: Moodymann, Masters At Work, Dilla, Q-Tip . . . when I hear music like that, it makes me want to jump in the studio and work harder. And then there are acts like Stereolab. With them, I can just listen and enjoy because they're not even on a scale of achievable, in a certain sense. They're magical, impossible—like marrying Jane Fonda when you're fifteen. There's very few forms of music that fall into that category for me—I'm always analysing, listening for tricks that I can apply myself, but not with them. With Stereolab, I just sample them instead.

JIM O'ROURKE (musician and producer) I'm really happy with the end section of 'Puncture In The Radax Permutation'. I think those string arrangements are the best ones I ever wrote for a pop record. I really wish that it would just go on for an hour.

DEBBIE BALL (Electrelane) If I had to pick the ultimate, ultimate, ultimate Stereolab favourite song, it would be 'French Disko'. But there are the same reasons that I love 'Sadistic' on *Refried Ectoplasm* (*Switched On Volume 2*). It's that combination of it being so propulsive and something you can dance to, and there are lots of interesting textural layers of different instrumentation going on. I used to DJ that song out quite a lot as well.

I also like 'Sadistic' because it also connects to my guitar playing/aping of Tim Gane. He's got a really interesting rhythm guitar style where he's both really on the beat but a bit sloppy in his actual strokes. That's the way that I interpret it, anyway. And I used to like the way that he would get into a bit of a trance, and his fringe would flop around.

The vocals on 'Sadistic'—I like that about Stereolab as well. Either you tried, with your best A-Level French, to translate what Laetitia was saying, or you just went with it. I love music that has vocals as another texture, I suppose a *layer* in the music. It's like an instrument. There was a lot of rhythm and percussion and energy in how Laetitia would sing. So that comes across in that song as well.

11

'REFRACTIONS IN THE PLASTIC PULSE' ELECTRONICS

In 1988, when Tim Gane and Laetitia Sadier met in Paris, rave fever was breaking out in the UK, as the second Summer of Love brought thousands of young people to huge outdoor parties where they would dance all night to house music, then freshly minted in Chicago.

Dance music became huge in the UK, breaking through on radio, in clubs, and in the charts via international acts like Steve Hurley and Marshall Jefferson and domestic producers like S'Express and 808 State. Britain's guitar bands were soon getting in on the act, as artists like Primal Scream, Happy Mondays, and The Stone Roses mixed up dance production with indie sounds to create the Madchester/baggy/indie-dance hybrid. (New Order had already been doing this for years, which might explain why people don't really consider them an indie-dance act.)

By September 1989, when Sadier moved to London, the rave scene had calmed slightly, as the British police clamped down on outdoor parties. In fact, as Sadier told *Chick Factor* in 1993, she had never actually been to a rave, but she did love techno. Similarly, it is hard to imagine Tim Gane losing his mind at an illegal Orbital rave, though he did tell tales of attending all-night parties at London's Scala.

Stereolab weren't ravers, and they certainly weren't a Madchester band. But electronic music has had a profound impact on their work. As noted earlier, techno pioneers Kraftwerk were an early influence on Gane, and as he told *Synth History* in 2023, he bought his first sequencer and Moog around the same time as his first guitar. In 1983, he and his friends formed Uncommunity, a power-electronics band that played 'atonal electronic noise music'.

The electronic side of Krautrock/kosmische music also appealed to Gane's tastes. If you listen to *Kollektion 01: Sky Records*, which Gane compiled from the Sky Records archive, it is heavy on proto-electronics and low on guitars. Talking to *Electronic Sound* about the record, he explained that Sky's output represents 'the later period of Krautrock', when 'the rock elements had pretty much gone and an enormous amount of captivating music was being produced'.

Stereolab weren't an indie-dance act as we would typically understand the genre. But they *did* make dance tracks, like 'Metronomic Underground', and they often incorporated electronic music into their work. This helps to explain why the group built up a cult following among music fans and producers more typically keyed into electronic music, to the point where both *DJ Magazine* and *Resident Advisor* ran news of the band's return in 2025.

Robin Rimbaud, aka experimental music producer Scanner, is a huge fan of the band, despite (or perhaps because of) not knowing where to place them. 'Despite using synths, their sound is most certainly still closer connected to Motorik garage pop, I feel,' he explains. 'Having seen them live, my ears were most certainly damaged by the guitars more than anything else, too. But their interests, especially Tim's, come from an exploratory industrial background. I know, as I'm familiar with his music before Stereolab, and we were even on compilations together in the 80s!* So, they certainly offer an interesting challenge to anyone trying to label them.'

* Uncommunity featured on the 1984 compilation From Down Yondah alongside Rimbaud's The Rimbaud Brothers.

Stereolab's electronic leanings were expressed in their early music through Moog synth effects that, though important, initially felt like garnish rather than the main meal. Moogs, Gane once explained, were mainly used for 'siren sounds' in the early days of the band, before being employed as the basis of chords.

'Au Grand Jour', from the *Super 45* EP, actually starts with a synth burble, but this is soon submerged below waves of guitar. This balance changed in 1992 with the release of the Moog version of *Peng!*'s 'Super Falling Star', in which the synth's electronic hum comes right to the foreground. But it was a relatively obscure song, originally released on the fourth edition of the *Volume* compilation series. It wasn't until *Emperor Tomato Ketchup* that electronics became a fundamental part of the Stereolab sound.

'It was on this LP where we really started to investigate the treatments made possible by electronic devices of all kinds—electronic rhythms and pulses, filtering, vocoding, electronic effects, synth chords and riffs,' Gane writes in the sleeve notes to the 2019 reissue. Some of the credit for this goes to John McEntire, who recorded parts of *Emperor* in Chicago and encouraged the group to explore new sonic possibilities. They would return to him in 1997 for *Dots And Loops*, which became one of their most acclaimed works.

Like *Emperor*, *Dots And Loops* is an album of two parts, recorded in two locations—Chicago and Düsseldorf—that calls back to the past while looking forward to the future. And yet, like its predecessor, it also feels remarkably coherent.

In March 1997, Stereolab, now with Richard Harrison on bass after the departure of Duncan Brown, decamped to Idful studios in Chicago, where they had recorded some of *Emperor*, to work with McEntire again. In the year between the two records, however, things had changed: Idful had installed the powerful digital audio workstation Pro Tools, which was then becoming an industry standard. This, it turned out, would be fundamental to the development of *Dots And Loops*.

'*Emperor* was kind of an outlier in terms of what I'd said about them [Stereolab] being rehearsed and everything . . . I don't think we were even using click tracks or anything at that point,' says McEntire. 'And then it changed really radically with *Dots And Loops*. That was the beginning of putting everything together one element at a time.' (Well, perhaps not *quite* the start, as there was certainly an element of this to the recording of *Emperor*.)

The band had started out working with good old-fashioned tape, as they always did. But after two days working on the drum track for 'Miss Modular', Andy Ramsay and John McEntire decided that something wasn't working and they should record the drums in loops, using Pro Tools.

The vital difference between Pro Tools and tape comes in the editing process. With tape, you can splice together takes and move sections of your music around, but this comes with a certain physical effort: you literally have to cut the tape and re-attach it, which puts limits on how many changes you can make and how extreme you can go. Pro Tools, however, is infinitely malleable. You can move and loop sounds to your heart's content; the only limit is your imagination.

'Digital audio recording seemed like a child's toy, making lots of little loops of the bass, guitar and drum parts, not having to play everything through from beginning to end, plopping things in where you wanted them and moving things around to see how it sounded,' Gane writes in the sleeve notes to the reissued *Dots And Loops*.

'Tim does all his demos on four-track cassette, the Fostex. He probably still does to this day,' says McEntire. 'So, he had everything—all the ideas are present in their most basic form. And then we literally wrote the arrangements in Pro Tools. So you snip, snip, snip, loop, move around.'

This was one inspiration behind the album's title. The other was cinematic, with *Dots And Loops* being influenced by experimental animation and cinema. 'Brakhage', the opening track, takes its name from filmmaker Stan Brakhage, while the album's title refers to *Dots* and *Loops*, two works by Scottish Canadian animator Norman McLaren.

You might think that Stereolab, rooted as they were in the wild improvisational sounds of Krautrock, would hate using loops in this way. But it actually fits very snugly with the band's compositional theory of interlocking musical cells, which they developed while writing and recording *Emperor Tomato Ketchup*. It's not like they fumbled clumsily over the use of brief musical snippets when recording to tape, but it is far easier to move these loops around when using Pro Tools.

You can hear this new confidence on a track like 'Diagonals', where John McEntire's circling marimba riff appears to drift in from another song to sit beautifully on top of Andy Ramsay's drums. Far from betraying their Krautrock forefathers, Stereolab's adventures in Pro Tools can perhaps be seen as a continuation of Can's technique of recording long, improvised musical passages and then editing them together in the studio.

When I spoke to Sean O'Hagan for *Radio Primavera Sound* in 2024, he talked about how Stereolab transformed the source material for *Dots And Loops*. 'I recorded the stuff and then I went away, back to the UK, back to The High Llamas,' he recalled, having contributed piano, Rhodes piano, Farfisa organ, and brass and string arrangements. 'And then I heard the mix of the record, [and it] was kind of upside down. Because you may have recorded a song, and the verse . . . when the mix happened, the verse was the chorus and the chorus was the verse, and the intro was the coda and the coda was the intro. It's just like, *Wow. Okay, that's dramatic*. But it was really, really, really exciting. The mix on that record is just so exciting.'

Recording Ramsay's drums as loops might sound like a recipe for repetitive, unadventurous beats. But *Dots And Loops* is actually home to some of his best work. On 'The Flower Called Nowhere', he brings an enchanting shuffle to the music, his drums dancing around the song's airy chord sequences, bringing a sense of spring-hearted joy. There is not a single Motorik beat to be found on *Dots And Loops*, in what was one of the album's radical departures from the band's past, while Stereolab's latent jazz influences frequently come to the fore.*

As well as jazz, McEntire says that the Brazilian influence emerged

* It is worth mentioning, however, that McEntire plays the drums on album highlight 'Brakhage'. 'Andy kept calling that song *the Tears For Fears tune*,' he recalls. 'Because, if you could imagine that song with the half-time *boom-tsh, boom-tsh, d-doom tchau* . . . that's how they were trying to run it down,' he explains, imitating a lounge-style 80s beat. 'Nobody liked it, especially not Tim. So, one day, I got fed up, and I was like, *Well, if we're going to make this work, we have to do something completely different*. So I set up a bass drum, a snare drum, a cymbal, and a hi-hat in the control room, played that beat for thirty seconds and looped it . . . it gave everybody the impetus to want to work on the song.'

strongly on *Dots And Loops*. 'We were trying to mine all these interesting things from the past, and somehow the floodgates just opened at around that time, and everybody was listening to Jorge Ben, Caetano Veloso, and Gal Costa,' he explains. 'It was just so refreshing to hear those chord changes, those melodies. It was very different from anything that we had really heard before. I think Tim especially saw the way the writing went in terms of the chord progressions. He's always been very keyed into that.'

Some sharp-eared listeners claim to be able to hear the difference in audio quality between Pro Tools and tape. I'm not one of them. But *Dots And Loops* does undoubtedly sound sharp, bright, and shiny. Too shiny for some people: there are Stereolab fans who believe that the band lost it with *Dots And Loops* and never got back into the groove. Even Tim Gane has said the album was 'too smooth', telling *The Ringer* in 2019, 'There was something about that that I didn't like.'

He repeats these complaints in the *Dots And Loops* sleeve notes, writing that he doesn't much like 'Prisoner Of Mars'—one of three songs recorded in Düsseldorf with electronic duo Mouse On Mars, aka Jan St. Werner and Andi Toma—because it sounds 'way too slinky and smoooooooth!'

McEntire disagrees with this assessment. 'Is it too smooth? No. If anything, I think that was an aesthetic choice. I think it was an outgrowth of the material, too. I think the songs really lent themselves to that kind of sound. It went there. There was plenty of analogue on that record. We cut all the drums and bass tracks and probably some of the guitars too on the analogue machine and just moved them over. We would have mixed it to analogue as well.'

On the subject of 'Miss Modular', a McEntire production that became the first single from *Dots And Loops*, Gane is far more positive. Pro Tools, he writes, gave the band added control over the record's sound. 'We managed to add a wonderful glistening sheen to the basic drums, bass, and acoustic guitar backing track to "Miss Modular", they seem glued together and the whole track seems to be in a state of artificially derived delirament [sic],' he writes, while also praising the 'dripping and melting' sound of the song's brass arrangements, the result of 'electronic treatments'.

'Miss Modular' is one of Stereolab's best-loved songs and was one of their biggest chart hits in the UK, reaching #60 in September 1997, just before the release of *Dots And Loops*. It also gave a very telling indication of the new influences at work on the album, featuring an ultra-bright mixture of acoustic guitar, jazz chords, bossa nova lilt, prominent brass, and electronic touches, all balanced with Stereolab's familiar vocal acrobatics.

Elsewhere on the album, Pharrell Williams favourite 'The Flower Called Nowhere', which was influenced by Polish jazz pianist and film composer Krzysztof Komeda, has a similarly jubilant lustre, as does the gorgeously yearning 'Rainbo Conversation'—one of several songs to feature the none-more-lounge sound of John McEntire's marimba.

Using Pro Tools also allowed Stereolab to go even further into collage, particularly on 'Refractions In The Plastic Pulse', a seventeen-and-a-half-minute track divided into four distinct sections. Among the most adventurous songs in the Stereolab catalogue, it is also perhaps the closest the band come to contemporary electronic music. Twelve minutes in, the electronic sounds that have been glimpsed throughout the track come to the foreground to create a glitchy IDM stroll that sounds a little like Autechre's experiments into obscure rhythm and sound. You can imagine this two-minute section of the song coming out on Warp Records in 1997, to enthusiastic chin scratching and proto-internet praise.

Andy Ramsay is one of three songwriters credited on 'Refractions', alongside Gane and Sadier, and his influence looms large over the record. When I spoke to Sean O'Hagan in 2024, he praised Ramsay's work on *Dots And Loops*. 'I just remember being in the studio with John McEntire and Tim and Andy Ramsay. The brass sessions were just incredible,' he said. 'And the organ—the keys—sessions were always amazing because we found a way of putting the organs through a bunch of filters. I think there were ATC Tone Chameleon filters. And that was just so exciting.

'We just thought we would blow the top off the studio with the sounds, they were just incredible . . . Andy was doing such great work. He had a couple of Doepfer modular synths set up. And he was just coming up with these bizarre electronic rummagings.'

'Parsec', which follows 'Refractions', is another moment that brings to mind the electronic music of the time, in this case the rhythmically tangled, drum & bass-influenced sound of drill & bass, as heard on two landmark albums from 1996, Aphex Twin's *Richard D. James Album* and Squarepusher's *Feed Me Weird Things*. You wouldn't confuse 'Parsec' with the work of either producer—it is far too *Stereolab* for that, with its lush brass arrangement and delicate French-language vocals—but the intricate drum programming and pulsating bass line feel like cousins of the British pair, even if this was a path Stereolab would not travel down again.

McEntire compares 'Parsec' to the 1998 Tortoise track 'Jetty', which has similarly skittering drums. 'Those are just a couple things that are a little bit dated, in terms of that [drum & bass],' he says. 'I mean, it was just in the zeitgeist, for sure. I think it works. But again, it's a little bit too specific to that time.'

Journalist Simon Reynolds, who interviewed Stereolab several times in the 1990s, was interested to hear the band turning toward drum & bass. 'When I interviewed them for *Emperor Tomato Ketchup*, I said, Hey, come along with me to Speed—LTJ Bukem's club for the floaty, jazzy, ambient-y side of jungle,' he recalls. 'I thought they would dig the sound, and as it was a fairly decorous spot, right in the centre of London, it wouldn't be too hardcore for them. But Tim and Laetitia made up some excuse. Another in my long line of unsuccessful attempts to influence musicians and widen their horizons.'

One of the many odd things about *Dots And Loops* is that two of the album's most electronic tracks—'Refractions In The Plastic Pulse' and 'Parsec'—were recorded in Chicago in early 1997, *before* Stereolab went to record in Düsseldorf with Mouse On Mars, the influential electronic music duo whose first album, *Vulvaland*, was released on Stereolab's old label, Too Pure.

'There are two parts to that record,' O'Hagan told me in 2024. 'There's the part that was done in Chicago and the part that was done in Düsseldorf with Mouse On Mars. And I think it was defining, halfway through the 90s. It was a really exciting time, because there was that whole German electronic, celebratory movement: Markus Popp, Fennesz, Mouse On Mars. It was just a really buzzy time.'

The band recorded 'The Flower Called Nowhere' and 'Prisoner

Of Mars' in MOM's studio, Academy-Of-St.-Martin-In-The-Streets. But the duo's influence is probably best heard on album closer 'Contronatura', another MOM production, which starts off as an enigmatic jazz stroll before accelerating in its second half into a disco/house groove, loaded with what Gane calls a 'strange jungle of sounds'.

'On this track, which gestated over a two-week period (most of the tracks gestated over time here), he [Jan St. Werner] would gradually add layers to his insect horns, as I called them (sounds produced from his sample/filter keyboard) and load them onto an Emagic Notator,' Gane writes. 'This is how he built up the strange jungle of sounds heard on this track.'

Dots And Loops was preceded by the *Miss Modular* EP, which added the summery, brushed drums of 'Allures', the percussion-heavy jazz of 'Off-On', and the calm melancholy of 'Spinal Column' to the EP's title track, creating a charming but hardly world-shattering release.

Perhaps more exciting—and certainly more daring—was the Japanese edition of the EP, released in 1998 to celebrate the group's first tour of the country. This record would cement Stereolab's association with electronic music by bundling together three remixes of *Dots And Loops* tracks with a single edit of the EP's title song. Given the electronic directions in which Stereolab were travelling in the late 1990s, it was a record that deserved a wider audience.

Admittedly, the results of these remixes were a mixed bag. US hip-hop producer Dan The Automator's remix of 'Miss Modular' doesn't really work, as he tries to impose a lumpen beat on a song that doesn't need it. Kid Loco's 'Prelude To The Autumn Of A Faun' mix of 'Contronatura' never really raises its head above the barrier of *okay*; and Jon Spencer Blues Explosion drummer Russell Simins' take on 'Rainbo Conversation' is lost in the fog of history, one of very few Stereolab songs it is nigh-on impossible to find online.

It is telling that none of these remixes has ever been included on any of Stereolab's numerous odds-and-sods compilations. The one track that *has* been compiled from the Japanese EP is Autechre's 'Feebate Mix' of 'Refractions In The Plastic Pulse', which was released on the 2022 *Pulse Of The Early Brain* compilation and more than justifies the band's excursions into remixing.

You can see why Autechre, an entirely uncompromising electronic duo who are prone to playing in the dark, would appeal to Stereolab. And the hook-up works incredibly well, with shades of Sadier's processed vocal poking through a dense mesh of percussion and electronic noise.

In many ways, the Autechre remix is reminiscent of the sprawling electronic collage of 'Simple Headphone Mind', Stereolab's second collaboration with Nurse With Wound, which was released in April 1997, as the band were recording *Dots And Loops*. In another world, you could imagine Stereolab and Autechre forming a symbiotic relationship of the kind the group enjoyed with Nurse With Wound and going on to release whole EPs of finely balanced electronic freak-outs.

Perhaps inevitably, though, by the time of the Japanese EP, Stereolab were moving on again. *Dots And Loops* would prove to be their electronic peak—the album that techno heads, night owls, and IDM freaks frequently reference. It is the Stereolab album where electronic sounds are most prominent, and—more importantly—it is a record where electronic music came right to the core of the group's working methods, changing the way they worked and radically expanding their vision.

This change in working method is less sonically distinct than simply bolting on the electronic blurt of the Moog, but you could argue that the emergence of Pro Tools on *Dots And Loops* allowed Stereolab to fulfil a kind of destiny, whereby rock music could be reduced to its core elements—its dots and its loops, if you will—then moulded, shifted, and transformed, like Charles Long playing with plasticine in his New York studio.

Given Stereolab's frantically creative minds, it was no surprise that the band's next record, 1999's *Cobra And Phases Group Play Voltage In The Milky Night*, would be a reaction to *Dots And Loops*, with the group shunning click tracks in favour of a looser, jazzier approach that threw up only a handful of electronic-tinged tracks. Gane would go even further on 2001's *Sound-Dust*, seeking out acoustic instruments like the celeste and the harpsichord and using far fewer electronic sounds. But the group's electronic adventures didn't stop there. Stereolab might turn away from certain influences and techniques from album to album, as the muse takes them, but they rarely abandon a particular sound entirely, their influences slowly piling up into an infinitely sophisticated strata of thought.

Sound-Dust's 'Gus The Mynah Bird', for example, has a drifting ambient coda that reminds me of The Orb. Writing on gearspace.com, Andy Ramsay says that the band 'probably made a lot of use of the EMS Synthi A'—a classic modular synth as employed by Pink Floyd, Tangerine Dream, and Jean-Michel Jarre—on the song. 'Me and Jim [O'Rourke] both had one,' he writes. 'Also, we liked the Wiard modular that John [McEntire] had at Soma [where *Sound-Dust* was recorded]. A lot of the sounds that you hear are basic organs heavily processed through modular synths or just whatever pedals kicking around that took our fancy.'

'Free Witch And No Bra Queen', a 2001 single, combines electronic effects with a jazz loop to hilarious if unsettling effect. 'Mass Riff', from the 2003 EP *Instant 0 In The Universe*, starts from a base of rushing drum machine rhythm and rippling electronic bass, and 'Cosmic Country Noir', from 2004's *Margerine Eclipse*, introduces itself to the world with astral synth sweeps and electronic pops and clicks.

The band's 2025 album, *Instant Holograms On Metal Film*, features an incredible wealth of electronic instruments, including (deep breath) the EMS Synthi, Roland Jupiter 4, Electro Harmonix DRM15, Vox Drum Machine, TR606, Korg MS20, Moog Matriarch, MicroMoog, Prophet 5, Roland Jupiter 4, Oberheim SEM, and more. These might seem like slightly superficial examples of electronic influence after the sweeping changes of *Dots And Loops*, but they show that the spark remained.

Dots And Loops was well received on the whole and sold respectably, charting at #19 in the UK and #111 in the USA. While the album is not universally loved, it is generally seen as part of Stereolab's Imperial Phase—the brief period of time in which they could do no wrong, stretching from *Mars Audiac Quintet* to *Dots* and forming a mighty run of form and creativity.

Things were about to change, however, and change radically, with the birth of Tim and Laetitia's distinctly analogue baby son, Alex.

12

'PEOPLE DO IT ALL THE TIME'
CREATION

Stereolab were a rampant creative force until their initial split in 2009. Over nineteen years, they produced ten studio albums, three mini-albums (if that is how we are counting* Space Age Batchelor Pad Music, Music For The Amorphous Body Center, *and* The First Of The Microbe Hunters*), and around thirty singles and EPs, the non-album work being enough to fill five* Switched On *compilations. That's a Beatles-esque rate of creation, making them true draft horses of the avant-garde.

Speaking to *Uncut* about 'Jenny Ondioline' in 2020, Laetitia Sadier spoke of the importance of creativity to the band. The song's lyrics are inspired by a book about German painter George Grosz, in which someone—it may have been Grosz himself, but Sadier couldn't remember—talks about how important it is to remain creative, whatever is going on around you.

'This song is about shifting the perception, saying that we are not the victims, but that we are the creators—we're not here to cry over our desolate fate, we're here to create the world that we desire. If you look at things from that point of view, then it's optimistic,' she explained.

'The message [the song] carries is very central to our work, or at least to my lyrical work, that we're all creative beings and we're all implicated in the course that humanity will follow.'

Running alongside the band's recordings, we have Stereolab's music videos, hand-made record sleeves, and a rich vein of side projects and guest appearances. The group—and especially Tim Gane and Laetitia Sadier—are always making things. In 1998, however, nestled between *Dots And Loops* and *Cobra And Phases Group Play Voltage In The Milky Night*, they enjoyed what some people might consider the ultimate act of human creation: making a child.

I am not, of course, suggesting that Laetitia and Tim's son, Alex, was the *equivalent* in any way of the band's music, much less some kind of side project. Parenting is hard work. It's just that I like the idea of Alex—from conception to education—existing somewhere in the brilliantly creative line that has marked Tim and Laetitia's lives: another mode of creation, alongside the records, very different in its own way and certainly more important. But creation nonetheless.

Maybe it is because I am a parent myself, but I find the influence of parenthood on Stereolab's music a fascinating subject. The old, tired idea of the writer Cyril Connolly that 'There is no more sombre enemy of good art than the pram in the hallway' is thankfully given short shrift these days. But I can't imagine writing, recording, and releasing an album with a new child to attend to, as Stereolab did while making their sixth studio LP, *Cobra And Phases Group Play Voltage In The Milky Night*. And I certainly can't imagine taking a young child on tour.

Generally—and very unfairly—having a child doesn't fit into the idea of the rock'n'roll life, which is full of clichés about drugs, booze, and extreme behaviour. But then neither do Stereolab, in many ways, and it sounds like the band enjoyed having a baby on tour.

Morgane Lhote, who played keyboards in Stereolab from 1995 to 2001, says that it was 'awesome' to tour with a baby. 'What was really cool about Stereolab is that it was cool being in a band with women. And I remember touring in the States when Laetitia was pregnant, and I was like, You don't see that often. First of all, touring with women in a band, and also a woman that's pregnant. I just loved it,' she says.

Going on tour with Alex, she explains, 'was almost like being a family. We had the nanny, but sometimes I would put him to sleep and wait until he was asleep,' she says. 'I think it was a continuation of being in a band that was a good environment to be in, as a young woman, because nothing crazy would happen on tour. It was safe.'

In her book *Connection Is A Song*, Anna Doble mentions interviewing Stereolab for the *Leeds Student* magazine before they played the Cockpit in the autumn of 1999. I asked Doble about this when I interviewed her around the release of her book, intrigued by the idea of being parents on tour. 'I'm pretty sure they joked about Tommee Tippee cups being scattered around their dressing room instead of booze,' she says, 'and said it had changed their view of how to travel/tour, because sleeping was now the priority.'

Alex was born 'a few months before recording started on *Cobra*', according to the sleeve notes of the 2019 reissue. The year 1997 had been a busy one for the group. As well as writing and recording *Dots And Loops*, they played forty-one gigs in Europe and the USA. To mark the occasion, they released the traditional tour seven-inch single, which paired the sumptuous stroll of 'The Incredible He Woman' with the rolling, percussive groove of 'Iron Man', one of those brilliantly danceable but controlled Stereolab freak-outs.

The same year also saw the release of *Simple Headphone Mind*, the band's second collaboration with Nurse With Wound, although in this case Stereolab's involvement was limited to handing over the master tapes of 'The Long Hair Of Death', from their 1995 split single with Yo La Tengo, and letting Steven Stapleton get on with his de/reconstructive work.

The following year, 1998, was quieter, in terms of touring and releases. The band played fifteen dates in the UK, Oceania, Japan, and the USA, and released the *Uilab* collaborative EP with American post-rock group Ui, the band led by journalist Sasha Frere-Jones, as well as a split seven-inch single with Soi-Disant.

The band's biggest release of 1998, however, was *Aluminum Tunes*, aka *Switched On Volume 3*, which rounded up twenty-five offcuts, rare songs, and otherwise unavailable material that they had originally released between 1994 and 1997. The album is a beautiful selection of artistic idiosyncrasy whose eclecticism shows the magnificent range of the band's musical thinking.

For the recording of *Cobra*, the band once again called on John McEntire to produce, alongside Chicago musician and producer Jim O'Rourke. Richard Harrison had left the band by this point, so the bass was now being handled by Simon Johns (who would soon join full-time) as well as the ever-adaptable Sean O'Hagan and O'Rourke himself.

'We were all in the same circle of people,' says McEntire of the decision to bring in O'Rourke. 'They had a great admiration for Gastr Del Sol [O'Rourke's group] and Jim's solo work. Jim was really coming into his own as an artist at the time, too, and as a producer. And I feel like it made total sense. We complemented each other.'

O'Rourke's introduction to Stereolab's work came via *Transient Random-Noise Bursts With Announcements*, but he had also been aware of Tim Gane's work with the power electronic group Uncommunity in the 1980s. 'If you were into the underground, cassette noise, trading mail thing that was happening in the 80s, which I was, that's where the first things I put out were,' he says. 'Uncommunity was on a label, Broken Flag, which was one of the big players in that tiny world.'

O'Rourke was unaware that Stereolab were fans of Gastr Del Sol. Instead, he and Tim connected as record collectors and lovers of obscure music (although Gane would never accept O'Rourke's love for 10CC). O'Rourke doesn't remember meeting Stereolab when Gastr Del Sol supported them in Chicago in 1994—although he says it could well have happened—but by the time of the recording of the band's sixth studio album, they were friends, having got to know each other when Stereolab recorded *Dots And Loops* in Chicago in 1997.

O'Rourke says that the invite from Gane to record part of the album was very casual. 'Tim just asked me one day—they were in Chicago for a show or something. He said, Oh, thinking of asking you and John to do the next one [album], do you want to come over to London for a little while? And that was my first big—I don't want to say production job, but recording/producing job for anybody who played for more than fifty 50 people. So it was kind of a big deal.'

This would be the third album in a row where Stereolab used two different producers ('producers', incidentally, isn't the word Stereolab tend to use, but it seems to fit), and O'Rourke says it made sense for him to work on the same album as McEntire, who had different skills and specialities. 'There's a very specific technical sound that John is very, very good at getting, that I can't do, and quite frankly, I wouldn't want to do,' he says. 'It's not what I like. It's not what I do. But I don't mean that in the way that I don't like what John does.'

There is, in fact, a huge amount of mutual respect between these two Chicago musicians. O'Rourke, McEntire explains, is 'a really good arranger. He could also play basically anything.* And I'm a little bit more like a technical guy: the synths and the tech stuff, that's my world. He's more the instrumentalist, arranger, the writerly person. He's got tech chops for days, obviously, too.'

There would be very little crossover between the two when working on *Cobra*, however. Gane would apparently decide from his demos which songs each man was to work on, and O'Rourke says he didn't even *hear* McEntire's productions until the album came out.

Meanwhile, Simon Johns came into the band's orbit thanks to his involvement with Clear Spot, a band he formed with My Bloody Valentine drummer Colm Ó Císóig, who released the seven-inch 'Moonman Bop' / 'Psycho's Blues' on Duophonic Super 45s in 1998. He says that joining Stereolab was 'a bit daunting, because I'd gone from being in a band that played to one man and his dog in the local pub. So it was a big step up in terms of professionalism. It was nerve-wracking. They had known each other for almost ten years.'

McEntire's presence provided continuity for the band as they prepared to record their sixth studio album, but Alex's recent birth meant they opted to stay in London, rather than fly out to Chicago to record, eventually settling on Wolf Studios in the heart of Brixton, when their usual London studio, Blackwing, was unavailable. (They did, in fact, record one song at Blackwing: 'Italian Shoes Continuum', in February 1998.)

McEntire says that Alex wasn't a problem during the sessions. The studio, however, was a different matter. 'It was a guy—the first

* On *Cobra*, he contributes bass, guitar, keyboards, percussion, and string arrangements.

or the ground floor of the guy's flat, basically, was a studio,' he says. 'He [studio owner Dominique Brethes] had a big analogue desk in there and the twenty-four-track machine and all the outboard gear. It was extremely uncomfortable and really oddly kind of configured, so everything was a bit of a struggle. Then the drum room was like a tiny bedroom, basically. So that's why all the drum sounds on that record are super, super dead, and it wasn't a really pleasant experience overall. But I think the record turned out great.'

There were certain time pressures, too. O'Rourke says that the 'filter freak-out solo' on the last section of 'Blue Milk' 'is literally me playing it while I'm putting down the final mix. Because the guy wanted all of Stereolab's gear out of the studio on the last day, and I was still mixing. So they were literally pulling all the gear out of the studio while I was mixing "Blue Milk".'

Brethes himself says that the band had booked his studio because it was local. 'They were in the process of building a studio, using a similar choice of equipment, but it was not ready in time for this album,' he says. 'My studio is on the small size, particularly the live room, but they came to inspect it and were happy with it.

'What I remember is that Tim and Laetitia had a newborn, and there seemed to be a little tension between them at times,' he adds. 'The band members, including Sean, were very nice, though Laetitia kept her distance.'

The studio was one enforced change for the band. They also decided to record without a click track to mark time, which gave the music a looser feel. O'Rourke says he never uses a click anyway. 'There's lots of stuff you can't do [if you don't have a click], but there's a lot of stuff you *can* do that people think you can't.'

'We used Pro Tools,' says Johns, 'and I think we were all quite dazzled by the fact you could quantise live drums. So we did a bit of that, moving stuff around,' he adds, noting that, as a result, *Cobra* has 'a more constructed feel than the previous records'.

This is another of Stereolab's magnificent contradictions. Johns calls the album 'constructed', but it is also one of the band's freest, most sprawling records. Gane, speaking to *The Guardian*, called it his favourite Stereolab LP, alongside the follow-up, *Sound-Dust*, as well as 'the weirdest album'. That may be pushing things somewhat, but *Cobra* is significantly different to what came before, with electronic sounds pushed to the back and jazz influences brought to the fore.

'The Free Design', the album's first single, is wrapped tightly around a jazz riff; 'Fuses' is an orgy of decadent jazz feel; 'Blips Drips And Strips' reminds me of the big-band standard 'Take 5', allied to one of the band's most unusual vocal arrangements; and 'Italian Shoes Continuum' has the kind of racing jazz drums that you can imagine your bohemian grandparents getting down to in the swinging 1940s. Given that these songs all come in the album's first half, you can understand why some fans were put off by what feels like a radical shift in focus.*

The second half of the album sees the latent Beach Boys influences in Stereolab come into focus. After the wonderful 'Puncture In The Radax Permutation', which Jim O'Rourke says is his favourite song on the album, thanks to the gorgeous string arrangement in the song's end section, 'Caleidoscopic Gaze' combines 'California Girls' piano boogie—the studio had a stand-up piano, which the group attacked with drawing pins in order to get an authentically 60s tack piano sound—with a 'Good Vibrations'-esque musical saw.

The album closes with 'Strobo Acceleration' (a rare mid-period Stereolab song to feature a Motorik beat), the twinkling romance of 'The Emergency Kisses', and the lustrous 'Come And Play In The Milky Night', which Gane considers one of the band's best ever songs. It was also a favourite of late American hip-hop producer J Dilla (aka Jay Dee), who sampled it for Busta Rhymes' 'Show Me What You Got' and two Jaylib songs: 'The Message' and 'Poisonous'.

•

Cobra was released in September 1999, two years after *Dots And Loops*—an unusually long gap for a group as prolific as Stereolab. Talking to the *Washington Post* around the time of its release, Gane said that the gap 'appears longer than it is', adding, 'We tour a lot more now. In the early days, we could go right back into making a new record. After *Dots*

* It's worth mentioning, though, that the cosmically lustrous 'Infinity Girl', one of the best-loved—and perhaps most typically Stereolab—songs on the album also falls in *Cobra*'s first half.

And Loops, we toured for like seven months. Then we had our child. Obviously, we were caught up in that, but we carried on doing some recording, small pieces, remixes, and some music for other things here and there.'

You can feel the influence of new parenthood on *Cobra* in several ways. The group's decision to record in London clearly had an influence on the record's sound, although, without the benefit of easily accessible parallel universes, it is impossible to say how *Cobra* would have played out in Chicago.

Certainly, the album often has a gentler sound than most previous Stereolab records, but the band were already moving in that direction on *Dots And Loops*. I like to think, too, that the sleep-addled minds of Gane and Sadier, struggling with the demands of a young child, as all parents do, also influenced the rather disjointed sound of *Cobra*, which works well when the listener's own mind is unfocused and open to diversion. The tightly coiled chaos of 'Fuses', for example, sounds exactly like the inside of a new parent's head, rushing to get the baby ready and out the door without forgetting the nappies, wipes, milk bottles, and other essential supplies for even the shortest trip into the outer world.

Lyrically, too, parenthood appears to have had an influence. 'Caleidoscopic Gaze' and 'Strobo Acceleration' both examine the role of women in society, with the former making a reference to the 1978 book *Woman And Nature: The Roaring Inside Her*, by feminist philosopher Susan Griffin, and the latter looking at the liberty of women. These songs are by no means the first time that Sadier has examined these themes in her lyrics—1997's 'The Incredible He Woman', for example, tracks Mary's transformation into Jesus—and it may be entirely wrong to link these preoccupations to Laetitia becoming a mother. But it feels worth a mention.

'The Emergency Kisses', meanwhile, reads like a yearning for past romance, a time of kissing on a park bench and the revelation of desire, a nostalgic feeling many new parents can relate to as romance becomes a waking dream among the hard reality of dirty nappies and sleepless nights.

But it is 'People Do It All The Time' that really brings home the delightful shock of parenting to *Cobra*. The song's lyrics focus on parenthood as an act of creation, the wonder and happiness that a new child brings, as well as the slightly dazed feeling that marks the first few months of a baby's life. At one point, Laetitia directly addresses her joyful new baby, in what feels like one of the most open-hearted and revealing moments in the band's catalogue. The song vibrates with a vivid humanity, the love for a fellow human being shining through.

Stereolab songs are often oblique, full of political ideas and obscure references. 'People Do It All The Time', by contrast, feels remarkably straightforward: it is a song of love and wonder, in which Laetitia looks forward to the future of her young son. It reminds me of the first few moments I spent with my own children and the promises I babbled to them: serious and sincere, but also dangerously drunk on hormonal love. I adore the song's title, too, with its casual downplaying of the wonders of birth: because, yes, people *do* do it all the time. But that doesn't make every single birth any less magical.

Sadier also deals with the subject of pregnancy in Monade's 'Cache Cache', a song released in August 1998 on a seven-inch single, with 'Calimero', Stereolab's collaboration with Brigitte Fontaine, on the other side. 'Cache cache' translates into 'hide and seek' in English, and Sadier told the Red Bull Music Academy that she wrote it because Alex 'was supposed to come out on a certain due date, and he took much longer to come out'.

'It was a song, well, don't be scared of coming out, even if the world might seem like a sombre place,' she added, after the interviewer, Nick Dwyer, had played the record. 'To come out and play. Yes, it's very emotional to hear this, because now I know why I don't play my records because it makes me want to cry. Mary [Hansen] is all over this. She's playing the keyboard and she's singing. I totally remember being pregnant like this, and Mary playing the keyboards and me engineering.'

Monade started in 1996. In Stereolab, Gane wrote the music and Sadier penned the lyrics and vocal melodies, a division of labour that she eventually found frustrating. (It is telling that Sadier contributed a great deal, musically, to *Instant Holograms On Metal Film*, Stereolab's post-reunion album of 2025.)

'That was the contract that I did not know I was signing with Tim:

that he would control the music absolutely and entirely,' Sadier told *The Guardian* in 2019. 'There were other things in Stereolab that were frustrating me, too. It was always too layered—I would hear the songs on a four-track demo and their power and their essence, and I felt: This is beautiful. There was a way of working that was very industrial and mass produced, that was really driving me crazy. And we weren't laughing that much.'

Monade was a reaction to this, as well as an outlet for her own creativity. 'It was extremely liberating and very fun,' she told the Red Bull Music Academy. 'I would say that the Monade projects—I did three albums—were really like a playground, because I had to construct my own identity, but within a school that was Tim's school of music, as I called it. I had to find my own voice, who I was.'

'It was quite healing to be in a band: ah, you can be in a band and have a lot of fun!' she later explained to *The Guardian*. 'And be really friendly and love each other! Not that we didn't love each other in Stereolab, I think we did very much. But it was not really expressed somehow—people were grumpy.'

Cobra came at a new period in Sadier and Gane's lives. But it also marked a fresh phase for the band: the heavy guitars of *Transient Random-Noise Bursts With Announcements* had long disappeared; electronics retreated from the mix now too, as jazz and lounge music came increasingly to the fore. Stereolab also felt slightly unfocused, with the furiously concentrated rush of songs like 'John Cage Bubblegum' replaced with the meandering of 'Caleidoscopic Gaze'. From now on, the band's frantic release schedule would ease too, with at least two years passing between albums.

The decision to ease up sonically was a conscious one, with the band aiming to produce a looser style of music. Talking to *The Guardian* in 2019 about *Cobra* and its follow-up, *Sound-Dust*, Gane says that he likes 'things that are sprawling and not identified really easily, not easy to digest but there's a lot of possibilities in them'. This is *Cobra* in a nutshell.

These possibilities didn't exactly go over well with the critics, who gave *Cobra* a mauling. In the *NME*, journalist Johnny Cigarettes awarded the album 0/10 for its 'bad jazz and progressive rock', claiming that the band hadn't written a good pop song since 1993.

Pitchfork, meanwhile, gave the album a score of 3.4, criticising the band's 'socialist cocktail jazz schtick'.

'I still carry around the fact that the *NME* gave it a zero out of ten for no fucking reason,' says McEntire. 'They just want to be reactionary. It's a good record. It's *great*. I thought that was total bullshit. But for some reason that kind of clouds my feelings about it.'

There were positive reviews too, but even among Stereolab fans, *Cobra* remains divisive. Some claim it is the band's best work; others—perhaps the majority—feel it is overly long and lacks that one *killer* song.

What's frustrating is that the three extra songs on the *Free Design* EP, which preceded the release of *Cobra* by two weeks, are uniformly excellent and could perhaps have improved the album. 'Escape Pod (From The World Of Medical Observations)' is a bizarre, collapsing boogie with a lovely melody; 'Les Aimies Des Memes' has a delicious bass line; and 'With Friends Like These' is a classic duet between Sadier and Hansen, their two vocal lines fluttering off each other with character and affection, like a cotton-candy take on Lee Hazlewood and Nancy Sinatra.

Cobra didn't sell particularly well, either, making only #92 in the UK charts and #154 in the USA. There was still time in 1999 for the release of the tour single *The Underground Is Coming*, which includes the tough dance number 'The Super-It', as well as the downright bizarre 'Fried Monkey Eggs And Monkey Jelly.'

'The Super-It' would later be released as a single to promote the release of *Electrically Possessed* (*Switched On Volume 4*) in 2021. In a press release, Gane called it 'a kind of lost song in a way . . . written not for an LP but around the same time as the Brigitte Fontaine "Caliméro" seven-inch (in which, I think, it shares a big similarity) and recorded at the same time as the tracks for the abandoned *Charlie's Angels In Space* video game ("Fried Monkey Eggs" etc . . .) although this track was never intended for that project.*

'In our earlier days, it would have ended up as a single itself,' Gane

* I can only apologise to the reader that I have discovered *nothing* about the *Charlie's Angels In Space* video game. Even Stereolab band members who played on 'Fried Monkey Eggs' appear to know nothing about it.

added of the song, 'but this was now the LP period of the Groop, and so we ended up releasing it as part of a tour single EP. Immaculately recorded by Fulton Dingley, it sounds wonderful and certainly one of the best from the period. Maybe we should have waited a bit and put it on *Margerine Eclipse*.'

There are perhaps more ifs, buts, and maybes around this period of Stereolab's life than any other, as the group changed their sound and (arguably) shrunk their audience in the process. *Cobra And Phases Group Play Voltage In The Milky Night* might not have been a commercial or critical hit; it is a chaotic, turbulent record that gives few easy answers. But I value it as a rare album that speaks to the loving chaos of early parenthood, without resorting to cliché and babble. (Which new parent hasn't experienced the turmoil of a milky night?) It would also go on to make some interesting waves in the USA, as we will see in the next chapter.

13

'COME AND PLAY IN THE MILKY NIGHT'

RECYCLING

The roots of sampling—that is, using a portion of someone else's music as part of your own composition—can be traced back to the none-more-Stereolab sound of* musique concrète*, when French composer Pierre Schaeffer started creating elaborate sonic collages in the 1940s, using recordings of the human body, trains, and kitchen utensils.

Stereolab favourite John Cage experimented with similar techniques on his early 1950s composition 'Williams Mix', which uses various recorded sources on tape, divided into six categories: city, country, electronic, manually produced, wind, and 'small' sound. Meanwhile, Can's Holger Czukay would splice tape recordings into the band's music before the birth of digital sampling.*

The first use of sampling in pop music was, according to the slightly odd source that is *The Guinness Book Of World Records*, 'He's Gonna Step On You Again', a 1971 song by South African musician John Kongos that used a sample of African drumming. Others claim

* See, in particular, the 1977 album *Saw Delight*.

that the good people at Guinness have confused 'He's Gonna Step On You Again' with 'Burundi Black', a 1971 song by Burundi Steiphenson Black, aka French composer Michel Bernholc, which uses a drum sample from the 1968 album *Musique Du Burundi*.

Whatever the case, by the time Stereolab lurched onto the London scene in the early 1990s, sampling was a well-established tool of musical production thanks to the advent of hip-hop and dance music, both of which rely heavily on borrowing pieces of other people's records.

Given Stereolab's love of musique concrète, the avant-garde, and collage itself, it was inevitable that they would lean toward sampling, and yet it's not generally an element of the Stereolab sound that gets much attention. I wonder if there is a certain snobbery at play. In the early 1990s, when Stereolab started, the use of sampling in rock music was generally concentrated on indie dance, which was about to become very unfashionable indeed as musical trends moved on.

To certain music fans, sampling was (and even perhaps still is) seen as laziness, as earning your musical satisfaction on the back of someone else's hard-worn creation. Maybe that is why I almost prefer to think of what Stereolab did as *recycling* other people's work, which gives it a kind of virtuous sheen, as well as a more open meaning.

Whatever term you want to use, Stereolab employed sampling/recycling/reusing extensively. To take an early example: 'Enivrez-vous', from the group's debut album, *Peng!*, doesn't just take its lyrics and title from a poem by Baudelaire; it also includes what Gane, in the album's sleeve notes, calls 'a small sample' of 'Miss Fortune', a 1971 song by Krautrock pioneers Faust, 'which was layed [sic] over the top almost at random'. You can hear this at about the 2:24 mark—a soupçon of wah-wah organ that adds texture and tone to the Stereolab original.

'You Little Shits', another *Peng!* track, features what may be another Krautrock sample, this time courtesy of Neu!'s 1972 track 'Super'. Gane says that he doesn't remember if the song's beat is Joe Dilworth playing or not, but other sources have claimed it as a borrowing from Neu!, pitched down significantly.

By the time of *Transient Random-Noise Bursts With Announcements*, Stereolab's use of sampling was in full swing. The album's cover lists four samples, and there could have been more, with Stereolab having to re-record 'Pack Yr Romantic Mind' at the last minute after they were refused permission to use a portion of George Harrison's *Wonderwall Music*.

According to WhoSampled, which is generally accurate, there are sixty-seven samples in Stereolab songs. This is almost certainly too high a number, and it includes samples used in songs that Stereolab have remixed. But the list's incredible range offers a fascinating insight into what people think makes Stereolab tick.

Some of these alleged samples are from predictable sources: Neu!, Kraftwerk, Cluster, and so on. Others are from far less obvious places. 'The Free Design' is said to use the brass arrangement from ABBA's 'Dancing Queen' (which would be an interpolation rather than a sample, but still); 'Jump Drive Shut-Out', a 2006 tour single, apparently samples Loose Joints' much abused disco classic 'Is It All Over My Face?'; and another single from the same year, 'Interlock', is said to sample Sharon Scott's 1966 northern soul classic 'Could It Be You?'*

Stereolab's samples can be divided into two categories: garnish and building blocks. The former, such as the Faust sample on 'Enivrez-vous', add a layer of interest that the songs could have probably lived without. Sometimes, as on *TRNBWA*'s 'I'm Going Out Of My Way', which uses a portion of Perrey & Kingsley's cover of Antônio Jobim's 'One Note Samba', the sample is basically there to act as a transition between tracks.

Building block samples, which are rarer in the Stereolab world, are fundamental to the song in question. One of my favourite examples of this is 'Free Witch And No Bra Queen', one half of a 2001 tour single. The song's opening section essentially consists of Stereolab making fun with a jazzy bossa nova sample, twisting, twerking, echoing and layering it into a particularly groovy type of submission. Similarly, I'm not sure 'Jump Drive Shut-Out' could exist without its disco loop. That both songs appear on tour singles is probably no coincidence: this is Stereolab at their most playful, letting their collective hair down

* I make no claims about the accuracy of this list. Sampling can be a tricky matter, so let's just say that we don't know *for sure* what Stereolab have sampled, unless they have confirmed it themselves.

in the name of musical fun, without the hassle of an album to think about.

Using the term 'recycling' rather than 'sampling' for this chapter is deliberate, as it allows me to dig into the different ways in which Stereolab have used other people's art for inspiration. Of course, all bands borrow, and all bands are inspired. But Stereolab do so in a very enlightening way. It is often said of Gane in particular that he is very skilled at borrowing from other people's work in order to reinvent it.

To pick just a few recyclings: *Emperor Tomato Ketchup* takes its name from an experimental film made by avant-garde Japanese filmmaker Shūji Terayama, while the album's cover artwork is inspired by the LP cover of a 1964 recording of Bartók's *Concerto For Orchestra* by the Bamberg Symphony.

Cliff, the cartoon figure who appears on a number of the band's early record sleeves, was borrowed from a Swiss political comic, and 'Elektro (He Held The World In His Iron Grip)', the final song on the *Low Fi* EP, takes its name from the cover of a 1961 issue of the comic book *Tales Of Suspense*. None of these is obvious; all of them are intriguing. They feel like breadcrumbs for the intrepid Stereolab fan to follow, half parlour game, half library tip.

In turn, Stereolab's music has been recycled by other artists, with hip-hop producers proving particularly keen. At the time of writing, WhoSampled lists fifty songs that have sampled Stereolab and, if some of these don't really count—Stereolab and Nurse With Wound 'sampling' Stereolab on their collaborative releases, for example—it is still a surprisingly high number for a band that emerged from London's shambling early 90s indie scene. Th' Faith Healers—and I don't mean to pick on them, but it is an obvious comparison—have never been sampled, according to the WhoSampled database, while Tortoise, who would seem more hip-hop friendly, have only been sampled three times.

When I asked Tim Gane about this in 2008, he said that he saw a certain connection between Stereolab's working methods and the hip-hop artists who have sampled them. 'I identify with the way they make music,' he explained. 'Rather than a band that makes songs, like them, I tend to pick and mix. Everything is there to be used.'

It is not just the number of times that Stereolab have been sampled that is impressive. The *quality* of acts to have sampled them is high, too, reflecting a respect for the band that exists among some of the world's most celebrated hip-hop producers.

The late J Dilla, for example, sampled 'Come And Play In The Milky Night' on Busta Rhymes's 'Show Me What You Got', as well as using 'Refractions In The Plastic Pulse' on Slum Village's 2000 track 'Untitled/Fantastic'. In a 2001 interview with BBC Radio 1's Gilles Peterson, Dilla mentioned Stereolab as one of his favourite bands of the moment, alongside Radiohead.

Madlib, another hugely respected US producer, is also a Stereolab fan. He sampled 'The Flower Called Nowhere' on his 2014 track 'Ra Ash' and used 'Velvet Water' on his 2003 production for Wildchild, 'Hands Up'. Jaylib, the duo formed by Dilla and Madlib, sampled 'Come And Play In The Milky Night' on 'The Message', while Madlib's unreleased 'Stereolab Flip' is a wonder of parallel musical thinking, as he squashes 'The Flower Called Nowhere' (again) into a lolloping hip-hop beat.

There are plenty more examples, too: one of my favourite Stereolab flips is Brandy's 2012 track 'Slower', on which British producer Switch transforms 'Fluorescences' into a sublimely sensual R&B song.

'I had been playing Stereolab to an intern at the time,' Switch, aka Dave Taylor, explains. 'We had been referencing Jackson—the French producer—and the way he utilises samples. We were trying to do that. It didn't come out as planned at all, but we landed on something cool with a loop from the "Fluorescences" track. The next day, I was in a session with Chris Brown, who co-wrote "Slower". I was playing with it, and he just started dancing and fake-falling over. It was odd: that fella's quite a presence when he gets up—brilliant in the studio. He started singing on some Michael Jackson steez, and Brandy literally just pounced. We ended up with something a bit different for her—but still fitting. She was well on it.'

Pharrell Williams and Flying Lotus are avowed Stereolab fans, with the latter praising *Dots And Loops* and the 2005 compilation *Oscillons From The Anti-Sun* in a 2012 interview with *Westword*. 'I love that sound,' he said. 'I feel like it's very California. It feels like where I live. It just feels like it was made in the sunshine.'

It wasn't, of course. But it is notable that the Stereolab music that hip-hop producers sample comes largely from the *Dots And Loops/ Cobra And Phases Group* era, when the group eased up on the guitar velocity and allowed their jazz influences to seep through, with only the occasional artist reaching further back into the group's catalogue.

I said in the last chapter that Stereolab's audience arguably shrank around *Cobra*, and in terms of dedicated listeners, it probably did. At the same time, hip-hop producers' sampling of Stereolab's music from this era has probably given it a bigger passive audience than anything else that the band has released.

Taylor says that Stereolab are popular among hip-hop and R&B producers because their songs have 'moments': 'You have to listen to everything, every turnaround, drums, pre-chorus, the ramp, outros because it's always surprising,' he says. 'Like Matthew Herbert or something, there are loops and stings all over the place. It's worth the hunt—which is what separates the best hip-hop producers, in my opinion—hunting in the unlikely places. Stereolab falls into that because they're a lot of everything—with a common thread of soul and funk.'

Taylor names Madlib's 'Ra Ash' as his favourite use of a Stereolab sample. 'Not really for the sample, which is a very, very, very tricky spot,' he says. 'But that a Stereolab record is playing in the background of one of the most textbook Madlib beats—cheeky.'

Of all the producers who have sampled Stereolab, J Dilla is probably the most significant. The producer, composer and rapper, born James Yancey in February 1974, has become a hip-hop eternal, his reputation soaring after his death in 2006 from a combination of TTP and lupus. Although he did rap, Dilla was best known for his production style, which brought a behind-the-beat looseness to drum programming that has gone on to influence producers and drummers alike.

His second studio album, *Donuts,* released three days before his death, is considered one of the best hip-hop albums of all time, and his production work for the likes of Common, Busta Rhymes, A Tribe Called Quest, The Pharcyde, De La Soul, and his own group, Slum Village, is legendary. So, to have J Dilla sample your song not once but *thrice*, and to keep your production largely intact, as the producer did with 'Come And Play In The Milky Night', is a major feather in the

Stereolab cap—a sign that their music was capable of resonating far beyond the universe of alternative guitars. And it has helped 'Come And Play' become one of the group's biggest, most-loved songs, especially in the USA.*

Morgane Lhote says that being sampled was a 'logical conclusion' to Stereolab's work. '[Stereolab] borrowed from a lot of people. So, it is the logical conclusion that people would borrow from them,' she says. 'To me, that seems like a good circle.'

Sean O'Hagan, who worked on *Cobra And Phases Group Play Voltage In The Milky Night*, returned the favour to James Yancey in 2024 with the release of The High Llamas' eleventh studio album, *Hey Panda*, on which the influence of Dilla runs strong. 'This record had to address what I have come to love,' he said, when announcing the album's release. 'Dilla reshaped the world. We live in the finest non-judgemental musical times, where the legacies of soul, jazz and lo-fi indie have produced a hybrid of generous and stunning creativity. I want *Hey Panda* to be of this generation.'

When I spoke to O'Hagan for Radio Primavera Sound in 2024, he praised J Dilla's musical appeal. 'The thing about Dilla was, people talk about his beats, and they talk about the fact he was off the grid,' he said. 'And when he was presenting his ideas, there were people, hip-hop producers, who were just saying, Is it me, or does this sound wrong or does it sound new?

'That's what he was doing rhythmically. But he was a very musical guy. As a kid, he was very musical, very naturally musical. I think he was a cellist as a kid, and his household was quite musical. His uncle and his dad, they were avid record collectors and possibly DJs, and he loved harmony and he loved jazz, and he loved reaching for great sounds. He wasn't just going to reach for a beat that was visceral and was going to affect people physically. He wanted to reach for great chords.'

When I interviewed Laetitia Sadier in 2024, I asked her why she thought hip-hop acts loved Stereolab's music. 'I think our music appeals to music lovers,' she said. 'People really have this kind of melomania

* In one of those weird algorithmic quirks, the two-minute demo version of 'Come And Play In The Milky Night', released as part of the 2019 *Cobra* reissue, has become one of Stereolab's most popular songs on Spotify, its warm, jazzy softness lending itself to playlists.

[a deep love of music]. And the chords and melodies and rhythms, you know, maybe it's put in a way that no one's quite done it like that before? It suscitates images, and maybe they find that attractive: very, very musical and dark, but optimistic, somehow. It's a blend of two forces, of masculine and feminine and darkness and light. Maybe it speaks to certain types of artists.'

Being sampled brought Stereolab's music into the mainstream in a way that had never really happened before. Busta Rhymes' album *Anarchy*, which is home to 'Show Me What You Got', charted at #4 in the USA and sold more than a million copies, while Brandy's *Two Eleven*, on which 'Slower' appears, made it to #2—chart placings way beyond anything Stereolab ever achieved on their own. The group's popularity among hip-hop producers would also lead to some intriguing collaborations, as the group continued to show how brilliantly unusual they could be.

14

'NOTHING TO DO WITH ME'

DADAISM

For all their political views and love of the avant-garde, Stereolab can be pretty ridiculous when they want to be.

If you take a step back, many of their song titles are laugh-out-loud funny. 'Moogie Wonderland', anyone? 'How To Play Your Internal Organs Overnight'? 'The Noise Of Carpet'? 'Italian Shoes Continuum'? 'Daisy Click Clack'? There is a website that features people's best fake Stereolab song titles that always makes me laugh because, frankly, you can easily imagine Stereolab calling a song 'Beanbag Exit #9' or 'Box-Prong Modulator'. It is very much to the band's credit that some of their song/album titles manage to be both insightful *and* funny: see *Space Age Batchelor Pad Music*.

The band's record sleeves can be pretty silly, too, notably when they featured Cliff and his shit-eating semi-grin, and some of the band's outrageous musical fusions—prog-jazz lounge or Krautrock glam, for example—are frankly absurd, even if they always manage to pull them off.

We can perhaps trace this back to their love of Dadaism. Dadaist artists employed nonsense and irrationality to reject the steely logic of modern capitalism, using techniques such as performance art, collage, sound poetry, cut-up writing, and sculpture to renounce violence, war, and nationalism. Dada was a precursor to surrealism and an influence on the Situationist International, as well as on musicians like Frank Zappa and David Bowie, who used William S. Burroughs' Dada-inspired cut-up technique for lyric writing.

It was also a huge influence on Stereolab. Speaking to *The Arts Desk* in 2023, Sadier explained that the Dada movement 'echoed my desire for freedom . . . but also the transgression of the straitjackets that a big part of humanity has either been made to wear or has worn on behalf of their ancestors without questioning its wider implications.'

We can see a link, too, between Dada and the absurdist thinking of Camus, whereby the absence of god creates a void at the centre of existence. 'Something needed to break free, and they started chipping away at it unseen,' Sadier explained to *The Arts Desk*. 'Those post-modern ways brought the artistic discourse to a whole new level, which made us observe ourselves with a fresh set of eyes that could penetrate corners of the psyche that hadn't been reached in that godless way before. God was not in charge anymore. Technology was making huge breakthroughs. So, it made us ask that question: Who is in charge?'

In the same interview, Gane declared his favourite Dada artist to be Germany's Hannah Höch, citing in particular her photomontage work. 'Her collages bedazzled me long before I understood the wider meaning of Dada as a reaction to bourgeois society in general and the First World War,' he explained. 'As a (sort of/kind of) musician only, it's sometimes hard to analyse how something from a different medium affects your ideas in another.' Photomontage, he added, 'has the most direct affinity with the music I was into because of the whole punk and post-punk thing. It's quick to reassemble everyday images into hidden meanings and open up a whole new world of possibilities.'

It is inevitable that once you become aware of the influence of Dada on Stereolab, you start to see it everywhere. Dada, Sadier told *The Guardian*, was about 'putting one thing against another and seeing what happens and maybe you find a deeper truth in that collision'. On a fundamental level, Stereolab do this in their absurd musical combinations—Krautrock meets Yé-yé, bossa nova meets drone—and in their song titles, where depth and ridiculousness combine.

Indeed, the band's whole *existence* sometimes feels like a Dadaist experiment in rejecting societal norms. Whoever heard of a radically left-wing guitar group who signed to a major label and went on to influence the biggest hip-hop stars in the USA? How do you get to a situation where Pharrell Williams identifies 'The Flower Called Nowhere' as 'the best fellatio music there is'? And what are the band's collaborations with Nurse With Wound other than pure Dada instinct, a musical round of Exquisite Corpse?

On a more macro level, you can see the influence of Dada in some of the band's sonic collages, which sometimes—on '(Varoom!)' or 'Blue Milk'—jam together two bits of music that don't seem to have anything to do with each other, just because.

For me, though, the band's most Dadaist song came on their 2001 LP *Sound-Dust*, the band's seventh studio album and, I would argue, among their least understood records.

After the relative commercial failure of *Cobra And Phases Group Play Voltage In The Milky Night*, Stereolab returned to the fray in May 2000 with the fantastic EP *The First Of The Microbe Hunters*. The EP—Morgane Lhote's favourite Stereolab record—combines dazzling *Dots And Loops* offcut 'I Feel The Air (Of Another Planet)' with six new tracks recorded in January 2000: the Miles Davis electric-period grooves of 'Outer Bongolia' and 'Barock-Plastik'; the airy bossa nova laments of 'Intervals' and 'Nomus Et Phusis'; the 'Free Design'-ish 'Household Names'; and the awkward layers of 'Retrograde Mirror Form', a self-consciously ugly experiment in which Sadier begs to be left alone.

It is a fascinating record both musically and lyrically, offering an insight into Sadier's state of mind as the new century ground into gear. 'Barock-Plastik' is a reflection on the childhood promise of romance, while Household Names also tackles the subject of love, albeit through a thick fog of obfuscation. On 'Nomus Et Phusis', meanwhile, Sadier directly addresses her baby son, encouraging him to fight for freedom and truth and not let other people dictate their laws to him, bringing up again the idea of autonomy as liberty.

More than a year passed between the release of *The First Of The*

Microbe Hunters and the *Captain Easychord* EP, which hit the shelves in July 2001—a huge amount of time between releases for a band as relentlessly active as Stereolab. *Captain Easychord* is notable for the lead track's rollicking piano line and a country feel, relatively fresh territory for the band (after 'Tone Burst (Country)'), as well as the nightmarish, almost Shakespearean lyrics to 'Long Life Love'.

Mostly, though, the EP served as an introduction to *Sound-Dust*, Stereolab's seventh studio album and Gane's joint favourite. As on *Cobra*, production duties were split between John McEntire and Jim O'Rourke, although this time Stereolab travelled to Chicago to record—a decision that resulted in a host of guest musicians appearing, including Rob Mazureck on cornet, Chad Taylor on percussion, and Wilco's Glenn Kotche on crotales (small tuned bronze disks that you can hear on 'Captain Easychord' and 'Gus The Mynahbird').

Morgane Lhote had departed the band by this point. 'I got fired,' she explains, when I ask about her departure. 'It was in 2001. It was hilarious because it was April Fool's Day, and I got a phone call from Tim. And he said, I don't want you to play in the band anymore.'

Lhote was almost relieved, having spent a couple of unhappy years in the group due to personal tensions. 'I had some of the best times of my life in Stereolab, but also some pretty miserable times,' she says. 'I felt pretty bullied at some points.'

Simon Johns, meanwhile, had formally joined on bass. 'We stayed at John McEntire's house, and that was fun,' he says of the recording of *Sound-Dust*. 'Chicago's a good city. We were in Soma Studios, which is next to the Rainbo Club bar, where the post-rock people hung out. That was fun, meeting people I admired musically.'*

Johns says that the recording process for *Sound-Dust* was particularly long. 'Initially, it was me, Tim and Andy, the first few weeks,' he says. 'Tim was there for months and months.'

O'Rourke says that Gane wanted to do something consciously different with the band's new studio album. 'He actually asked me to go a bit hard on him: *If you think we're doing what we've done before,*

---

* The group were perfect house guests, according to McEntire, although he says they weren't at all prepared for the freezing Chicago winter.

you could tell us,' he explains. 'And I remember I kind of told off Sean [O'Hagan], which is really not my style. It was probably just me being young. I was like, If I hear you play that Beach Boys chord progression again . . .'

O'Rourke also worked with Sadier on her vocals for *Sound-Dust*. 'Like *crafting*, *pacing* of how to sing the lyrics,' he says. 'And I think she really, really appreciated that. I don't think anyone had done that with her before. Sit down with the lyrics and, *Okay, the phrasing of this here, you know, when this comes in . . . on this part of the word, pull away from the mic*. Things like that.'

This coaching, he says, is most obvious on 'The Black Arts', the album's theatrical centrepiece and one of its strongest songs, on which Sadier gives a gorgeously expressive vocal performance. '[*Sound-Dust*] was also where I was really starting to become the producer I would be,' O'Rourke says. 'I really think of [recording] as, like, doing the staging of a play. There's the lighting and there's the marking on the stage, all that stuff matters. And the key thing with that stuff, with certain types of music, is the vocals. That's the person doing the monologue, if you will.'

I wonder what made him decide to do this. 'It was probably because I was finally starting to feel confident,' he replies, after a moment's thought. 'And also, I had never really worked with anyone who's really *a singer* before.'

Sadier wasn't the only Stereolab member to benefit from O'Rourke's inspirational methods. In an interview with *Tape Op*, the producer mentioned that when recording *Sound-Dust*'s 'Nothing To Do With Me', Mary Hansen 'really had to sing out, because the character was supposed to be this bigot. . . . So she's singing it like she usually sings her back-up vocals. I thought that she really needed to step up to this. She wouldn't do it. So I ran into the live room with a stick and chased her out into the street and then back into the room and immediately pushed *record*. When she sang the part again, she was out of breath . . . she sang differently, and it worked.'

Johns remembers the *Sound-Dust* sessions as the first time that the band experimented with the 'dual mono' technique that they would later dive into headfirst on *Margerine Eclipse*. This essentially involves making different recordings for the left and right channels of the song's final mix. It's not *particularly* obvious on *Sound-Dust*, but you can just about make it out on 'Nothing To Do With Me', which features both Chad Taylor and Andy Ramsay on drums. 'Half the music is completely different to the other side, left and right,' Johns explains. 'They're complementary, but they're two distinct compositions that work together at the same time. That was fun, quite an intellectual challenge.'

'That was just Tim's MO,' says McEntire. 'He's like, This is how we're going to do the tracks. And I was like, That sounds amazing. Let's push the boundaries. Absolutely.'

It's no surprise, given the personnel involved, that *Sound-Dust* is often compared to *Cobra*, and certainly, both records have a loose, jazzy feel. Personally, though, I think *Sound-Dust* has more emotional depth, which is reflected in its very downbeat feel, particularly on songs like 'The Black Arts', where Sadier sings of being lonely, and 'Hallucinex', where she looks forward, rather ambiguously, to the show stopping. The brass-led intro to 'Baby Lulu', meanwhile, is one of the saddest sections of music that Stereolab ever committed to tape.

I ask McEntire if he thinks the Chicago winter might have been to blame for the album's dejected feel. 'I don't know about that. My big takeaway with that album was Tim was really kicking in with the contemporary classical stuff, which I was able to completely get on board with, and Jim as well,' he says, mentioning Ligeti, Bernard Herrmann scores, and Jacques Lejeune's *D'Une Multitude En Fête* as particular influences.

'Double Rocker', for example, has a 30-second section around the two-minute mark that is directly inspired by Ligeti's *Continuum* for harpsichord. 'It seemed like he [Tim] was taking a lot more chances,' McEntire says. 'And I thought that was fantastic.'

In the reissued album's sleeve notes, Gane describes the initial demos for *Sound-Dust* as 'rather claustrophobic and uniformly downbeat' and 'decidedly one paced', which led him to insert a number of upbeat sections into the songs, such as the Beach Boys-ish final section of 'Space Moth' and the 'groovin'' final half of 'Double Rocker'.

This is, perhaps, a curious thing to do with a band's songs. Most bands would either let the album's gloomy feel lie or write whole new songs, rather than new sections. But it shows how Stereolab benefited from their affinity for musical collage and the ability to flip genres. It doesn't seem unusual at all for 'Space Moth', for example, to end on a different emotional note to where it started, given Stereolab's history of in-song switches.

Without wanting to speculate too much, it is notable that Sadier and Gane separated as a romantic couple fairly soon after the release of *Sound-Dust*. It is possible, then, that some kind of romantic unhappiness can be heard in the album, particularly as it came at a time when O'Rourke was encouraging Sadier to refine her vocal technique. If that *was* the case—and this is pure conjecture—you can imagine why Gane would feel compelled to insert some levity into the album's demos.

On a happier level, Gane calls 'Suggestion Diabolique', the album's penultimate song, 'the culmination of everything we were trying to do with this record as a collective', writing that Sadier and Hansen's vocals 'have never sounded better together . . . Mary in particular brings great character to her vocal parts.' McEntire's production is 'amazing', the studio sounds wonderful, and the various sounds and effects 'integrate themselves so well with everything else going on', including 'Andy's tape slapback drums'.

Among such melancholy, the album's standout is 'Nothing To Do With Me', a surreal, outlandish riff that is the band's Dadaist masterpiece. Very different in tone to the majority of *Sound-Dust*, it's a lilting, Beach Boys-ish number that is full of sunshine, introduced by Mary in great voice. The song is really all about the lyrics, though, which are delivered in Hansen and Sadier's unflappable (if slightly breathless) style. They were derived from *Blue Jam*, a BBC radio show by British comedian Chris Morris, and *Jam*, its TV offspring.

Morris is a fascinating character. His early work on the news satire *On The Hour* and its TV spinoff, *The Day Today*, had an anarchic spirit, lampooning the norms of broadcast media and British society as a whole. One episode of *The Day Today*, for example, features passengers trapped on a train reverting to animalistic states, ostensibly as part of a report into an ongoing rail crisis. In another, Morris provokes a war between Australia and Hong Kong.

But this was nothing compared to the impact of *Brass Eye*, a TV series that aired in 1997 (with a 'Paedogeddon!' special following in 2001), in which Morris again parodied TV news. This time, he was pulling precisely no punches. The 1997 'Drugs' episode—in which Morris warns of the dangers of 'Cake', a new drug from the then non-existent Czechoslovakia that affects the user's 'Shatner's Bassoon', while also giving them the dreaded 'Czech neck'—was bad enough for the moral majority.

The 'Paedogeddon!' special was a genuine sensation, reportedly the most objected-to programme in British TV history at the time, with various politicians speaking out against Morris after it aired. The *News Of The World* tabloid published the names of all the writers of the show in a 'Role Of Shame', while *The Sun* said that all involved in the programme 'must never work in television again'. It gives some idea of Morris's character that he was apparently totally unmoved by the moral furore.

In 1997, around the same time that *Brass Eye* was bringing Morris to mainstream attention, he created the BBC Radio 1 show *Blue Jam*, a bizarre mixture of music (including Stereolab's 'Cybele's Reverie'), dark comedy, and horror. Morris is said to have described it as 'like the nightmares you have when you fall asleep listening to the BBC World Service'. Recurring sketches on the show included 'Doctor', who suggests bizarre treatments to his patients, such as prescribing heroin for a cold; and 'Bad Sex', in which two lovers make increasingly surreal demands of each other, such as to 'shit your leg off'.

In 2000, Channel 4 broadcast *Jam*, a televisual successor to *Blue Jam*, featuring a series of disconnected sketches, many of them taken straight from Morris's Radio 1 show, played out over ambient music. It was these sketches that provided the lyrics to 'Nothing To Do With Me'. The song's lyrics include a reference to an infamous Jam sketch in which a bereaved mother asks a plumber to 'fix' her dead baby, several allusions to the doctor and a mention of 'TV Lizards', in which a couple finds lizards in their television, all delivered in Sadier and Hansen's chillingly off-hand delivery.

Morris's work is often called surreal, but I consider it closer to Dada. There is a comparable anger and anarchy to his humour, and his work is outward-looking, with an eye on the modern world, while the surrealists tended to look inward.

Take the example of 'Paedogeddon!' This was a show that, under several levels of satire, was ridiculous: popular radio DJ Neil Fox, for example, was duped into telling viewers that 'paedophiles have more genes in common with crabs than they do with you and me'. But it was also *angry*: angry at the way that the British media treated the subject of paedophilia; angry at the media's hypocrisy, in which British newspapers *themselves* sexualised children); and angry at the vacuous—if largely well-meaning—way in which celebrities would be prepared to spout utter nonsense on television, without bothering to investigate the facts.

Jam and *Blue Jam* retain some of this anger, coming in response to the intense work that Morris had put into *Brass Eye*. 'It [*Blue Jam*] was so singular, and it came from a mood, quite a desolate mood. I had this misty, autumnal, boggy mood anyway, so I just went with that,' Morris said in 1998, in a rare interview. 'But no doubt getting to the end of something like *Brass Eye*, where you've been forced to be a sort of surrogate lawyer, well, that's the most creatively stifling thing you could possibly do.'

You can hear this anger in 'TV Lizards', where the affected couple get increasingly irate at a repairman's failure to address the issue of the lizards in their television set. *Jam* and *Blue Jam* made for dark and often uncomfortable consumption, a desolate disgust oozing from every pore.

You can see why this appealed to Laetitia Sadier. Both Sadier and Morris are drawn to constantly question why things have to be this way, and both deploy a dark, Dadaist humour, born of frustration at the world around them.

Simon Johns says that Stereolab definitely had a sense of humour. 'We weren't serious people—not all the time,' he says. 'I think the reason why we look sort of po-faced and serious is because when we're onstage, everyone's concentrating. We don't look very jolly because we have to concentrate to make songs happen properly.'

Jim O'Rourke, who remembers watching *Brass Eye* with Laetitia at her house when they were recording *Cobra And Phases*, agrees, although he struggles to define where the band's sense of humour lies. 'There's a little bit of the naughty schoolboy, getting something past the proctor,' he says, after a long pause. 'There *is* a sense of humour. There's a satirist take, especially in the lyrics.'

On 'Nothing To Do With Me'—for which Morris received a co-writing credit—putting images from a TV/radio sketch show into a pop song is, in itself, a Dadaist act that calls on the techniques of collage and cut-up writing.

Juxtaposition is important, too. 'Nothing To Do With Me' is a sweet and rather tender-sounding song, the kind of thing you could imagine young lovers putting on in their car as they drive to the beach for a healthy day out. To this, the group add lyrics about bed wetting, heroin, and fixing dead babies.

You can ignore these if you like. But they lurk underneath, undeniable. In this way, the song feels like a rejection of the strait-laced and buttoned-up demands of everyday life, using society's own cultural tools to shine a light on its dark underbelly, much like *Brass Eye*'s appropriation of modern broadcasting techniques. There is something distinctly Dada, too, in the methods that Jim O'Rourke used to inspire Mary Hansen's vocal technique, chasing her into the studio with a stick.

Ironically, as Stereolab were making one great Dadaist statement with 'Nothing To Do With Me', they put an end to their semi-regular habit of including a side-length collage of musical ideas on their albums. This is a practice that has always struck me as Dadaist in its approach in that it brings together contrasting and sometimes even unconnected musical ideas in the name of a greater whole, the listener being discombobulated by the accumulation of detail. To listen to 'Blue Milk'—*Cobra*'s eleven-minute epic—is to be confronted by an almost illogical collection of different musical thoughts that reminds us of the cruel and often random nature of life, like Camus staring into the godless void.

Stereolab do use collage on *Sound-Dust*. 'Captain Easychord' has a second section that sounds almost totally unconnected to the first, while Gane, as mentioned above, inserted more upbeat sections into many of the album's songs. But the LP doesn't have that *one* epic sound collage that listeners may have come to expect (and nor too would the three studio albums that follow).

Perhaps this is one of the reasons why *Sound-Dust* feels strangely overlooked. I was going to say it is underrated, but it feels more *un*-rated than under-appreciated. Some of the reviews at the time were strong—UK rock mag *Q* called it the band's 'best yet', while *Mojo* said it contained 'Tim Gane and Laetitia Sadier's prettiest songs since '95's *Music For The Amorphous Body Study Center*'—but it didn't perform well in the charts, making its heavy way to #117 in the UK and #178 in the USA. These days, *Sound-Dust* is rarely mentioned by fans in discussions about the band's best albums, even though it was part of the 2019 reissue campaign.

Sound-Dust was also the last album that Stereolab made with Jim O'Rourke and John McEntire. O'Rourke says he was meant to be part of a new Turn On record with Gane, Ramsay, and O'Hagan, but this never came to pass (a turn of events that might be related to him joining Sonic Youth and relocating to New York in 2000).

It feels strange to talk to O'Rourke and McEntire, two men with huge musical pedigrees, about their work with just one band, a bit like chatting to Pythagoras about vegetarianism. But the two Chicago musicians are clearly fans of their work with Stereolab. 'It sounds weird, but I really do think their two best albums are the ones I worked on,' O'Rourke concludes. 'It's not because I worked on them, it's because they're more like *albums*. [*Cobra* and *Sound-Dust*] are what they are because each song builds a character that is then contrasted by the next one or added to by the next one,' he explains. 'So they work as records. And maybe that's why, at the time, if I remember correctly, those two weren't that popular when they came out. I think it's because they don't have that overarching *sheen* of, like, *This album is the THIS album*.'

It's a very tempting theory. One of the reasons I love Stereolab is because they are so hard to classify. But even within this perplexity, you can generally find some kind of album shorthand. *Peng!* is the indie record; *Transient* the noisy one; *Mars Audiac Quintet* the pop LP; *Emperor Tomato Ketchup* the groove-led masterpiece; *Dots And Loops* the electronic experiment; and so on. It is, admittedly, an extremely limited viewpoint, but it kind of works. So what, then, are *Cobra* and *Sound-Dust*, if you had to sum them up on the back of a cigarette packet? I don't really know.

Stereolab did innovate on *Sound-Dust*. There is the excursion into country music glide on 'Captain Easychord', while their borrowings from modern classical composers and both jazz and bossa nova come increasingly to the fore. It is also home to the group's first experiments in using different recordings on left and right channels—something they would explore in much greater depth on their next LP, *Margerine Eclipse*.

But these are subtle tweaks, rather than great leaps forward, à la *Mars Audiac Quintet* or *Emperor Tomato Ketchup*. And *Sound-Dust* isn't an album to *demand* your attention. You can read this in some of the record's reviews, which feel more like an exhausted shrug of the shoulders than an in-depth reaction. *The Wire*, long a supporter of the band, claimed that *Sound-Dust* had 'nothing to grip or to engage the senses . . . Stereolab have now defined and refined themselves to a point where they are almost invisible', while for Launch.com, 'It all sounds nice, but little sticks.'

It is hard to get people excited about *any* band's seventh album. And perhaps Stereolab suffered in this respect from the outrageous levels of imagination and creativity that characterised their early years. For me, though, *Sound-Dust* is a magnificent, little-understood work of emotional maturity, where the sadness of everyday life pokes through the band's retro-futuristic machinery with a Dadaist twist, and it is well worth a revisit.

15

'NEW WAVE' COLLABORATION

Ten years on from the Queen of England's terrible 1992, 2002 was Stereolab's own annus horribilis. It was around this time that Gane and Sadier split as a romantic couple, and in December 2002, Mary Hansen was killed while cycling in London, a tragic loss of life that has inevitably overshadowed everything the band have done since.

On a more mundane level, 2002 was also the first year since their debut with no new Stereolab music, the year's only release being *ABC Music*, a CD compilation of the band's Radio 1 sessions over the years. It was also the group's quietest year for gigs since 1991, with just fourteen concerts, half of them in Australasia.

That's not to say that Stereolab were idle. In 2002, they started to build their own Instant Zero studio in the Médoc region of France, northwest of Bordeaux. It was here that they would record their next album, *Margerine Eclipse*.

The year also saw the release of one of the group's most brilliantly illuminating collaborations: 'New Wave', from Chicago rapper Common's fifth album, *Electric Circus*. This isn't strictly a Stereolab collab—only Laetitia Sadier is billed on the record—but Common does (sort of) reference the Stereolab name in the song's lyrics, and photos of the group (minus Andy Ramsay) appear in the cover artwork.

Collaboration is written into the Stereolab DNA. At the most fundamental level, Tim Gane writes the band's music and Laetitia Sadier the words and vocal melodies—a pact established in the earliest days of the duo's working relationship, albeit one that Sadier started to chafe against as the years passed.* For the listener, though, this was a divine combination: during the band's split, you would have had to be a saint to listen to Gane's work with Cavern Of Anti-Matter and not occasionally wish for Sadier's vocal to come floating in over the top.

Gane and Sadier have always been the core of Stereolab. Expanding outward, you have the group: Andy Ramsay, Mary Hansen, and (in 2002) Simon Johns and Dominic Jeffery, who replaced Morgane Lhote on keyboards in 2001. Each had their own instrument—drums, guitar/vocals, bass, and keyboards—but they would also contribute in other ways, like Ramsay's synth work on *Dots And Loops*. To this you can add Sean O'Hagan on a variety of instruments, plus string and brass arrangements; producers like John McEntire and Jim O'Rourke, who also added their own instrumental touches; and a slew of additional musicians, as befit the demands of each song.

Beyond that lay a world of collaborations, and what is striking is not just the range of collaborators that Stereolab have had over the years but the variety of ways in which they have worked with them. With New York artist Charles Long, they provided the music for an art exhibition, full of rubber and Day-Glo colours; with flautist Herbie Mann, the group sent off the master tapes of 'One Note Samba / Surfboard' for Mann to giddily dash with flute; with Brigitte Fontaine, the group provided the musical backing for the French musician to dance muckily over, like a phlegmy serpent, the result being the 1999 single 'Caliméro'. In each case—and there are many, *many* more—the resulting piece of art is very much a meeting of minds, like *Stereolab Plus*.

Stereolab have kept a tight rein over their music, but they weren't

* It is worth noting that on the band's 2025 album *Instant Holograms On Metal Film*, Sadier had a greater input on the band's music, beyond words and lyrics.

a group to impose their will on a collaborator. Their two records with Nurse With Wound, *Crumb Duck* (1993) and *Simple Headphone Mind* (1997), were especially notable for their liberty and lack of artistic ego.

Gane was a long-standing fan of Nurse With Wound, which centred around industrial pioneer Steven Stapleton. When Gane was only fifteen, he formed Uncommunity to make 'power electronics'—'sort of a cross between Whitehouse and Nurse With Wound,' as he later told *Tape Op*.

Stereolab initially asked Stapleton to produce *Peng!*, but he declined—although not, as has been reported, because he felt the group were 'too rock'. 'I thought they were too derivative of the German band Neu! at the time,' Stapleton explains. 'I was getting quite a few offers to produce, and I just wanted to stick with music that I really liked, rather than being a professional producer. That's probably when I heard some of the demos or a couple of singles or something and decided that I didn't want to do it.'

Undeterred, Stereolab came back with an intriguing proposal. 'They came up with this offer, which I couldn't refuse,' says Stapleton, 'which was: *We'll send you a multi-track. You can do whatever you want with it, can mix it however you want to mix it. And I want you to design the cover, title the record, and have it manufactured. And then we want to go into a shop and buy it without knowing what it's going to be like*. So, I thought, *That's amazing!*'

The result was the *Crumb Duck* EP, a ten-inch record released on the none-more-indie Clawfist label in October 1993. It's a fascinating record in many ways, largely because it shows the almost undilutable strength of the Stereolab melodic core.

The record features two songs. 'Animal Or Vegetable (A Wonderful Wooden Reason)' is a thirteen-and-a-half-minute track in which Stapleton takes a still-unreleased Stereolab song, tears it into pieces, then reassembles it in his own image.* 'Exploding Head Movie' is shorter and more straightforward: a five-minute track that's actually a pretty straight remix of a section of 'Jenny Ondioline'.

---

* 'A Wonderful Wooden Reason' is a Faust reference, taken from the chorus of their 1971 song 'Meadow Meal'.

Stapleton might not be a particular fan of Stereolab, and he says he didn't get—or even *want*—to decide which songs he would be working on. But the music the band sent over was 'fantastic', he says. 'Me and my engineer spent three or four days just manipulating it and changing it and adding bits and turning it into what it is at the moment. It was a great success.'

He also found certain parallels with his own work. 'I was amazed to find that they had almost done a homage to Faust and to Krautrock music in general. Going through the multi-track, I was really, really amazed to hear the drums. It was so Faustian. The drums were like "Sunshine Girl".* That's when I saw that there was some kind of kinship between what we're doing.'

And it was this that he wanted to expand upon. 'It was the Motorik element: I'm drawn to that. I'm a great fan of Neu! and early Kraftwerk. I wanted to bring out that and add textures to that. At the time, I remember there was, on most of the pieces, lots of vocal. But for ninety percent of the time, I left that out to keep them instrumental.'

Perhaps this helps to explain why Stapleton's work on *Crumb Duck* feels almost like a tribute to Stereolab's strengths. Stapleton is credited on the record with organ, guitar, harmonica, percussion, loops, mixing, pedals, tapes, ring modulator, and generator, and he obviously threw himself into the project. But the two tracks still ended up sounding very much like Stereolab themselves.

'Exploding Head Movie' resembles 'Jenny Ondioline' with a few added layers of texture. 'Animal Or Vegetable (A Wonderful Wooden Reason)' is more extreme, but the four fundamental drivers of the song—collage; propulsion; Sadier's vocal melody, which is looped and reversed in the song's opening minute; and the influence of Krautrock—were already well-worn Stereolab tropes.†

Simple Headphone Mind was similarly bold, although in this case Stapleton says Stereolab *did* hear the music before it was released—but only as the record was being cut, as he wanted them 'to hear it at its

* 'It's A Rainy Day Sunshine Girl' is the opening song on the second Faust LP, *Faust So Far*.

† Of course, some of these influences may have come to Tim Gane via Nurse With Wound themselves, with Stapleton having used collage techniques on his debut album, *Chance Meeting On A Dissecting Table Of A Sewing Machine And An Umbrella*, in 1979.

best'. It consists of two songs, the title track and 'Trippin' With The Birds', both of which are based around 'The Long Hair Of Death', from Stereolab's 1995 tour single with Yo La Tengo. In each case, Stapleton pulls his focus right in on the song's bassy pulse, which is looped ad infinitum, and then gradually pulls out to reveal a cosmic universe of detail, like Neu! at their most spacey.

Both songs are extremely hypnotic, drawing the listener in as they build and mutate. Much like the music on *Crumb Duck*, 'Simple Headphone Mind' and 'Trippin' With The Birds' are outliers in the Stereolab catalogue, but they didn't sound out of place when they were included on the band's 2022 compilation *Pulse Of The Early Brain*. Stereolab, you feel, could have got to 'Simple Headphone Mind' on their own, if required, but Stapleton's intervention helped speed them on their way.

'When I was working on them, I kept the integrity of their music,' Stapleton says. 'I did fuck it up quite a lot on *Crumb Duck*. The "Wooden Reason" track, I certainly took a lot of advantage of. But with *Simple Headphone Mind*, I pretty much kept a lot of their essence in there.'

Sadier's 2002 collaboration with Common was equally daring in its own way, an ostensibly unlikely meeting of minds. I've already talked about Stereolab's popularity among US hip-hop producers. All the same, contributing vocals to a big rap record was an unusual thing for Sadier to do in 2002. A lot is made of listeners in the streaming era being far more open to different types of music, rather than listening along strict genre lines. And while this view does rather exaggerate the not-actually-*that*-closeted listening habits of the pre-streaming public, there was undoubtedly more musical tribalism in the '90s and early 2000s. Few 'indie' singers appeared on hip-hop albums at the time, and, if you look at the guest list for Common's *Electric Circus*—Mary J. Blige, Jill Scott, Erykah Badu, et al—there aren't a lot of artists who feel obviously aligned to Stereolab's work.

At the same time, appearing on a Common album wasn't like guesting on Lil Jon & The East Side Boyz' *King Of Crunk*, to cite another big 2002 rap record. Common saw *Electric Circus* as an album that would go beyond hip-hop. 'I wasn't feeling hip-hop,' he said at the time, in the Mobo Awards' tenth anniversary brochure. 'So, my motivations for that album were other genres of music, like Pink Floyd and Jimi Hendrix.'

The influence of rock music on *Electric Circus* comes across in a number of ways. The grungy 'Electric Wire Hustler Flower' features a vocal by Sonny Sandoval from the nu-metal band P.O.D., while Hendrix himself is saluted on the guitar-driven 'Jimi Was A Rock Star'.

'Common came to one of our shows,' Sadier explained when I interviewed her in 2024. 'I think we were playing in New York with Stereolab. And he came and spoke to me. He was so nice and, really, the way he put it and his enthusiasm for music and, I don't know, *chords*, he was just so enthusiastic and so clear and beautiful. It was impossible to look him in the eye and say, No, I'm not doing that. So it's like, Yeah, sure, I'll do something.'

The song that emerged is not just an album highlight but one of the best hip-hop tracks of the era. Produced by J Dilla alongside his Soulquarians associates Questlove and James Poyser—all Stereolab fans—'New Wave' is the perfectly simpatico midpoint between Common's soulful rap and Stereolab's Krautrock/French pop mélange.

Sadier is the only Stereolab member to be credited on 'New Wave', but it feels like the whole band could have been involved, with the song riding along on a hypnotic piano and drum machine loop, together with a swirling organ that could easily have featured on *Sound-Dust*. It feels strangely inevitable when Laetitia appears in the chorus, her voice multi-tracked over itself in ornate layers, to sing about humanity.

'The part that Common was rapping over, that was the whole song, and we were like, We're going to send this to Stereolab!' Poyser said on the *Questlove Supreme* podcast in 2024. 'And then you [Questlove] came in the studio and was like, No, man, it needs a different hook!'

'I was always listening to *Dots And Loops*, and then I put Dilla onto it,' Questlove replied. 'I went and brought all their CDs. And, like, *This is the kind of happy shit they sing to, so you guys got to find a way to amalgamate that into this song.*'

Once again, we see how powerfully adaptable Sterolab's music can be, its sound remaning strong among so many different ingredients, like a super-strength gin that always cuts through the mixer. This is part of what makes the band such effective collaborators: singular vision meeting collective strength; open-mindedness encountering supreme confidence in their own ideas.

'New Wave' was an artistic triumph, and I had always thought of *Electric Circus* as a commercial success too, but in fact, when the album was released in December 2002, it stalled at #47 in the US charts, thirty-one spots lower than Common's previous album, *Like Water For Chocolate*. It would eventually sell about three hundred thousand copies in the USA, which is a lot, but not for a rapper on a major label.

The reviews were varied, too, with critics varying wildly in their appreciation of Common's new sound. Nick Southall, in *Stylus Magazine*, compared the album to Richard Ashcroft's solo work, which seems provocatively harsh. *Mojo* was more positive, calling it 'a record of startling breadth'.

Electric Circus's reputation has improved considerably since then, as hip-hop has embraced a freer range of influences. A 2017 *Pitchfork* review called it 'a flawed but classic album' that helped to advance Black popular music, while some fans see the influence of *Electric Circus* in Kendrick Lamar's stunningly eclectic 2015 LP *To Pimp A Butterfly*.

Tyler, The Creator, who is one of the most influential figures in modern hip-hop for the way he has expanded the genre's aesthetic horizons, is certainly a Stereolab fan, explaining during a press conference in 2013 that he had been in love with the band since high school. He sampled the group's 2005 single 'Plastic Mile' on his unreleased 2009 song 'Plastic Cup', and he would later work with Sadier on 'Campfire', from his 2013 album *Wolf*.

'Quite simply, he [Tyler] asked me, and he said, Here's the music, you can write what you want. You know, Blah, blah, blah, blah, blah.' Sadier explained, when I asked her about this in 2024. 'And I was happy to write something life-affirming in something that is otherwise quite dark and *mortiferous*.'

It might be a stretch too far to say that 'New Wave' set up the Tyler collaboration. But, like *Crumb Duck* and *Simple Headphone Mind* before it, the Common song proved a stirring example of Stereolab's collaborative audacity, as well as providing a rare shining light in a horrible year for the band.

INTERSTITIAL THREE
OUR FAVOURITE STEREOLAB SONGS

NIGEL HOUSE, SEAN FORBES, CHRIS SUMMERS (Rough Trade)

[NH] I'm going to go for 'Simple Headphone Mind'.

[SF] The one with Nurse With Wound? We did an exclusive on that, with that foil sleeve that was a fucking pain in the arse to open. Because he gave us all the copies but didn't tell us which ones were the coloured ones.

[NH] You had to open it to find out which one it was. Then you couldn't reseal it. I could have chosen quite a lot of different songs from them, but I really like that one. It's maybe a bit more out there. Nurse added a few weirder bits to it.

[SF] I like 'Lo Boob Oscillator'. It's the most obvious pop song … until the last fifteen minutes. It's like a pop song, and then at the end they're like, *Oh yeah, we've done a pop song. We'd better go back into some noise-like repetitiveness.* So, when I play it, I always take it off before the end gets going. But I really like that. I also like 'Super-Electric'. I think Joe Dilworth plays drums on that. And he's quite … not groovy, but he's got a certain style that just reminds me of that era a lot.

[CS] 'Metronomic Underground'. Because it's a banger. I just like the way it feels. And it gets noisier and noisier. Fantastic.

XYLITOL (musician and DJ) I suppose the one that had the biggest effect on me, really, was 'Simple Headphone Mind', the collab with Nurse With Wound. I just think the amount of space in that! They did a few collaborations together, and each time they worked together, they brought out the best in each other.

Stereolab is generally five-minute-long, kind of chirpy songs with harmonies, as well as the experimental thing. But this is, like, they've got space, they've got a twenty-minute canvas in which to really explore the nuances within this repetitive refrain and go at it from every kind of angle, like it's kind of helicoptering over this terrain. It's beautiful.

ROBIN RIMBAUD (Scanner) I am indeed a Stereolab fan, been friends with them for years. I must say that 'Simple Headphone Mind' with Nurse With Wound is an absolute favourite of mine, a truly transformative tune! Psychedelic space rock at its best, and Steven Stapleton offering up the weird and wonderful wrapped around a great groove.

MARGEAUX LABAT (marg.mp3) It's a tie: 'Les Yper-Sound' has always been a top song for me because I think it's a perfect pop song. I feel like I know myself and I know what I like, when it comes to music that I really, really love now. And I just love music that has strong melodies. I love a great pop song that's catchy and melodic but also deeply musical and weird. There has to be an element of eccentricity in the music that I really gravitate towards. I love weird pop music, so it's a perfect weirdo pop song.

To me, I think ['Les Yper-Sound'] is the perfect blend. I love the repetition of what Laetitia is saying and Mary's overlapping harmonies. I think it's a perfect, perfect song.

But I think my *favourite*—the Stereolab song that really changed my life, what 'Les Yper-Sound' is tied with—is 'Refractions In The Plastic Pulse', because that just totally shifted my perception of what a song could be, with its ambitious length. The song could be divided into four different sections, and this is a clichéd, corny phrase, but it really is like a sonic journey, taking you to places that I hadn't been taken to before.

I think of me listening to the song for the first time, and it really redefined my perception of what a song is and what it *could* be. A lot of Stereolab songs gradually build up to the main part of where the song kicks in. They're a very patient band. A lot of the music that I gravitate towards is patient songs.

One of my favourite sections of any song that I've ever listened to is around the twelve-minute mark when it's really, really minimal—the kind of IDM section where all of the musical elements are pulled out, and it's just this weird beat that eventually morphs and transforms into the final part of the song. When it's just the pure electronic segment, where it hits at the runtime of the song, I think it's perfect. It scratches this itch in my head that I'm like, *Wow, this is hitting so, so hard.*

16

'... SUDDEN STARS'

HARMONY

I never met Mary Hansen, and she didn't give many interviews, so it is hard for me to construct an image of her. Those who did know her, however, spoke very highly of Stereolab's guitarist and singer.

Hansen was born in Australia in 1966, moved to London in 1988, and joined Stereolab in 1992. Prior to that, however, her first entry into British indie music was as a backing vocalist in The Wolfhounds, contributing to the band's 1989 album *Blown Away*. 'I was sharing a house with Paul Sutton, who was McCarthy and The Wolfhounds' manager, and our bass player and a woman called Janet, who was dating one or other of us at the time,' says David Callahan, the group's singer. 'We used to be quite regular attendees of the Scala cinema [in London] when they used to do the late-night, transgressive, sort of drugs and soft porn screenings. Mary had come over from Australia not long before and was working in the ticket office there. And somehow, we got speaking, and Janet eventually offered her our kitchen floor to sleep on, because she didn't have anywhere to stay.'

Hansen soon graduated from the kitchen floor to a spare bedroom.

'And it turned out she was a pretty good singer,' says Callahan. 'Our voices really went together. I don't know if it was the Cockneys-being-transported-to-Australia history that made the voices blend, but we certainly could harmonise together.'

In the title of this chapter, I reference the harmony that Hansen brought to Stereolab. I mean this largely in the musical sense. But everyone seemed to like Hansen, too, which brought a certain unity and togetherness to the Stereolab family.

'The best way to describe Mary was to say that at her wake there were hundreds of people,' says Callahan. 'She was incredibly popular… a very, very open person. Really very, very lovely, very warm. I don't think there's anyone who disliked her. Really, no one.'

Gane and Sadier certainly had warm words for their bandmate. Speaking to the *Chicago Tribune* in 2004, Gane said that Hansen 'was a very central, major part of the group… she was the kind of personality who summed us up, in a sense.'

At the Red Bull Music Academy in 2015, Sadier said that she and Hansen were 'both feminists, not with-the-hat feminist but in the sense that we're women and we want to do it . . . there was a real conscious effort behind the fact that we're doing it and we had to do it as women, because we were,' she added, while discussing the recording of Monade's 'Cache Cache'. 'There was the Riot Grrrl movement, and it was like, *Hey, girls, get up and do it!* There's also all this behind it, like, *Yeah, we're women and we're doing it.*'

Bass player Simon Johns says that Mary initially felt slightly cold to him, perhaps because she thought he was a muso. 'But eventually she warmed up, and we got very friendly,' he adds. 'She was a really lovely, friendly, happy-go-lucky woman who lived her own life. She lived alone in a little flat in London and had lots of friends. She made a lot of friends in other bands. When we would be sitting in the dressing room, eating crisps and drinking lager, she'd be out in the central kind of space where all the portacabins open out, making friends.' Mary was also, he says, 'a brilliant singer . . . and a good musician'.

Hansen created an incredible body of work before her death at the horribly young age of thirty-six. Nearly all of it was in bands; her one solo release came out posthumously in 2005. The *Hybird* EP contains four tracks, three of which had apparently been released in some form before Hansen's death—although I have struggled to find evidence of this—and one song that was completed by Stereolab drummer Andy Ramsay. All of the songs—but particularly 'Twenty Feet Behind'—are Stereolab-ish, mixing delicate vocal textures with synth-heavy backing. 'The Horizontalist Remixes Rose Giganta Mary Rose Mix' has an unusually disjointed and almost humorous feel to it, like The Beach Boys' 'Heroes And Villains' bounced through a sci-fi comic book.

Hansen was in several other groups during her time with Stereolab, including Blips, a one-off project with Tim Gane and former Spacemen 3 lynchpin Sonic Boom; Europa 51, with Andy Ramsay and Simon Johns; Schema, with Seattle band Hovercraft; Splitting The Atom, with Ramsay; and The Horizontalist, again with Ramsay. She also contributed vocals to other bands, including The High Llamas, Callahan's Moonshake, and Mouse On Mars. And all of this while still 'holding down a job in the box office at the now defunct Scala cinema in London', according to journalist Dan Glaister, who wrote Hansen's obituary for *The Guardian*.

'She had a knack, a natural talent, for finding good harmonies,' says Callahan. 'With what I did and definitely with what happened in Stereolab, she could throw herself into solving a musical conundrum very quickly and easily.'

Callahan recommends 'Rite Of Passage', from The Wolfhounds' *Blown Away* LP, as the best example of the work Hansen did with his band. But it was in Stereolab that she really shone. She is often described as a backing vocalist (as well as guitar and keyboard player), but the reality was never quite so straightforward. Backing vocals provide many things that are evident in Stereolab's music, notably harmony and countermelody, but by their very nature, they are *secondary* to the main voice, and this kind of hierarchical status doesn't feel right for the democratic sound of Stereolab's work.

Writing in the sleeve notes of the *Cobra* reissue, Gane explains how the group's vocals were typically arranged, with Hansen singing the higher lines and Sadier the lower ones, as this best suited their voices: 'At least half the songs Stereolab recorded never had a lead vocal and a backing, just two or more lines that were divided up between them.'

This is part of what makes Stereolab so different to other bands. It's not exactly unusual for a band to have more than one vocalist, but this kind of fluidity is rare, with the role of 'singer' being a fixed position in most groups.

Ray Dickaty, who played saxophone on *Emperor Tomato Ketchup*, says that Stereolab's twin vocals were 'quite sublime . . . and the fact that they [Laetitia and Mary] can find melodic ideas within what at times could be considered chaos, like, *Well, where do we go? Which notes of the chord are we looking at to go here?* It's really quite remarkable that they were able to find that in this music.'

What's more, Hansen was often singing in French, a language she didn't understand. 'Singing in French is just so different,' she told *Pitchfork* in 1996. 'There's certain things that don't even come into the English language, and it's interesting for me to sing in French. There's a lot of space for you to sing what you want to sing, depending on your mood. Sometimes you don't sing anything. Some of the French-language songs are very abstract because the French are very philosophical about things. They philosophise all the time.'

Gane would later compare Stereolab's vocal mix to the band's post-'96 musical structure of interacting melodic cells. 'Since *Emperor Tomato Ketchup*, many songs consisted of interlocking melody parts that were sometimes sung or sometimes played on an instrument, it was never really defined,' he writes in the *Cobra* sleeve notes. 'It's amazing that they got these lines to work so well as sung parts, but they were used to it and over the years became very skilled at personalising them with their voices.'

While I understand what Gane means about the vocals being an intricate part of the Stereolab jigsaw, I think he overlooks the fact that human beings instinctively react differently to the human voice. The voice is such a personal thing—pure human expression, delivered directly from the lungs—that listeners generally respond more profoundly to the voice than to an instrument, however well played. This means that the voice will always be more than just one part of the musical mix, however much the band might intend it as such.

I feel like I know Laetitia and Mary through their voices: Laetitia feels deep, thoughtful, the worrier of the pair; Mary is more happy-go-lucky, a dreamer perhaps, always ready with a comforting word. Their voices bring personality. And this is why the Stereolab albums where Sadier has to provide her own supporting vocal lines—*Peng!*, or the post-Hansen LPs—don't feel quite as satisfying, however brilliant the vocal arrangements might be. One voice is never as captivating as two. There are moments on 2025's *Instant Holograms On Metal Film*, for example, where Sadier sings solo and sounds strangely abandoned, the songs feeling ever so slightly *empty*.

By contrast, consider 'Blips Drips And Strips', from *Cobra*: Mary's initial vocal is highly unusual, a kind of casual 'oh wey' that has been cut off in its prime; it doesn't *mean* anything, as far as I can tell, and there are no actual *words* in evidence. But human beings are driven to find meaning, and I can't help but probe that strangled 'oh wey' for some kind of hidden significance, even if there isn't any. Is Hansen agreeing with Sadier? Or undercutting her, using the sarcastic 'oh yeah' of the recalcitrant teenager?

Stereolab employed their dual vocals in many different ways over the years. On songs like 'The Noise Of Carpet' or 'Wow And Flutter', Hansen's vocals offer wordless counterpart and harmony—the group's famed 'ba da ba's—which alternately lift up the 'main' vocal line and coil around it attentively, like lions waiting to spring.

Stereolab's vocal arrangements can be more intricate than most but never overly flashy or at the expense of the song. 'The Noise Of Carpet' is a guitar song; no one is trying to call attention to the massed voices, exactly, but it still has one of the band's most dazzling vocal arrangements.

On the 1996 single 'Fluorescences', Hansen's vocals sound supremely conversational, her vocal lines a response not so much to the words Sadier is singing but to the concerned tone of her voice, like an arm around the shoulder. 'Fluorescences' wouldn't be half the song it is without Hansen's vocals, which bring solace and warmth in a way that is incredibly moving. On 'With Friends Like These', from 1999's *The Free Design* EP, Laetitia and Mary trade vocal lines like two old friends duetting at a karaoke night. You can feel the human spark, the connection between the two women, that was the bedrock for their musical relationship.

Journalist Pierre Perrone, who wrote Hansen's obituary for *The Independent*, commented on the way her 'playful nature and mischievous sense of humour came through in the way she approached the backing vocals.' He quotes Hansen as saying, 'Instead of singing a particular "la-la-la", you can sing "chew-ba-cca", you can sing almost anything because people don't really notice. It's a thing between Laetitia and me. We play little games. It's always a bit different.'

If you do want to talk about 'lead' vocals, then there are a few Stereolab songs where Hansen is to the fore, including *Cobra*'s 'Puncture In The Radax Permutation'; *Emperor Tomato Ketchup*'s 'Tomorrow Is Already Here'; the masterfully unsettling 'Long Life Love'; 'Seeperbold', originally released on a cassette with *Select* magazine in 1995; and 'Metronomic Underground', where Hansen's brilliantly off-hand vocal drives the song ever forward.

Given Hansen's importance to Stereolab, you can understand why some people think the band were never the same after her death. David Callahan said as much in a 2021 interview with freelance writer Malcolm Wyatt. 'I like all the Stereolab albums, but I think a little bit of their soul dropped out when she died,' he said. 'I think they'd probably say that themselves, to a degree.'

Hansen's death was a massive loss for Stereolab on a personal and artistic level. Not only did the band lose a voice, but they also lost her instrumental contributions (guitar, percussion, and keyboards), which were hugely important to the band's live shows. In a review of a 2004 gig in San Francisco, the *Oakland Tribune*'s Jim Harrington wrote extensively about Hansen's absence and its impact on the band, noting, 'The band's latest release, *Margerine Eclipse*, is a tribute to the fallen friend. And, in a way, so was Monday's concert. Stereolab had enough instruments and players to cover Hansen's absence. But the British band seemingly made the deliberate choice not to go in that direction. The group left the holes once filled by Hansen as if to say, The music goes on without her, but it will never be the same.'

•

After Hansen's death—and Gane and Sadier's romantic decoupling—Stereolab's once prodigious output slowed considerably. The group only released two more 'proper' albums before they went on hiatus in 2009: 2004's *Margerine Eclipse* and 2008's *Chemical Chords.**

The group themselves have acknowledged that Mary's death changed something fundamental within the band. 'It's Stereolab, but it's really quite a different band,' Gane told the *Chicago Tribune* in 2004. 'It has to be. If we don't do that, I don't think it's right that we should keep doing it.'

Simon Johns assumed that Hansen's death would be the end of the band. 'I thought, *We can't carry on without her*,' he says. 'I just assumed that we would break up, she was such an integral member. She was one of the original members of the band, not totally original, but in almost from the beginning. And she was so loved. It seemed like the natural thing to do was to call it a day. And we didn't, and that was a surprise.'

Not only did Stereolab keep going after Hansen's death, however, but they found strength in returning to music. 'It was a relief to be working on music again,' Gane told the *Chicago Tribune*. 'It's good to get back to doing something, not cruising along gently but really having to think about music.'

'It was very difficult,' Sadier said at the Red Bull Music Academy in 2015, in response to a question about how the band carried on after both Hansen's death and her romantic separation from Gane. 'It was a very difficult time of separation and loss, one for which music can be a very real help, where you can pour your sadness. Or when it came to losing Mary and we were writing *Margerine Eclipse*, and I ended up having to sing all her parts, because she was gone. It was really, really sad, really sad time. It took me a few years really to assimilate and recover, but I'm still extremely sad over losing Mary. I don't know if I've actually completely accepted her death. To me, she's still in the room right next door.'

Margerine Eclipse, Stereolab's eighth studio album, was the first LP to be released after Hansen's death. Before that, though, came *Instant 0 In The Universe*, a six-track EP issued in October 2003.

Instant 0 was also the first music to be recorded in the group's new

* *Fab Four Suture*, from 2006, is a compilation, while 2010's *Not Music* features material recorded during the *Chemical Chords* sessions.

Instant Zero studio in France. It is very much a sister record to *Margerine Eclipse.* Two songs, '. . . Sudden Stars' and 'Hillbilly Motobike', appear on both releases and all four of the additional songs from *Instant 0* were included on the 2019 reissue of the album.

After a terrible period for the band, recording a new album was a surprisingly positive experience. 'It was in their house in Moulis, which is near Bordeaux, it was like a shed in the back garden, a big sort of barn/garage that was half built by the time we turned up,' Johns says. 'It was really good. Pro Tools was really slow back then. Fulton Dingley was engineering and producing when we first went there. He would render these drums in Pro Tools, and it took ages. So we'd have a few overs of cricket in the back garden. It's the way you dreamed of being a band, of recording in some country manor, like in the 70s: drinking wine and eating duck, playing cricket, making rock music.'

Both *Instant 0* and *Margerine Eclipse* highlight Stereolab's new innovation in sound, which they refer to as 'dual mono'. For every song, the group made two recordings with slightly different arrangements, which would be used in the left and right channels of the song's final mix.

'Obstacles and puzzles always open up what to do to try to get around them,' Gane told *Seattle Weekly* in 2004. 'I always try to set up a new way of thinking about the music before we record. If we carried on recording the same way, I'd think we were guilty of what people say, that it always sounds the same.'

If the technique sounds complex, well, it *is* and it isn't. The human brain is perfectly used to interpreting different signals in each ear, and you can enjoy both *Instant 0* and *Margerine Eclipse* without being aware of any studio trickery. Most people will also be familiar with this kind of stereo separation from listening to records from the 1960s that were recorded in mono, played back through modern stereo equipment.

When you pay close attention to it, though—especially with headphones—the effect is intriguing. I hear the separation best in the vocals and the drums. Different vocal lines are typically divided between the two channels, which, when you notice it, makes it feel a little like there are two Laetitias creeping around your cranium. Needless to say, Mary's presence is sorely missed—it would have been fascinating to have a different vocal tone in each ear, with the disjointing effect this could bring.

'Vonal Declosion', the first song on *Margerine Eclipse*, kicks off with a snare drum intro that starts in the right channel and is then taken up by the left, as if Stereolab are showing their cards right from the off. Seven songs later, on 'Margerine Melodie', you can clearly hear, about three minutes in, the drums in the left-hand channel break into a more frenzied, rattling beat while the drums in the right continue to plod along. And so on.

The original idea for *Margerine Eclipse* was for everything to be recorded live, much as the band had done early on in their career. But this idea was eventually shelved. 'We made a few spontaneous decisions when making the LP on how we should go about recording it after our original concept of doing it "live" in the studio was dropped,' Gane writes in the sleeve notes. 'I remember standing in the studio the night before we started recording and talking about panning the speakers extreme right-left and having nothing in the middle. This eventually led to the idea of having one version of the song on the left speaker and a second version on the right speaker and the third 'version' would be the two combined.'

The band had gone partially down this route on *Sound-Dust*, something Gane only realised when listening to the albums again for the 2019 reissue series. On *Margerine Eclipse*, however, the group wanted to push the technique as far as it could go.* Gane believes that dual mono is at its most effective on '. . . Sudden Stars', as it helped to give the band's music a new kind of thrust, revitalising that key Stereolab ingredient in a way that I imagine was vaguely comforting.

'Andy had the idea to record basic drums on one side and make a delay of these and put them on the other side,' Gane writes. 'He then replaced the delayed drums with a live played version of exactly the same thing. The effect on the music was totally different—a very strange propulsion.'

Much like *Sound-Dust* before it, *Margerine Eclipse* is an album full

* Gane doesn't mention it, but you can hear a similar kind of hard panning on 'Analogue Rock', from *Transient Random-Noise Bursts With Announcements*, which suggests the idea had been floating around since 1993.

of collage-style sections with separate—and sometimes apparently unrelated—constituent parts cropping up like musical mushrooms. This got even more complicated when the album was reissued in 2019, with some tracks getting what Gane calls 'slightly altered or additional intros and outros here and there'. For example, 'La Spirale', initially a bonus track on the Japanese edition of the album, was restored to its original place as the mid-section of 'Hillbilly Motobike'.

For me, however, the technical achievements are less important than the album's humanity and emotional heft. On 'Hillbilly Motobike', Sadier seemingly alludes to her romantic separation from Gane, which happened shortly before work started on the album, singing about a couple who loved each other but who tore each other apart. She has never talked about the meaning of the song, whose galloping opening section doesn't suggest your typical break-up lament. But the song's themes of romantic separation and eternal change seem unlikely to be pure coincidence.

There are several other songs on *Margerine Eclipse* that could also be about Sadier and Gane's fractured relationship, including 'Vonal Declosion', which touches on the suffering of love; 'Margerine Rock', with its frustratingly paradoxical central character; and 'Margerine Melodie', which looks at the dynamics of two people locked into a project. But the reference (in French) to 'my lover' in 'Hillbilly Motobike' makes the relationship interpretation seem most likely, and it is perhaps telling that it is the only song whose lyrics are not printed on the album sleeve.

Naturally, Mary Hansen's death hangs over *Instant 0* and *Margerine Eclipse*. In his sleeve notes, Gane says that all the music was written before Hansen died, and the album already had its name, which was inspired by a sign for margarine in a Spanish supermarket. The lyrics, however, were not completed until after Hansen's death, and many of them undoubtedly refer to the band's former singer. The most obvious reference comes in the wistful, whimsical, and deeply sad 'Feel And Triple', in which Sadier says goodbye to Mary and traces some of their shared history.

'I was reflecting on my years with her,' Sadier told *The Independent* in 2004. 'Reflecting on how we sometimes found it hard to express the love we had for one another. What made it difficult? Oh . . . two girls in a band. You can imagine. You project your neurotic stuff and voilà! Around 1997, though, we overcame this, and it was beautiful. I'm very happy we managed to do that.'

I can hear Mary, too, in '. . . Sudden Stars', the opening song on the *Instant 0* EP. The song is a cosmic ode to letting go that resides on a sublime and seemingly unresolved chord sequence. It is fitting that '. . . Sudden Stars' has gorgeous harmonies, a latticework of 'la's wrapped around the central voice, like woven silk.

'. . . Sudden Stars' is one of the most touching songs I have heard about coming to terms with grief, its various musical sections passing through depression, anger (as distorted guitars rip through the hitherto tranquil musical mix) and finally acceptance, like a musical Kübler-Ross model. In the song's closing section, Sadier's two vocals seem to call back to each other, like an echo over an idyllic mountain pass—a reminder that harmony isn't just a musical term.

Speaking to *The Independent*, Sadier explained that, though she isn't religious, 'I feel Mary's energy is still around somewhere. It didn't just disappear.' It is this that we hear in '. . . Sudden Stars': grief laced with hope, acceptance, and sadness. The idea of mortality reigns over '. . . Sudden Stars', of life coming to an inevitable end. But it is not a depressing song; instead, it seems to suggest that mortality is a consequence of life, which must end at some point, but memories will remain.

Simon Johns says the band never really talked about Mary's death. 'We didn't come together and say, *That was bad, wasn't it? How's everyone feeling about that?* It's not really the way we operated at any point,' he says. 'I know that Laetitia sorted out her grief with writing some lyrics about her [Mary]. But I don't know what the lyrics say. I mean, I never looked.'

Is 'Dear Marge', the album's closing song, about Hansen, too? 'Mary' being called 'Marge' isn't out of the question, and that would also support my theory that *Margerine Eclipse* is itself, in a way, named after the band's singer. It's a stretch, though, and I am perhaps on stronger ground with the naming of *Instant 0 In The Universe*: 0 is *nothing*, total absence, like the instant loss brought on by Hansen's death.

Margerine Eclipse saw new forces arrive in the Stereolab orbit. Dominic Jeffery, who joined the band in 2001, is credited with organ, electronic piano, harpsichord, and celeste on the album (although he doesn't remember the last instrument), while Fulton Dingley, who was one of the in-house engineers at London's Blackwing Studios, really comes to the fore. After recording additional material for the seven-inch single version of 'Wow And Flutter', Dingley had first produced Stereolab in February 1998, when they cut 'Italian Shoes Continuum' at Blackwing. On *Margerine Eclipse*, alongside engineering and mixing, he is credited with drum machine, synthesizer, MIDI, and percussion, marking a big step up. Naturally, Sean O'Hagan is also present on the record, while Mouse On Mars' Jan St. Werner added electronics to 'Vonal Declosion' and 'Feel And Triple'.

Margerine Eclipse charted at #108 in the UK and #174 in the USA, roughly in line with Sound-Dust. Ultimately, it is another strong album, outside of the band's imperial phase, thanks to the innovation in dual mono and some brilliant songwriting. It might, in fact, be the band's most *human* album, alongside *Sound-Dust*—a record that is rooted in actual people and lived experience, rather than political theory and intellectual games. I go back to *Margerine Eclipse* a lot when I am feeling sad or otherwise put off by the world, and it is always a welcoming experience.

Of course, the recording of *Margerine Eclipse* was guided by necessity. It would have been wonderful to hear Hansen sing these songs, her dual vocals with Laetitia offering contrasting tones on different speaker channels. But we shouldn't wish an album away for what it's not and could never have been.

I sometimes wonder how Stereolab made *any* kind of record in these circumstances, but they appear to have found solace—and perhaps even harmony—in music. Working in dual mono was a challenge for the band—a strictly unnecessary musical puzzle that focused the collective mind, helping to steer them out of what was the most difficult period of their existence and into the slightly deflated peace of their final phase.

17

'NEON BEANBAG' JAZZ

In 2005, a lot of people expected Stereolab to disappear. Instead, they came back with brass.

Margerine Eclipse was the band's last record for Elektra; the next Stereolab album release, *Oscillons From The Anti-Sun*, a three-CD, one-DVD box set of EP tracks that came out in April 2005, was the kind of record that bands often put out *just* before they split, drawing an elegant line in the sand under their career. *Pitchfork*'s review summed up the set's appeal when it concluded that *Oscillons* was 'just as good as the albums, only different'.

Instead, a creative left-turn was on the cards. Stereolab released three seven-inch singles in 2005: 'Kybernetická Babička', 'Plastic Mile', and 'Interlock', which were followed in 2006 by three more: 'Whisper Pitch', 'Excursions Into Oh, A-oh', and 'Eye Of The Volcano'. All of these were then rapidly compiled onto the *Fab Four Suture* compilation, which was released in March 2006.

If *Fab Four Suture* gets overlooked by Stereolab fans, this is, in part, down to the way it was released. Even after all these years of digital music, playlists, and the glory of the *song*, albums are still viewed as the most important thing in an artist's career—the tent-pole event around which the rest of a campaign is hung. Young bands still dream of releasing a classic album, while older acts such as The Rolling Stones often plan their touring campaigns around the release of a new LP, as if *that* will make any difference to ticket sales.

Fab Four Suture isn't strictly a studio album, then, in the classical sense. It's a compilation, and it is billed that way on streaming services, even though it bears all of the other hallmarks of a 'normal' studio album. The same basic group played on it, and it has a consistent sound, even if it was recorded in different studios, including Instant Zero and Press Play, the South London studio owned and managed by Andy Ramsay.

So why release the band's music this way? My guess is for a combination of comfort and ease, and perhaps a desire to shake things up. Stereolab had been releasing conventional albums since *Peng!* in 1992; *Margerine Eclipse* was their eighth studio LP, and there was arguably a chance of diminishing returns if they continued to do things the same way.

So, why not try something new? The iTunes download store had opened in 2003, and by 2005, when the first of the *Fab Four Suture* singles was released, people were starting to talk seriously about the death of the album, now that fans could pick and choose the songs they wanted to download. This hasn't happened, of course, but the time for experimentation was ripe.

Writing in *Comes With A Smile* in 2006, Adrian Pannett noted how Gane 'loves the economics of singles and EPs', while Sadier 'prefers the length of long-players'—conclusions that were apparently based on recent conversations with them both. In a way, *Fab Four Suture*'s staggered release allowed both of them to get their way.

After leaving Elektra, Stereolab returned to their label roots in 2005, agreeing a deal with Too Pure, the London indie label that had released many of their early records and was now part of the Beggars Group indie monolith. Perhaps releasing a series of seven-inch singles felt like a throwback to the previous Too Pure days. Certainly, recording a series of singles, rather than *an album*, meant that the pressure was lowered. Stereolab would be free to follow their muse, cocooned away within the homely environments of Instant Zero and Press Play.

I see *Fab Four Suture* as a kind of comfort release. The record's very name suggests it: 'Fab Four' alludes to The Beatles, while a suture is a row of stitches that holds together the edge of a wound. So, we have the image of music—and in particular Liverpool's favourite sons—holding Stereolab together, at what was clearly still a difficult time for the band.

Fab Four Suture isn't a record of grand innovation, exactly, but it's not a simple retread of past glories, either. Instead, it is the band's brass album, where they got heavily into the bassy sounds of the French horn, as played by new member Joe Walters, who came on board in 2004.

By this point, Stereolab had been using brass instruments for a decade. Their 1994 album *Mars Audiac Quintet* includes tenor saxophone, trumpet, and trombone, with brass arrangements by Sean O'Hagan. But *Fab Four Suture* is where they really come to the fore, with Walters being the first full member of the band to focus on brass.

Simon Johns says that Stereolab initially used Walters as a session musician. 'They tended to use the same people over and over again,' he says. 'Sean would have done the arrangements for the brass. Joe would have been available, and Sean probably would have liked the sound of the French horn and arranged a load of deep parts for the French horn. It's such a gorgeous sound. When you hear it in the music, it really fits.'

Dominic Jeffery, who played Fender Rhodes and clavinet on *Fab Four Suture*, says that the French horn 'gives the music another flavour', but he didn't see anything particularly preplanned or deliberate about bringing the instrument on board. 'We thought about the tunes and the sound that would fit with them,' he says.

While saxophone and trumpet are common in pop music, the French horn is less so. You can hear its solemn, deep tone on everything from The Beach Boys' 'God Only Knows' to Kanye West's 'All Of The Lights', but it is perhaps a little too pompous-sounding to have much wider use in pop. I associate the instrument more with brass bands, big-band jazz, and rousing, if slightly staid classical music. Stereolab's decision to push the French horn to the fore on *Fab Four Suture* seems brilliantly perverse.

It works, too. Album opener 'Kyberneticka Babicka Pt 1' (and its 'Pt 2' reprise, which closes the compilation) is a rare example of brass drone in pop music, a steady horn pulse driving the band ever onward, in a kind of doomed momentum that seems to always come back to where it started, locked-groove style. The song's vocals are fascinating too, a never-ending, never-breaking series of 'ah's that suggest paint smeared in thick layers across a canvas.

This brass obsession continues throughout the album. 'Eye Of The Volcano' has a wistful French horn opening, with various brass instruments then driving the song forward in a deep sonic thrust; 'Plastic Mile' starts with a huge—and ever so slightly comic—brass riff somewhere between aging circus clown and trombone heavy metal; 'Widow Weirdo' has a stately brass motif that recalls of Dvorak's *New World Symphony*, as rearranged for brass in the famed Hovis ad from the 1970s. Overall, the use of brass gives *Fab Four Suture* a warm, comfortably *aged* tone, an instant familiarity that reaches out to embrace you, like The Beatles' French-horn heavy 'For No One'.

There are other moments of understated innovation on the record, too. The treated, rattling drums of 'Vodiak' suggest the scrambled drum breaks of producers like Squarepusher and Aphex Twin—not *virgin* territory for Stereolab exactly, but certainly not habitual. 'Interlock' uses a filter effect in its closing section that reminds me of classic French Touch productions, and on 'Widow Weirdo', the band decide, for some bizarre but very welcome reason, to recreate MF Doom's 'The Hands Of Doom', from his 1999 album *Operation: Doomsday*—a callback to the love that Stereolab have received from the hip-hop world.

•

Stereolab would release another seven-inch in 2006, the tour-only single 'Solar Throw-Away' / 'Jump Drive Shut-Out'. More significant, though, was the release in August of *Serene Velocity*, a sixteen-song anthology of the band's Elektra years that was a greatest hits in all but name.

Compiled by the label with some input from the band, *Serene Velocity* does a decent job of summing up the band's decade with the US label. All Stereolab fans will have their own favourite songs from this period, but the band's big-hitting tracks—'French Disko', 'Ping Pong', 'Come And Play In The Milky Night', 'Infinity Girl', et cetera—are all present and correct, and all the studio albums from this period are represented. The album has a lovely title, too, with *Serene Velocity* the best auto-description of Stereolab's perverse beauty since *Space Age Batchelor Pad Music*.

Perhaps a greatest-hits LP seems a strange move for a band so obsessed with forward motion, but Stereolab are also a group for whom accessibility is important—one who had, at this point, released three volumes of their *Switched On* compilations, allowing fans who hadn't managed to get their hands on the limited tour seven-inches to delve into their music.

Stereolab didn't end with *Oscillons*, and they didn't end with *Serene Velocity*, as many reviews thought they might. But they didn't exactly spring out of the traps after the album's release, either. They released no new music in 2007 and didn't play any gigs—their first entirely fallow year since forming in 1990. Instead, they spent 2007 beavering away on what would be their two final studio albums: 2008's *Chemical Chords*, and 2010's *Not Music*, which would be released after the band went on hiatus in 2009.

Alongside *Mars Audiac Quintet*, *Chemical Chords* is Stereolab's big 'pop' album, if we think of 'pop' as viewed through the group's kaleidoscopic focus. When I interviewed Tim Gane about it in 2008, he described the album as fourteen tracks of 'purposefully, short, dense, fast pop songs. I was very interested in making the tracks short but very tense. A lot of 60s pop songs, within the three-minute form, with a lot of things going on.'

Those fourteen tracks whizz by in just forty-eight minutes, with only three breaking the four-minute barrier; the title track is the longest at a weedy five minutes and twelve seconds. 'I find seven-minute tracks a bit boring,' Gane told me—a surprising thing to hear from the man behind 'Jenny Ondioline'.

Shorter songs doesn't mean lighter songs, though. Speaking to *Wired* in 2008, Gane spoke of the density of *Chemical Chords*. 'I've been thinking in terms of "shortness" more as a kind of density—a lot going on, kind of a hierarchy of things, but going dense, going up—up towards the sky, as opposed to flat across the ground,' he said. There was, he explained, no particular reason for his aversion to longer songs around this time. 'I just felt that I would like to restrict myself to working with the songs in a very short time frame, a bit like pop music from an era like the 60s . . . because for me, 60s pop music is amongst the most complicated or complex music because it has so many resonances which strike you.'*

Chemical Chords' brevity and lightness of touch help to explain why the band's ninth studio album is often overlooked in the Stereolab catalogue. To those used to the band's sprawling, side-long epics, the record can feel slight, and it is surprisingly chirpy in a way that infuriates some fans. But it does have innovation at its heart: Gane worked up the album's songs from fifty or sixty small loops alongside Joe Watson, who had joined on keyboards in 2004.

'It wasn't really my intention to do it like this, it's just that I was running really late,' Gane told *Fact Magazine* around the time of the album's release. 'I was recording a soundtrack [for *La Vie D'Artiste*, with Sean O'Hagan] and it just dragged on and on—there were loads of little bits I had to do and re-do and cut. So I thought I'd have five or six weeks to work on *Chemical Chords*, but it turned out to be five or six days. I just didn't have time to make music as I'd done before, so I thought, *I'll cut up lots of little loops, beats from drum machines, stuff from records*.'†

As if to further infuriate fans of the old-school Stereolab Sturm Und Drang, *Chemical Chords* also goes heavy on jazz. Maybe it seems strange that this would be controversial, particularly after the acclaim of *Dots And Loops*. But in 2008—pre-*To Pimp A Butterfly*, Shabaka, Andre 3000, et al—jazz was a nebulous beast with an uncertain reputation. An *indie* band playing jazz, meanwhile, was often seen as a bit too clever-clever, particularly among the British rock critics of the time.

* Promo copies of *Chemical Chords* came with all songs cut off at the two-minute mark in a bid to combat piracy. It says something about Stereolab's oddball reputation that some people thought this was a deliberate ploy. 'In the US, a lot of people said they liked the way that the songs ended suddenly like that.' Gane told me in 2008. 'They expect some kind of messing about on each record. I actually quite got into the idea of doing that for real, doing a record where things did really stop. What could we do with it?'

† More on this in the following chapter.

Growing up in the UK in the 1990s, I had a strange relationship with jazz, which seemed to bounce in and out of fashion faster than a Dizzy Gillespie bop. When I first started to get into music, around the late 1980s, jazz was decidedly uncool, the music of torturous wedding bands and silk-suited fuddy-duddies who had probably never even *heard* of Jesus Jones. Then, in the early 1990s, the Transatlantic combination of A Tribe Called Quest's jazz-heavy *Low-End Theory* and the acid jazz movement in the UK swung things around, and suddenly jazz was cool. I started to seek out second-hand Miles Davis records, which were in plentiful supply in British shops, while dutifully trying to work out what on *earth* 'modal' meant.

Throughout the 1990s, a lot of the best—and, more importantly for a teenager, *coolest*—music was shaped by jazz, from the jazz-jungle of Roni Size, DJ Krust, and Photek to the dusty beats of the Mo' Wax label. Among indie/alternative bands, however, jazz simply wasn't *done* in the early 90s. From baggy to shoegaze to grunge to Britpop, barely a jazz beat cast a shadow on the indie charts, a situation that only changed toward the end of the decade. *Dots And Loops* was influential in this regard, while Tortoise certainly bore the influence of jazz. So too did Radiohead, on their 2001 album *Amnesiac*, which includes a collaboration with distinctly trad British trumpeter Humphrey Lyttelton.

Stereolab, then, were left to carry the indie jazz can for much of the early and mid-90s, which they did in a low-key fashion on songs like 'Stomach Worm' (perhaps their first excursion into jazz swing), 'The Brush Descends The Length', 'Young Lungs', and 'Percolator', before breaking into flagrant jazz-influenced grooves on *Dots And Loops*.

'Jazz was a dirty word, to be honest, among some of the musicians at that point in time—it was something to be sneered at,' says Ray Dickaty, the saxophonist who played on *Emperor Tomato Ketchup*. 'But there was a definite distinction between what I even now call *jazz* jazz, which is what we now know as bebop. And then there's spiritual jazz, which we might say [includes] Pharoah Sanders, Archie Shepp, even Joe Harriott. There was definitely a disdain towards jazz, but also a respect towards certain types of jazz.'

Simon Johns says that the influence of jazz bubbled away under the surface of Stereolab without necessarily becoming explicit. 'I don't think we talked about Miles Davis. I don't doubt that we all liked [Davis's legendary 1970 album] *Bitches Brew*, an amazing record,' he says. 'Jazz was something we were enthusiastic about, but we didn't have the ability to play at that point.'

Jazz, Johns adds, has a formula. 'The II–V–I [chord progression] and the turnarounds. There's a repertoire of moves, of musical tropes that you employ in jazz,' he says. 'You can't make jazz music without knowing what they are. And we didn't know what they were. But we certainly were influenced by jazz. Tim has a large collection of jazz records. He likes Duke Ellington and Miles Davis and Coltrane, and all that weird stuff from the 70s and 60s. He lifted sections of music from jazz records and then put them through his filter, and that came out the other side sounding like Stereolab. [Jazz] was an input, not an end goal.'

Perhaps the group's most obvious borrowing from jazz came in their use of swung rhythm. Dominic Jeffery, who came to the band from the world of jazz and blues, says that Stereolab typically played directly on the beat, which was a challenge to him when he joined. But you can hear a basic take on a swung rhythm in Stereolab songs from 'Stomach Worm' to 'Brigitte' and, if this basic shuffle doesn't seem so revolutionary, you'd be surprised at how few bands ever break from their devotion to rock's steady backbeat.

Going deeper, Stereolab often use time signatures that deviate from rock's sacred 4/4, in what feels like a nod to jazz. 'Diagonals' and 'Parsec' appear to be in 10/4, while 'Percolator', 'Rainbo Conversation', and 'Speedy Car' are in 5/4, the latter racing along like a jittery jazz dancer bugged out on Benzedrine. 'The Brush Descends The Length' is a waltz in 3/4; 'Iron Man' is in 8/8, with some 12/8 bars; and both 'Motoroller Scalatron' and *Not Music*'s 'Equivalences' are in 7/8.*

Similarly, Stereolab often use chord sequences that are unusual for rock music, in a way that points toward jazz. Some of my favourite examples of this include the undercut cheer of 'Ping Pong'; the slightly feverish 'Puncture In The Radax Permutation'; the bossa nova mope of

* Without an official score, of course, judging the time signature of a given song is not an exact science, and Stereolab often play around with the way they accent their rhythms, which makes working them out even trickier.

'Hallucinex'; and the brooding 'Immortal Hands'. Their instrumental choices, too, often feel jazz-inspired. The group frequently reach beyond the typical rock palette of guitar, drums, and bass, using instruments more often associated with jazz, such as trombone, trumpet, saxophone, flute, and vibraphone. (*Chemical Chords* is particularly heavy on the vibraphone.)

Taken on their own, these connections might seem slightly nebulous. Just using a trumpet doesn't make you jazz, of course, but Stereolab combine these elements—rhythmical adventure, melodic audacity and atypical rock instrumentation—with a love for improvisation and a penchant for using the studio as an instrument, in a way that is reminiscent of Miles Davis's electric period, when he and band would improvise live in the studio, the tapes then edited and spliced together into the songs we know today.

Dickaty says that Stereolab's jazz influences come across 'in the sense of harmonies, the extended harmonies, as well as the counter rhythms, working off each other,' he explains. 'Listening to, say, *Emperor Tomato Ketchup* and then going back and listening to Neu!, you can hear that they'd taken the Neu! idea and extended it by incorporating all these other facets of music, from the easy-listening records to the jazz records, the Latin jazz records and the spiritual jazz records, they were bringing all that in.'

Sometimes, the band's relationship with jazz is made more explicit. Speaking to *Seattle Weekly* in 2006, Gane explained that *Margerine Eclipse*'s '... Sudden Stars' was initially inspired by the rhythm of Miles Davis's 'Solea', from his 1960 album *Sketches Of Spain*, which Gane combined with a couple of other pieces of music that he had written.

Gane was also a fan of Sun Ra, the US bandleader who started out making traditional big-band jazz before blasting off into cosmic orbit with some of the most adventurous and outrageously far-out music the world has ever heard. Sun Ra was a particular influence on *Emperor Tomato Ketchup*, while Gane cited his deeply psychedelic *Cosmic Tones For Therapy* album (recorded in 1963 but not released until 1967) as one of his favourite records in an interview with *Digital Berlin*.

Chemical Chords is a *lot* less far out than this, being one of Stereolab's tidiest and most compact records. But you can hear the influence of jazz right from the off, with the opening song, 'Neon Beanbag', neatly synthesising a swung time signature, eye-catching chords, and vibraphone-heavy instrumentation, topped off by Laetitia's scat-like vocal patter.

'Neon Beanbag' doesn't feel like a particularly deep song, with its cheerful rhythm and jaunty brass riffs. But there is a melancholy undertow to its harpsichord trills, a kind of yearning inner voyage through the emotions, which makes sense when you consider that the song has its roots in a dream where Mary Hansen visited Sadier.

'I was crying [in my dream], and I was crying infinitely, infinite sadness, and she [Mary] said, Look, I'm sad to see that you're sad, but there's nothing to be sad about,' Sadier explained in a 2008 interview with *World Cafe*. Maybe the backstory to a song shouldn't matter in your appreciation of it. But since I learnt of its ghostly inspiration, of its glimpse into mortality, grief and acceptance, 'Neon Beanbag' has become one of my favourite Stereolab songs, a warm blanket in troubled times.

'Neon Beanbag' isn't just one of the best songs on *Chemical Chords*, it also feels like a model for the album to follow—albeit not always successfully. Its brisk, shuffling rhythm, which nods to northern soul as well as jazz, reappears on several other songs, including 'The Ecstatic Static', 'Self Portrait With "Electric Brain"', and 'Daisy Click Clack'—a sign, perhaps, of the album's hurried genesis in loops.

This eventually starts to wear. By the point that 'Daisy Click Clack'—which sounds like a parallel universe take on a World War Two showtune and is one of the few Stereolab songs I genuinely dislike—rolls around, I am quite ready for this rhythm to stop. Sadier seemed to share this frustration with *Chemical Chords*' repetitiveness, telling the *Village Voice* of the album, 'There's very little air and *ba-donk, ba-donk, ba-donk* all the way through practically.'

Chemical Chords ultimately suffers from this air of repetitiveness, with 'Neon Beanbag''s musical palette of brass, harpsichord, and vibraphone reappearing often. This is compounded by the fact that the typically intricate dual vocals of previous albums barely feature here. This was also the case on *Fab Four Suture*, of course, but that record cushioned the blow by being more adventurous and diverse.

Weighed against this, in *Chemical Chords*' considerable favour, is the fact that the album contains some of the band's greatest string arrangements (courtesy of Sean O'Hagan), as found on the stirring title track and the baroque pop of 'Cellulose Sunshine'. That both songs are eminently dramatic makes sense, given that Gane and O'Hagan had come to the album after working together on the soundtrack to *La Vie D'Artiste*, a 2007 comedy by French director Marc Fitoussi.

Elsewhere, Stereolab show that there is still experimental life in an old band. 'Fractal Dream Of A Thing' has a jazz-inspired 10/4 rhythm; 'Nous Vous Demandons Pardon' takes a hint from jazz in its circuitous and thoroughly unpredictable chord sequence and capricious drum lines; and 'Pop Molecule (Molecular Pop 1)' smashes forward and backward drum recordings into each other to gloriously climactic results.

Gane told *Wired* that 'Pop Molecule' was a telling example of the band's new way of working with micro-loops. 'Basically, what that is, is a tiny loop, one going forwards and one going backwards, and everything that we thought we could hear, we just reproduced with all the different instruments—keyboards, drums,' he said.

Elsewhere, 'Valley Hi!' feels a little like the Stereolab of shoegazing-not-shoegazing past, as rendered in dazzling 3-D by a band keen to show off the studio tricks they have learned over the past decade. It reminds me vaguely of Ride's 'Vapour Trail', rendered in splendid Technicolor.

Overall, however, *Chemical Chords* could easily have been better. One of the best Stereolab tracks of the era—and certainly one of the most plainly enjoyable—is the radiant and bubbling, De la Soul-esque 'Spool Of Collusion', which was only included on the iTunes version of the album and a limited seven-inch that came with the first five thousand physical copies—a decision that robbed the album of one of its best songs.

I thought I remembered *Chemical Chords* getting a roasting in the press, which it turns out isn't quite accurate. In fact, the album earned some pretty positive reviews—*Pitchfork*, for example, gave it a score of 8.1, calling it one of the band's strongest in some time—but there was a feeling in some quarters that the band were running out of steam.

Tiny Mix Tapes summed up this idea in a review that mentioned the band's 'now all-too-familiar sound', while *NOW* magazine said that *Chemical Chords* 'would make for a more engaging spin if Stereolab could mess with the equation now and again'.

I don't necessarily think this is the fault of the album, more a sign of how hard it is for a group to continue to engage after eighteen years and nine studio albums. Sure enough, *Chemical Chords* reached #102 in the UK charts and #170 in the USA—a resigned shrug of a chart placing in an era when even *Elbow* made it into the British Top 5.

From a band rapidly approaching the end of its first and most significant life, *Chemical Chords* wasn't a whimper, but it wasn't exactly a roar, either. Listening back to the album now, in particular 'Neon Beanbag', 'Valley Hi!', and 'Pop Molecule (Molecular Pop 1)', *Chemical Chords* is a timely reminder that Stereolab, like jazz itself, might float in and out of fashion but their quality lives on.

18

'SUN DEMON'
LOOPS

My last encounter with Stereolab phase one was on December 19, 2008, when the band played London's Koko, a venue once known as the Camden Palace—an indie stalwart.

The group were touring *Chemical Chords*, which had been released four months previously, and it didn't seem as though enthusiasm was particularly high. Koko has a capacity of fifteen hundred, but I don't remember it being sold out or particularly full. The band's brief UK tour that December saw them playing moderately sized venues—Concorde 2 in Brighton, the Black Box in Belfast—the likes of which they had been filling since 1994.

I don't remember much of the band's set that December night, either, but I do recall a general lethargy, which might have had more to do with me, as the Christmas party season ground on, than the band. *The Line Of Best Fit*'s review of the Camden gig mentioned that Stereolab 'take the stage to a ripple of applause, a muted welcome that belies the band's perennial success' before questioning why they aren't playing stadiums. The latter point was undoubtedly tongue-in-cheek, but it does give some idea of how big 'indie' music had become by

2008, with the inevitable swings of fashion transforming Coldplay, Kings Of Leon, and The Killers into stadium contenders.

I do remember enjoying the band's set, which balanced *Chemical Chords* songs such as 'Silver Sands' with classics including 'Lo Boob Oscillator' and 'French Disko'. But I wasn't as excited as I was when I first saw the group back in 1993. *Chemical Chords* was no *Transient Random-Noise Bursts With Announcements*, and I was a thirty-one-year-old man with a job and a tax return, rather than a sixteen-year-old music obsessive. I don't think I even had a look at the band's merch stand, where they were selling the inevitable tour seven-inch, 'Explosante Fixe' backed with 'L'Exotisme Intérieur', which would turn out to be the last new Stereolab music released before the band went on hiatus in 2009.

Had I known that the Koko gig would be Stereolab's final UK concert for eleven years, I would have paid more attention. But this was the band's curse. Stereolab were chronically undervalued at this time, a kind of musical Old Faithful who fans assumed would go on doing Stereolab things, to slightly diminishing returns, ad infinitum. They would, we thought, always be there. Until the day in April 2009 when they weren't. And even that, strangely, didn't feel like a shock, as if two Stereolab universes had been running in parallel since Mary Hansen died—one where the band were destined to stay together and one where they weren't.*

'I thought the band was coming to the end when Mary died,' says Simon Johns. 'And then I thought the band was coming to an end when Tim and Laetitia split up. So, when it did end, it was like, *Yeah, okay, all right, that's not a surprise.*' Dominic Jeffery, who joined the band on keyboards in 2001, said that by the time he left Stereolab in 2006, 'It had all died off.' The band weren't particularly active, and he had already taken a job at a food company.

Johns says that Stereolab 'could have struggled on for another few years' after 2009. 'I think the only reason why it ended when it did was because Tim got so bored with it, doing the same thing over and over again.'

* There is, perhaps, another parallel world in which Gane *didn't* discover a new way of writing songs after *Mars Audiac Quintet* and Stereolab split up in the middle of the 90s.

News of the split came after the band had played a short tour of Australia, New Zealand, and Japan in support of *Chemical Chords*, ending with two gigs at Tokyo's Shibuya Club Quattro on February 10 and 12. A month and a half later, long-serving manager Martin Pike posted a message on the Stereolab website entitled 'Hiatus / Sabbatical / Pause / Intermission / Breather', in which he said that the band were 'going to have a bit of a rest now after nearly nineteen years and work on a few other projects'.

'As we recently made #51 with *Emperor Tomato Ketchup* in the Amazon 100 Greatest Indie Rock Albums Of All Time, we feel that our work is done for the moment,' the note continued. 'We have had to cancel the last two shows that we were scheduled to play, apologies to all that had bought tickets, and there are no plans to record new tracks.' Duophonic, Pike added, was working on 'the release of *Chemical Chords 2*, we also have plans for a new *Switched On* and remastering of the back catalogue'. But there would be no *new* Stereolab 'product' for a while.

Perhaps inevitably, the various stories about Stereolab's demise don't always cohere. Speaking to *The Quietus* in 2015, Gane referred to it as a gradual winding-down. 'It definitely wasn't like any absolute split,' he said. 'We reasoned it out—very like McCarthy's demise, in fact.' He also rejected the idea of the band being on 'hiatus'.

'That's not the term I used,' he said. 'I said it stopped. It's a bit like . . . it doesn't seem to end anymore, does it? The idea was that there would be this other record coming out, and maybe if something really musically interesting [was offered to us], we'd maybe do it again. I'm not against the idea of it, I just wanted to stop, really. There are more complicated reasons, but the simple reason is just that.'

To *The Quietus*, Gane explained that Stereolab 'were as good as we ever were' live toward the end of phase one. 'In fact, much better than we were, very intense,' he added. 'I always judged it on intensity rather than playing well. From some point onwards, we never wavered.'

Later on, Gane's views on this seemed to have changed. In 2019, he told the *New York Times* that the band had split because he was tired of touring and 'couldn't see a way [the music] would develop. And I didn't have the spontaneity to make it work anymore. I felt the next record we made would be bad.'

Sadier took a more personal view of things, explaining in the same interview that 'the ambience in the band was really crappy and very stifling and I had no enjoyment being around the people in the band. . . . There was too much alcohol being consumed,' she added. 'Too much jadedness. Too many miserable people to be doing this.'

Gane disagreed, leading to what the *Times* journalist called 'a brief, tense back-and-forth' that ended with Sadier telling a tale of ending the band's last show 'in tears in a bar in Tokyo. I was bawling.'

I ask Simon Johns for his view on the *New York Times* version of the split. He pauses. 'It was never good, but it was never that bad, you know?' he eventually replies. 'You hear these stories of rock'n'roll monsters going on the road and turning up in separate limousines because they can't bear each other, they can't be in each other's company, but they still play a gig and still go on tour for months and months. I don't understand how you could possibly do that. We never had the luxury of that level of financial backing that we could turn up in separate buses, so you have to tolerate people's idiosyncrasies and behaviour.'

The band, he says, 'never really talked about our interpersonal relationships with each other'. But he can imagine Laetitia feeling marginalised. 'I think she found it difficult to penetrate the kind of . . . what she probably felt, and quite rightly felt, was a sort of a clique of the males in the band. It's unfortunate.'

Communication generally was a problem in Stereolab, according to Johns, who says he heard of the band's hiatus about ten minutes before the news was released. 'I think Martin probably sent me an email saying that we were stopping it for a while,' he says. 'I thought it was unlikely that we'd ever get back together again, in the back of my mind. I thought it'd be great if the opportunity arose. But it was almost twenty years.'

The end, he says, felt like 'a classic Stereolab communication breakdown. We were terrible communicators, really bad,' he explains. 'The seniors aren't good communicators. But, you know, it's not a business, just a bunch of musicians. No one expects you to have an exit interview.'

I don't remember any particular wailing, mourning, or gnashing of teeth at the announcement of the hiatus. Stereolab had, after all, had a very good run of it: nine studio albums, three mini-LPs, seven compilations, and numerous EPs and seven-inches over nineteen years is a hell of a creative streak. I think, too, that we can all imagine how hard it must have been to be in a band with your ex for seven years, which is no slight on anyone, least of all Sadier and Gane, but more a logical conclusion.

Stereolab deserved a rest and, ultimately, we had *Chemical Chords 2* to look forward to. This had been in the offing for a while: speaking to *Pitchfork* in 2008, Gane revealed that the band were already planning their next release. 'It will make an interesting kind of sibling or companion to the record,' he said. 'I think we won't release it like a normal record. We're not going to wait until next year, because it's too similar, it's from the same sort of sessions. We might do something like a tour album instead of a regular release.'

Sadier had a similar vision. 'The new record [*Chemical Chords*] is thirty-one songs; that's how I see it. It's thirty-one songs, which are split into two halves,' she said in the same interview. 'One is the day side, and one is the night-time side . . . I was happier with the mix on the second album, which hopefully will come out in a few months' time.'

Chemical Chords 2 turned out to be *Not Music*, the band's tenth studio album, and would be released on November 16, 2010, more than a year after the band had announced their break. At times, it really does feel like a secondary take on *Chemical Chords*. 'Pop Molecules (Molecular Pop 2)' is essentially 'Pop Molecule (Molecular Pop 1)' without all the thrilling backwards bits, while inessential remixes of 'Silver Sands' by Emperor Machine and 'Neon Beanbag' by Atlas Sound feel like born B-sides.

At other times, *Not Music* comes closer to Sadier's vision of the nighttime album to *Chemical Chords*' day. Songs like 'Two Finger Symphony' (which, beyond its title, doesn't appear to have much in common with *Chemical Chords*' 'One Finger Symphony'), 'Delugeoisie', and 'Aelita' are notably less chirpy than most of *Chemical Chords*, although they're not exactly dispatches from a long dark night of the soul, either.

Perhaps the most interesting thing about *Not Music*—something it shares with *Chemical Chords*, of course—is the way it was built up from loops. Stereolab have been here before: the genesis of their 1996 album *Emperor Tomato Ketchup* lay in Gane building what he called 'small melodic cells', from bass riffs to melodies, creating 'a mass of activity' from where a final song could emerge. But this method found its apotheosis in the sessions for *Chemical Chords* and *Not Music*.

'On the new record . . . I started an idea that's kind of like an excavation,' Gane told *Wired* around the release of *Chemical Chords*. 'What I do is I cut a very, very tiny loop/sample, and I just glue them together so there's maybe eight of them in a row, and that's maybe lasting about a second or a second and a half. And the kind of blurred sound gives it something you can't really precisely put your finger on, it's a strange kind of loop. And then I pitch-shift them up and down to make a chord. And then all we do with the band is we just listen really closely to what we can hear and try to reproduce it.'

Gane compared the process to Pop Art, 'where you're recreating a commercial product but in a painterly way . . . so instead of doing it with MIDI, we're actually playing these tiny little things that we think that we can hear, with real instruments,' he told *Wired*.*

At times, on both records, it feels like this method has put a slight drag on the band's music. It's hard to pinpoint exactly where the fault lies in the two albums' air of—to quote Sadier—'*ba-donk, ba-donk, ba-donk*'. But if you listen closely to a song like 'So Is Cardboard Clouds', on *Not Music*, the drums appear rather flat; it *sounds* like they are looped, or perhaps born out of loops, with the exact same rhythm playing out mechanically from bar to bar.

While promoting *Instant Holograms On Metal Film* in 2025, Gane hinted at this, telling *Mojo* magazine that on *Chemical Chords* and *Not Music*, 'I was probably playing games too much, and I think it may have unbalanced the music in some ways.'

Against this, there are two *Not Music* songs where the process of building up from tiny loops really pays dividends, creating a density, drive, and coiled excitement that is a new tool in the Stereolab armoury.

* It's worth mentioning that Gane's explanations of the composition of *Chemical Chords* and *Not Music* seem to vary slightly from interview to interview, although the idea of tiny musical loops is always there.

Both 'Laserblast' and 'Sun Demon' have a tightly spun, slightly manic energy to them, which derives from the interaction between the tiny musical coils. These are not just drum loops: you also have fragments of guitar, mouthwatering snippets of vibraphone, vocal amuse-bouches, and so on, all buzzing around each other like atoms in a reactor.

The two songs feel like a deconstruction of rock into its constituent parts, guitar music being torn apart and then flung back at itself to see what happens. It's an exciting, slightly nervous-sounding mix that reminds me of New Jersey garage producer Todd Edwards (best known for his Daft Punk collaborations 'Face To Face' and 'Fragments Of Time') and his use of microsampling, in which he rearranges hundreds of tiny samples, sometimes little more than a few nanoseconds, into exotic, highly rhythmical whirls of musical juxtaposition.

Stereolab don't go *that* far—the band's loops last seconds, rather than nanoseconds, and they all come from the group's own music. But this sonic micro-collage—related to but different from the kind of macro-collage we find on '(Varoom!)'—has the distinct air of Edwards's densely-packed musical bricolage.

It feels right that Stereolab should find something new, musically, on the final album before their split, as techniques that had previously been a part of their creative process are driven to their logical conclusion. *Chemical Chords* and *Not Music* do not represent the obvious forward leaps of some of the classic albums in the Stereolab catalogue, but they are not simple retreads. Rather, they are examples of a band firing on all cylinders, even as they circle the mortal drain.

Stereolab would go no further with this. By the time *Not Music* was released, they were already on a hiatus that not many people expected them to emerge from. And frankly, not *all* that many people cared. This wasn't The Beatles in 1970, this was the Happy Mondays in 1993—a band who felt like they had run their course, and who probably deserved a rest.

This they would get, over the following decade. But Stereolab were not done, by any means.

19

'VOID BEAT' INTERMISSION

Both Laetitia Sadier and Tim Gane had long established their musical lives outside of Stereolab by the time the band announced their hiatus in 2009.

Sadier's Monade project made their recorded debut in 1996, releasing two tracks on a joint seven-inch single with sometime Stereolab member David Pajo's M Is The Thirteenth Letter, in which Sadier was joined by Rosie Cuckston of Birmingham indie explorers Pram. Cuckston also features on the debut album by Monade, 2003's *Socialisme Ou Barbarie (The Bedroom Recordings)*—the name a reference to the aforementioned group of socialist libertarians co-founded by Sadier's beloved Cornelius Castoriadis—alongside Pram's Matthew Eaton, Tim Gane, Mary Hansen, and Jim O'Rourke.*

Monade—essentially a lo-fi and slightly shakier take on the Stereolab sound—would release two further albums, 2005's *A Few Steps More* and 2008's *Monstre Cosmic*, before Sadier announced in September 2009 that she was retiring the group. The heart-evaporating

* Though he is listed in the credits, O'Rourke says he has no memory of working on it.

'Étoile', from *Monstre Cosmic*, is the gem in the Monade collection.

This marked the start of Sadier's solo career in earnest. In September 2010, she released *The Trip*, the first album under her own name, and a record that felt like an emancipation from Stereolab in many ways. The only real link to Sadier's previous band, beyond Sadier herself, is the presence of Julien Gasc, who played keyboards live with Stereolab at the very end of the group's life; and the overall feel of the album is a lot gentler, especially on the devastating 'One Million Year Trip', which deals with the suicide of Laetitia's sister, Noelle.

Sadier followed this artistic triumph with a series of solo albums and collaborations. Her 2017 album *Find Me Finding You* was credited to The Laetitia Sadier Source Ensemble, a band name Sadier has continued to use since; she has also released albums with filmmaker David Thayer, as Little Tornados, and with Brazilian band Mombojó.

'Most albums I make, I orchestrate and I have collaborators, and so it's usually made, you know, bit by bit by bit by bit by bit by bit,' Sadier told me in 2024. My question, specifically, was about how she decided if an album should bear her name or that of the Source Ensemble, with whom she was then touring. 'We don't go as a band in a studio and record for two weeks or three weeks,' Sadier said. 'This is none of that. It really is more like an impressionistic painting, of just little touches, and I'm going to ask certain people to intervene if they're up for it.'

Sadier described herself as 'the composer' and 'the orchestrator' of her most recent album, the excellent *Rooting For Love*. 'But I like to stress also the fact that people contributed and that it wouldn't sound like that if they didn't,' she said.

Sadier has also lent the soft mystery of her voice to songs by a number of other artists over the years, starting in the early 90s and continuing to the present day, her guest appearances taking her from big commercial hits with Blur, Common, and Tyler, The Creator to working with underground artists like Giorgio Tuma and Marker Starling.

With Gallic cool in short supply in the London indie rock scene of the early 1990s, it was perhaps inevitable that Sadier would be invited to lend her voice to the Camden bands of the era, adding backing vocals to Gallon Drunk's 1993 album 'From The Heart Of Town' and to The Hair & Skin Trading Company's 'Go Round' single the same year. In 1994, she provided a deliciously theatrical, spoken-word counterfoil to Blur's 'To The End', which took her into the UK Top 20 as Britpop started to gather forces.

When I interviewed Sadier for *Line Noise* in 2024, she said she was happy about crossing over to the mainstream in this way. 'I love cross-pollination,' she said. 'When people ask me to collaborate, like [Italian artist] Giorgio Tuma, for instance, who is far less known, for me it's all about the song, or [Belgian singer] Benjamin Schoos. Let me hear the song, and if I have time and it speaks to me, then I'll contribute.'

•

If Laetitia got the harmonies in the Stereolab divorce, Tim Gane got the band's propulsion and experimental electronic tendencies. Like Sadier, he had already dabbled in extracurricular work while Stereolab phase one was still a functioning unit. In the 90s, he formed Turn On, an experimental trio heavy on improvisation, with Sean O'Hagan and Andy Ramsay (with input from Fulton Dingley). The group's only release, an eponymous album, came out in 1997.

According to an interview that O'Hagan did with *Magnet* magazine, Turn On was an attempt to 'break our recording habits in our respective bands', with nothing being prepared before the trio entered the studio. 'Everything had to originate in the room, with the four participants facing each other and approval had to be unanimous. There were plenty of rules. A bass sound could not be generated from an instrument that had already been used on that track. No pure electronic tracks and no purely organic tracks. The whole project was not allowed to exceed the appointed record time, five days. No consecutive speeds. No consecutive keys.'

The same year also saw the release of 'Blip ^ / Blip ~' by Blips, a one-off collaboration between Gane, Mary Hansen, and former Spacemen 3 mainstay Pete Kember, which appeared on the *Spooky Sounds Of Now* compilation. Four years later, Gane formed Alternative 3 with Andy Ramsay as well as members of Add N To (X) and Hairy Butter, to record 'an alternative score to *Alternative 3*, a fake documentary about alien threat'. The resulting record, 2001's *Original Soundtrack Recording*, is distinctly odd, a leftfield romp with its tongue firmly in its cheek. Gane and O'Hagan have also recorded soundtracks to two films by French filmmaker Marc Fitoussi—2007's *La Vie D'Artiste* and 2010's *Copacabana*—both of which are fun, if slight, when removed from their cinematic context.

Like Sadier, Gane has lent his distinctive musical talents to bands on the lookout for that mysterious Stereolab alchemy. In 2002, he remixed 'Another New Day' by German nu-jazz artists Jazzanova, and he has also reworked songs by the likes of White Lies and Welsh-Cornish psych pop explorer Gwenno.* However, his post-Stereolab musical career really took off in 2013 with the release of *Blood-Drums*, the first LP from Gane's new band Cavern Of Anti-Matter, which he formed with former Stereolab/Th' Faith Healers drummer Joe Dilworth and synth player Holger Zapf.

According to Gane, *Blood-Drums* was intended to be a low-key release. '[It] was just a limited-edition, vinyl-only pressing on a Berlin label, Grautag,' he told *Vice* magazine in 2016. '[Label founder Nicolas Moulin's] aim is to get experimental musicians to collaborate with him to make a record, which is always a double vinyl LP in a five-hundred edition, with a special cover he designs.'

This wasn't, Gane continued, 'a normally commercial record, although it was available ... I approached it like I would a soundtrack. It was a very specific thing, and I devised the sound of that record through conversations I had with the guy,' he explained. 'And then when it came out, I did what I could and played a few gigs, did some interviews, and it got some reviews, and then it went away.'

Well, not exactly. The band returned in 2014 with *Interlude Music*—'Recorded live to two-track half-inch tape between the hours of 22:00–23:00, January 7, 2014, in Berlin, Germany'—then made what most people consider their full debut, the dazzling *Void Beats / Invocation Trex*, released on Duophonic in 2016.

Gane wanted Cavern Of Anti-Matter to escape from under his shadow, telling *The Quietus* in 2015 that he would prefer it if people didn't even know he was in the band. 'I really don't want people to

* While writing this book, I was sent a 'Tim Gane / Stereolab Remix' of '1,000 Canciones' by the heavily Stereolab-influenced Pamplona garage band Melenas, as well as a new Thurston Moore single, 'Sans Limites', featuring vocals by Laetitia.

look at this and reference what I've done before, as that sets up another whole bunch of parameters,' he explained. 'I don't try to run away from the type of music I always end up messing around with, but, at the same time, I'm not pushing it. Not pushing any connections that people may make.'

His wish did not come true. As he acknowledged to *Vice*, Gane has a certain way with melody and a distinctive style of playing the guitar. As soon as this runs into a blazing Motorik beat on *Blood-Drums*' first song, 'You're An Art Soul', the jig is up.

Gane himself has described Cavern Of Anti-Matter's approach as 'setting up tiny rhythmic cells and expanding on them in certain ways, splitting the melody and stretching out'—with the idea of 'cells' taking the listener right back to the composition process of *Emperor Tomato Ketchup*.

Reviewing *Void Beats / Invocation Trex* for *Pitchfork*, journalist Philip Sherburne pointed out that the album's opening song, 'Tardis Cymbals', 'begins with a ringing E chord that longtime fans may initially mistake for the opening notes of *Mars Audiac Quintet*'s "Nihilist Assault Group" (or, for that matter, "Three-Dee Melodie" or "Transona Five" or "Anamorphose").' Elsewhere, Sherburne writes, 'The distorted organs of "Insect Fear" lend it a garage-rock feel that flashes back to the *Transient Random-Noise Bursts* era, while the swinging "Echolalia" recalls Stereolab's 60s fascinations.'

To be fair to Cavern Of Anti-Matter, the band do also call on many other influences, including Detroit techno and glassy electronica, while 'Automatic Morning', from the band's 2018 album *Hormone Lemonade*, evokes Dr Dre circa *The Chronic*. But you would have to be particularly resistant to Stereolab's music to listen to Cavern's records and *not* want Laetitia to suddenly appear, *ba-da-ba*-ing her way through Gane's dense musical arrangements.

This is why 'Void Beat', from *Void Beats / Invocation Trex*, is the song I have chosen to sum up the work of Cavern Of Anti-Matter. It is a sumptuous dream of a song, gliding around delicately on a layer of synth bliss, before Dilworth comes in with a ferocious beat to send the melody rushing off into the ether. Everything that is so special about Cavern Of Anti-Matter is contained in the song, but at the same time, 'Void Beat' reminds us—and I *am* being overly dramatic here, and probably unfair—of a hole at the heart of the band's music where Laetitia Sadier could be.

Cavern Of Anti-Matter continued to record after Stereolab re-formed in 2019, releasing the fantastically evocative *In Fabric* soundtrack in 2020 and the 'Temp Music' seven-inch in 2021. Gane has also released an album and a seven-inch single as Ghost Power, his duo with Dymaxion's Jeremy Novak, whose sound is not unlike that of Cavern Of Anti-Matter, but with an added dose of surreal humour.

The other members of Stereolab also kept themselves busy during the hiatus years, their bewildering variety of projects paying fitting tribute to Stereolab's eclectic career. Drummer Andy Ramsay runs Press Play Studios in Bermondsey, London, working with artists including Jamie T, Sky Larkin, and Wire, as well as composing music for film, TV, and radio. In 2011, he released two albums of sprawling cosmic rock as Anram, in collaboration with MV/EE, Flower, and Doozer, but he has largely remained behind the boards.

Joe Walters, the French horn player who once studied music at King's College, Cambridge, has leaned back into the classical world, playing with a dizzying array of prestigious orchestras, including the London Philharmonic.

Keyboard player Joe Watson is a lecturer in music at the University Of Sussex and has released two solo albums as Junior Electronics. His PhD in musical composition is 'a practice-based investigation into electronic music processes through performance, installation and recording using other-than-digital technologies such as modular synthesis and analogue tape', which sounds highly appropriate.

Bass player Simon Johns, meanwhile, revealed in a Reddit AMA in the summer of 2025 that he has Parkinson's disease but promised that new music is 'on the way (I hope)'.*

* Johns's profile on the website of *Lubes'n'Greases*, the 'flagship, award-winning, independent monthly magazine for and about the global lubricants industry', where he has worked since 2017, makes no mention of Stereolab, but it does say that he 'currently lives in Istanbul, where in his spare time he plays music and hosts a weekly radio program with his son'.

20

'I FEEL THE AIR (OF ANOTHER PLANET)'

REVIVAL

Absence suited Stereolab, in a way, as it does so many bands. It's an unfortunate logic, but musicians who are always around and always creating are very easy to take for granted.

It happened with The Fall, who only really got their dues after singer Mark E. Smith died in 2018 and we could look back on the band's work as a whole; and it happened with Stereolab, who were kind of always *there* during their first two decades, releasing new music and playing your local medium-sized venue.

If you didn't see them live this time, you knew they would be back. Until, of course, they *weren't*, and people started to realise what they had missed. It helped that artists like Pharrell Williams and Tyler, The Creator continued to sing the band's praises in the interim, introducing a new generation of music fans to the dazzling idea of Stereolab.

Was it obvious that the band would re-form? Is 're-form' even the right word for a group famously on a 'Hiatus / Sabbatical / Pause / Intermission / Breather'? Most bands re-form, and Stereolab have always treated their musical legacy with respect—the excellent *Switched On* compilations are a telling example of this. But Stereolab never were 'most bands', and their particular history of romantic and musical connection made getting back together seem unlikely. Until it happened.

The first news to break the Stereolab ice came in August 2018, when it was announced that the band would be releasing remastered editions of their *Switched On* compilation series on September 28. This was welcome news, but unlikely to get the pulse really racing, even on the newly launched Stereolab website forum.

The big news came four months later, on December 4, when it was revealed that the band would be undertaking 'an extensive reissue campaign' of all of their albums from 1993's *Transient Random Noise-Bursts With Announcements* to 2004's *Margerine Eclipse*.

'All seven albums will be reissued throughout 2019,' the announcement confirmed, before slipping in, casually, 'Keep 'em peeled for news of the live return of Stereolab.'

Excuse me?

The following day, it was announced that Stereolab would be playing the Primavera Sound festival in Barcelona in 2019. A full tour was confirmed in February 2019, with dates across Europe and North America during the summer and autumn, ending up at the Synästhesie Festival in Berlin on November 16. My excitement was through the roof.

In a 2025 interview with *Uncut*, Gane revealed that the reunion had come about because Warp Records, the UK indie label that was collaborating on the album reissues, had asked the band to play some gigs to promote the reissue campaign, which seems like a perfectly mundane reason for such an exciting event.

Stereolab duly played their first concert in almost exactly a decade on May 28, 2019, at the 140-capacity Music Hall in Ramsgate, a warm-up for the forthcoming tour. Sadier and Gane were joined by stalwarts Andy Ramsay and Joe Watson, with Xavi Muñoz Guimerá, who had played with Laetitia since her 2014 album *Something Shines*, joining on bass. (Simon Johns rehearsed with the band but did not join them on the reunion tour for health reasons.)

The setlist that night in Ramsgate included a fairly predictable array of the band's greatest hits, including 'Come And Play In The

Milky Night', 'French Disko', 'Metronomic Underground', and 'Ping Pong', with room for the odd deep cut, including 'Need To Be' from *Margerine Eclipse* and 'The Extension Trip' from *Music For The Amorphous Body Study Center*.

The band would largely keep to the same set throughout their 2019 tour. They played sixty-two gigs that year, performing 'French Disko' at fifty-eight of them. The only real surprise came at their June 9 concert at the Villette Sonique festival in Paris, where they apparently encored with a version of George Gershwin's classic 'Summertime', which Sadier had covered on her 2010 solo album *The Trip*.

As the band toured, the reissue campaign kicked into gear, with each of the expanded albums including an assortment of bonus tracks (largely unreleased demos) and sleeve notes by Tim Gane.* The albums were remastered from the original tapes by Bo Kondren, who had previously mastered *Chemical Chords* and *Not Music*. Kondren, Gane writes in the sleeve notes, is a believer in 'authentic mastering', a style that 'tries to preserve the inner musicality of the audio . . . Stereolab's music can often be quite impenetrably dense in the midrange, there is always a lot going on—lots of detail everywhere. We were both very keen to preserve this aspect of the sound and, at the same time, try to improve a little on resolution, spatiality and depth.'

The 2019 tour was a success, commercially and critically. Things might have come to an end there, Gane told *Uncut*, 'but COVID stretched it out for a couple more years'. In 2020, the band played seven gigs in Australia and New Zealand; in 2021, they played five UK concerts; in 2022, they embarked on a huge tour, with fifty-seven concerts in Europe and the USA; and in 2023, they played a modest seven gigs.

Bass player Muñoz, in an interview with *Valencia Plaza*, painted a harmonious picture of the touring band. 'It's a different budget and a different way of touring [to his previous experiences]. Very good sound conditions, a very professional backline and technicians and less physical strain,' he explained. 'We travel by bus, with a team of about

* Some of these demos had already appeared on the official-ish 2007 art project/album *Eaten Horizons Or The Electrocution Of Rock*, on the German label En/Of, of which only 130 copies were made

eleven people, each with a specific role, and at the end, you arrive at the venue much less tired. Plus, you have time to work on your own stuff during the trip. I get ahead on the album productions I've done for other bands on my computer; Joe Watson, who teaches composition at the University Of Brighton, takes advantage of the opportunity to grade his students' work, and Andy Ramsay, who has a recording studio in London, also manages things on his computer during trips between cities.'

David Callahan saw the band play at Earth in Hackney in December 2022, 'and they were fantastic. When I was a kid,' he adds, 'if bands reunited, you'd think it was awful. They'd just do it for the money, and they'd have no self-respect. Whereas nowadays bands re-form, and it seems like a communal effort to make sure it's worth the re-formation. Stereolab very much fit into that . . . they're doing the songs justice. They're playing them well and with energy.'

At the time of writing, I've seen Stereolab four times since they re-formed: at Primavera Sound Barcelona in June 2019; at Primavera LA in September 2022; at the Apolo in Barcelona in November 2022; and at Primavera Barcelona (again) in June 2025. I was incredibly excited to see the band in 2019, a decade on from my last Stereolab gig. But I was also working—if memory serves, I had to rush off to interview Danny L. Harle—and I couldn't quite absorb myself into their set as I wanted to.

I felt slightly divided about the setlist, too. It was packed with the hits—Sadier introduced 'Ping Pong' as 'a very nice song about the disasters of capitalism'—which covered the obvious bases of what I wanted to hear. But it seemed a touch too obvious for such a gloriously strange band, like The Velvet Underground returning for a romp through 'Sunday Morning' and 'Sweet Jane' with none of the avant nastiness.

Maybe I was just distracted. Melenas, an indie-rock quartet from Pamplona who are heavily influenced by Stereolab, were also there at the 2019 Primavera gig. 'It was a super-exciting and special concert for us,' they tell me. 'It was the first time we saw them and despite not being in the privacy of a room, it was exactly what we expected: impeccable sound, those very particular textures, that wave of repetition that enveloped us . . . and a really cool repertoire. There were even a few tears.'

Stereolab's LA gig, while brief and slightly stuttering, was stranger and—perhaps as a result—more engaging. Primavera LA was a peculiar event for a European to attend, with the festival public corralled off into separate sections of the Los Angeles State Historic Park, depending on whether they had hit drinking age or not, and it was all so *early*, with the headlining act signing off at 10:30pm. The crowd was young, well-dressed, and, as far as I could see, very sober, more focused on checking out Mitski and Clairo than pursuing the European (and, let's face it, *British*) festival tradition of getting out of their collective minds. Wandering through the crowd, random people would complement each other on their clothes, which I don't think you get at Reading or Leeds. This is a *good thing*, make no mistake. But it did create quite an odd environment in which to watch Stereolab, whose slightly grizzled faces and tendency toward the avant-garde didn't exactly feel in line with the festival's youthful crowd.

Rather than toe the line, crank out the hits, and try to draw the audience in, however, Stereolab got weird. Only one song remained in the set from the Barcelona festival gig—'French Disko', inevitably—with the crowd instead treated to the fairly predictable duo of 'Super-Electric' and 'Miss Modular', and the not-at-all-likely quartet of 'Refractions In The Plastic Pulse', 'Eye Of The Volcano', 'Delugeoisie', and 'Pack Yr Romantic Mind' in the slowly fading LA light. I am not quite sure what I expected of a re-formed Stereolab show in the heart of Tinseltown. But this wasn't it. *This* was far more interesting.

'I wanted to play so that you wouldn't need to know the songs before,' Gane told *The Ringer* in 2019, before Stereolab played the Pitchfork Festival during the first flush of their reunion. 'It's quite important that it does come across, even if people don't know us. That we're not just only about people who are familiar with our stuff pretty well and had seen us before and *remembering*. I mean, we're not interested in that whatsoever. No one's interested in that. No nostalgia. None of that stuff.'

The wonderful, almost illicit feeling that weirdness was back on the menu was confirmed at Stereolab's Apolo gig, two months later. Again,

'French Disko' and 'Miss Modular' were on the setlist. But so was 'Supah Jaianto', from the group's not-always-loved final album, *Not Music*; 'Laisser-faire', from the *Low Fi* EP, a record that was unavailable for two decades; and *Fab Four Suture*'s 'Eye Of The Volcano'. And these were just the opening three songs.

I loved them all. But it was 'I Feel The Air (Of Another Planet)' that really penetrated my skull. The song was first recorded in 1997 for *Dots And Loops* but missed the cut and was eventually released three years later on *The First Of The Microbe Hunters*, an eight-minute tumble and spin of circling 'bah's and cardiovascular rhythm that sounds like Yé-yé blasting off into space as the Earth collapses beneath it.

'I Feel The Air (Of Another Planet)' is well named: it feels familiar but displaced, hopeful but apprehensive, like removing your space suit on an unfamiliar planet and hoping for the best. And Stereolab reclaimed it that night as something like another greatest hit; not necessarily in sales, streams or renown but in artistic prowess, a reminder that the group's catalogue runs deep, wide and fascinating.

'I Feel The Air' is a song of revival, a work of reappraisal that shines new light on forgotten corners of the Stereolab universe beyond the obvious hits. It is a reminder that Stereolab, in their infinite variety, can be *that* as well as *this*. They feel the air of another planet. And if we stick with them for a while, then so too might we.

Stereolab's fundamental weirdness, their amiable obscurity, was underlined by the two compilations that they have released since re-forming. *Electrically Possessed* (*Switched On Volume 4*), which came out in February 2021, gathers up a brilliantly abstruse collection of songs from Stereolab's EPs and tour singles, the majority of which date from 1999 to 2009, in a riotous collection of leftfield electronics, disco, oddball collaborations, and mangled jazz. The album feels like a hymn to gleeful experimentation and colouring outside the lines.

Pulse Of The Early Brain (*Switched On Volume 5*), released in September 2022, gathers what's left of the band's catalogue, dredging the deep Stereolab seas to find what emerges. I use the word 'dredge' very deliberately: these songs are the deepest of Stereolab dives, the songs that have remained flattened at the bottom of the ocean where barely a light shines. And they are frequently some of the band's most esoteric work, from the feverish soundscapes of 'Trippin' With The Birds' to the space-ship jazz of 'Symbolic Logic Of Now!' These are the bioluminescent vampire squids and slowly crawling dumbo octopuses of the Stereolab catalogue. Autechre's gnarled and thorny remix of 'Refractions In The Plastic Pulse' certainly has a place in the Stereolab catalogue. And that place is on *Pulse Of The Early Brain*.

At the same time, perverse as ever, *Switched On Volume 5* is also home to some of the band's brightest songs—see 'Spool Of Collusion' and the previously unreleased 'Robot Riot'—as well as one of their most important works in 'ABC', which cleared the way for Stereolab to advance toward *Emperor Tomato Ketchup*.

Reunion—if that *is* the word—has worked well for Stereolab. Asked why they had returned by *The Guardian*, Gane said, 'We've got seven albums coming back out,' while Sadier, simultaneously, answered, 'For the money.' Laetitia, I am sure, was joking. But both things are probably true, to an extent, and those seven reissues gave the band the perfect excuse to tour without looking mercenary or profiteering.

Sure, some of the Stereolab reissues were relatively expensive in their exotic vinyl glory. But they are also available on streaming services and YouTube, where you can listen to them for nothing, decades of intense toil and inspiration for you, the listener, to pick and choose at your own glorified pace. Tickets for the band's Apolo show in November 2022 were €24; I paid €36 to see the Sisters Of Mercy the same year, and they were *terrible*.

Speaking to the *New York Times* in 2019, Sadier said she realised that people had been waiting for the band to come back all this time, 'and I feel really joyful that we can give it again to people, one more time', I've seen the reaction among four different crowds, in two different cities, to the return of Stereolab, and people were genuinely ecstatic.

Stereolab's reputation has also been bolstered by their time away, as if we needed an absence to make the heart grow fonder. *The Guardian* recently called them 'one of the best bands of the turn of the century'; *Pitchfork* went for 'one of the most exceptional and historically influential bands'; *Vice* has talked of their 'innovative and unparalleled discography'; *The Arts Desk* called them 'avant-pop icons'.

Well, that's *obvious*, you might think. But beyond a certain fanatical base, people weren't saying these things back in 2009. Re-forming didn't make this happen—decades of inspiration and sweat made it happen—but it has helped us all to see the band's genius, unburdened by the scourge of overfamiliarity.

This hasn't come without a cost, though. In the same *New York Times* interview, Sadier said that she saw the reunion tour as 'a shared enjoyment'—'I love this music and I'm so keen to be singing it and performing it again,' she explained—but she also had what the journalist called 'a brief, tense back-and-forth' with Gane about how and why the band had split up in the first place, which sounds like precisely the kind of thing that estranged couples who are brought together to discuss the end of their relationship *do*.

Toward the end of our interview, I asked Simon Johns what he thinks Stereolab will be remembered for. 'That's a good question,' he says, pondering his answer. 'For making interesting music? I don't think they'll be remembered for a particular song. The body of work is so large and varied that it's always coming up with interesting ideas, being open to trying stuff.

'One of our strengths, which was also kind of a weakness, was that we always played beyond our ability. So, at that interface between being in the comfort zone and going a bit beyond your ability, there was a kind of chaos and excitement there. It could all fall apart.'

Nigel House, the co-owner of indie music retailer Rough Trade, says that Stereolab have always sounded like Stereolab, even as their sound evolved, 'which I think is a really hard trick to do. You want a Stereolab record, you don't want a Rolling Stones record or something,' he adds. 'So, to stay like Stereolab but to be kind of different, not many bands can manage it. But I think they did it really well.'

David Callahan calls Stereolab 'one of the last great DIY bands. Obviously, they got signed to Elektra and other labels since. But they've always had control over running their own Duophonic label, and that literally started as a proper indie, where they were in the bedroom, folding the sleeves and sticking things on themselves,' he says. 'They've always retained their independence, even when they've signed to a major label and had big budgets for tours, for coaches and then employees on tour.'

Too Pure co-founder Richard Roberts believes Stereolab will be remembered as 'really influential'. At the same time, in what feels like a very Stereolab twist, he finds it hard to explain *who*, exactly, Stereolab have influenced over the years. 'There's a sound that's very definitely a Stereolab sound but there's no such sound as Stereolab, if that makes sense,' he says.

I nod in agreement. In truth, I don't quite know what he means. But the contradiction itself feels appropriate. When I ask Roberts which specific bands he thinks have been influenced by Stereolab, things don't get much clearer. He mentions DIIV and Beach House: 'That kind of new wave of post shoegaze, post rock, all of those types of things. But I don't think there's a particular band I'd say, *Wow, that's Stereolab*. Other than going back as far as Broadcast or something.'*

Maybe it is easier to go direct. Both Electrelane's Debbie Ball and Melenas are quick to acknowledge Stereolab's influence on their own music. 'Stereolab created their own style, totally recognisable, which has served as a source of inspiration for many other groups that came after them,' Melenas say, while adding The Notwist and Vanishing Twin into the inspiration equation.†

'As Melenas have evolved over time, Stereolab has become an increasingly important reference, especially in the exploration and incorporation of new sounds,' they continue. 'The use of analogue synthesizers, repetitive loops, hypnotic rhythmic patterns, as well as the mix of these sounds with drum machines... all of this is super inspiring when it comes to making songs. The variety of sound textures, the play of harmonies in the voices... the truth is that they always come up in conversations when we compose.'

Unrest's Mark Robinson goes so far as to compare Stereolab to one of the most influential bands in history. 'I feel like they should be remembered like The Velvet Underground or something like that,' he

* I don't dare mention that I don't think Broadcast sound that much like Stereolab, either, despite the connections between the two bands.

† To round out the list, I've heard Pram, Dummy, Komeda, and Fievel Is Glauque compared to Stereolab, all with some justification. Interestingly, most bands who are said to sound like Stereolab resemble early Stereolab. You never hear a band compared to *Chemical Chords*.

says. 'Maybe they haven't even hit their peak of popularity yet. Maybe in 2035 that's going to be the band everybody's going to be listening to.'

Musically, Stereolab are more relevant than ever in the 2020s, their genre-agnostic approach fitting squarely with the playlist era. Politically, too, their beliefs are more pertinent—more *necessary*, even—in a world where even supporters of capitalism seem to realise that something is wrong with the way we are living and the rampant demand for growth threatens the very air we breathe. What's more, in an age of consumerism and social media, Guy Debord's idea of 'The Society Of The Spectacle', in which images and representation eclipse direct experience—an idea that inspired Sadier and Gane right from the beginning—seems utterly germane.

Do young people love Stereolab? My obsession with the band tells me that they surely must do—for how could they not? Are Stereolab popular on TikTok? This is not something that a man in his late forties can answer. So, I google the question, and I am delighted to find a video on the platform by the popular music journalist marg.mp3 (aka Margeaux Labat), in which she talks about her love for Stereolab.

Busy as Labat is, she is happy to talk. '[Stereolab] are the culmination of all my favourite genres, which is why they are one of my favourite bands,' she says when we connect online. 'Pop music, indie rock, electronic music, 60s pop, Krautrock, 70s grooves.'

Do young people like Stereolab, I ask, slightly wary of shoving all young people into a dedicated pigeonhole?

'Yes,' Labat says. Kind of. 'They have a lot of younger fans now. Maybe not younger than me [Labat was twenty-seven when we spoke] but fans in their twenties,' she explains. 'In order to have really young, teen fans, I feel like TikTok has to play a part of it, for better or for worse. And I don't think they've had a TikTok moment yet.'*

Labat sees the Stereolab audience as being aged between their twenties and their fifties. 'But I think anyone has the potential to like Stereolab,' she adds. 'They're not an immediate band. Their music requires patience, and a lot of their songs are long. I remember listening

* Labat says she doesn't know how well her own Stereolab video on TikTok performed, as she doesn't tend to look at the numbers.

to *Dots And Loops* for the first time. One of my favourite Stereolab songs, "Refractions In The Plastic Pulse", I think it's fifteen minutes long or something.'

Young music fans, Labat explains, like immediacy. 'I feel like people aren't as patient listeners as they like to be or as they used to be,' she says. 'But I could be wrong. I feel like whenever I make these statements, I'm maybe overlooking how there's almost a reactive wave of music fans who are coming up right now that are, like, 'We're so tired of algorithms and TikTok and content that requires short attention spans. We want to listen to full albums.' They want to buy physical media.'

TikTok or not—hell, *young people* or not—Stereolab's second life has been an idiosyncratic triumph, much like their first. It has been a greatest hits canter when the band wanted it to be; an arty explosion when they didn't; and a reminder that Stereolab have never been your typical band of easy pigeonholes and one-dimensional sounds.

Stereolab today are still resplendent in their infinite variety, more than three decades since they formed; still weird, still wonderful, still gloriously unplaceable and still feeling the air of another planet, even after all these years.

INTERSTITIAL FOUR
OUR FAVOURITE STEREOLAB SONGS

MAXIM MOSTON (musician and producer) I love Stereolab! I think my favourite song of theirs is 'Pack Yr Romantic Mind', because that melody is an earworm.

A distant second would be 'Puncture In The Radax Permutation', because of the many stages of the song, each of them super catchy.

LEIRE, OIHANA, MARÍA, LAURA (Melenas)

[Leire] 'Pack Yr Romantic Mind'.

[Oihana] This question is very difficult. 'French Disko' is obviously a super hit, and it has all the ingredients that I like. Also, it is the song that introduced me to Stereolab, so it has that added memory. I also really like 'K-Stars', a more melancholic and ethereal side to the band. It is a super nice song to spend some time floating. And finally: 'Metronomic Underground', surprising, sexy, and that makes everyone dance almost without them realising it.

[Maria] 'Lo Boob Oscillator'. It is a party of choruses that envelop everything, as if you were inside a warm bubble. I like how the song grows until it transforms into an instrumental explosion with that Motorik rhythm that hooks you and drags you until the song ends, and you are left wanting more Stereolab.

[Laura] 'French Disko'. It's just that, really, when a song has the ability to take you so high and above everything in such an enveloping and beautiful way, I just give up, victim of the perfect hit.

BEN CARDEW (author) It was a scalp-tinglingly cold Barcelona morning in December 2024 when I realised that I was going to have to answer the frankly ridiculous question that I had been asking interviewees for this book, namely: what is your favourite Stereolab song?

When I am doing interviews, I don't tend to send over the questions in advance, as it makes for a laboured conversation. But this is the one question that I often give interviewees before we talk, so that they have time to ponder the incredible largesse of the Stereolab catalogue.

What I am presenting in this book is a list of twenty Stereolab (and Stereolab-adjacent) songs. But these aren't my *favourite* Stereolab songs, necessarily: often, they are among my favourites; other times, they play an illustrative role. And I am not going to choose one of those twenty.

Instead, let me go for a song that I barely mention in this book: 'Margerine Rock', from *Margerine Eclipse*, the band's eighth studio album.

Why?

The simple answer is that this song, with its indie-rock bounce, cascading melody, and array of bizarro sound effects, makes me very happy at heart, the ever-so-slight shade of melancholy to Laetitia's vocal melody paradoxically amplifying the joy. 'Margerine Rock' is a Stereolab song that will make me smile, whatever else is happening in the world.

The longer answer is that it *blows me away* that Stereolab could make a song this joyful-sounding at that stage of their career, when still reeling from Mary Hansen's death and Tim and Laetitia's split. Where the hell did this joy spring from?

'Margerine Rock' does another thing that I adore in Stereolab's music: it wears its experimentation lightly. Listen to it on a computer speaker or through crappy headphones, and you might not even notice the use of 'dual mono' production. And the song works fine without it. Plug in a good pair of headphones, though, and you can plainly hear different sounds coming from the left and right channels, a separate drum recording on each. I find this concealed innovation, this *stealth experimentation*, totally remarkable.

Which is why, for today—and perhaps today only—'Margerine Rock' is my favourite Stereolab song.

OUTRO
'INFINITY GIRL'
THE FUTURE

One day in April 2025, there was a package. Stereolab fans across Europe received a cardboard envelope in the post with the thrilling words 'Unsolicited Stereolab Material' stamped on the back.

Opened up, the envelope revealed a brown paper package with the Duophonic and Warp Records logos stamped on the front and a red sticker seal on the back. Inside *that* was a word search and a seven-inch single, home to 'Aerial Troubles' on side A and 'Aerial Troubles (Instrumental)' on side B. Stereolab, it appeared, were back.

To be fair, there had been warning. Speaking to the *New York Times* in 2019 about the prospect of new music, Gane was ambiguous. 'Don't know,' he replied when asked if there was any new Stereolab music in him. 'Maybe. That's the problem . . . there's the music that, as an instigator of the music, I'm interested in doing. That might not sound anything like Stereolab music. But can it become Stereolab music? That's the question.' Sadier, as a follow-up, asked what the hours would be—a joke and also perhaps not *really* a joke, when you get down to it.

There were other hints. Sean O'Hagan told Gilles Peterson on his BBC 6 Music show in 2024 that he hoped to see new Stereolab music sometime soon. And Mouse On Mars posted a picture to their Instagram on February 20, 2025, posing in the studio with Sadier and Gane.

What's more, Tim and Laetitia *had* worked on music together since Stereolab's split. 'Next Time You See Me', from Sadier's second solo album, *Silencio*, is a Gane co-write. 'I asked Tim to write a song also, which he did specifically, I believe, to that effect,' Sadier told *Freq* in 2012. 'He just proposed a demo, which sounded very different to what ended up on the record. He said that he was surprised at how it sounded, and he liked the final version.'

And so he should. 'Next Time You See Me' is a wonderful song, its jazzy chord sequence and lucid melody suggesting the best of both Gane and Sadier's worlds. The title is very sweet, too, for a couple who had recently ended their creative relationship, its hint of reconciliation giving hope that everything could *perhaps* be mended.

Phase three of Stereolab—a re-formed band with new material—moved relatively fast. Gane told *Uncut* in 2025 that the idea to record a new record came into focus around the spring and summer of 2023; most of the album was written in 2023, and the band started recording in January 2024. 'There were no rehearsals, as usual,' he added.

While all this was happening in secret, the band's public image ground into gear. On October 24, 2024, Primavera Sound announced that the group would be playing the Barcelona festival in June 2025. In February 2025, Stereolab announced a tour of Europe and North America. And on March 31, 2025, in one of the band's 'Interim Lab Report' emails, a discreet 'click here' link at the end of the message led to a picture of the brown envelope with 'Unsolicited Stereolab Material' printed on it.

The following day, a post appeared on the band's various social media channels with images of the paper package and sticker seal. Still, not many people dared to hope, particularly as the picture was published on April 1—April Fools' Day, the day for pranks, jokes, and deceptions.

A few days later, the cardboard envelopes started to arrive in the mail, and the questions multiplied. Was 'Aerial Troubles'—a bouncing pop number, sprinkled with the group's characteristic intertwined vocals—actually *new*, or a previously unreleased outtake? Could there be a genuinely new album on the way? The accompanying word search offered a few clues, giving up 'album', 'Warp', 'Disk', and more. People seized on the fact that 'Aerial Troubles' had several vocalists on it, including a male voice, as evidence that it *must* be new.

A week later, all was revealed: Stereolab would release *Instant Holograms On Metal Film*, their first new studio album in fifteen years, on May 23 via Duophonic UHF Disks/Warp. The album would feature thirteen new songs, including 'Aerial Troubles', written by Sadier and Gane and performed by the current touring line-up.

Instant Holograms had been recorded with admirable secrecy by Cooper Crain (of Bitchin Bajas and Cave) at Andy Ramsay's Press Play studio in London, with guests including Bitchin Bajas' Rob Frye, Ben LaMar Gay, Holger Zapf of Cavern Of Anti-Matter, Marie Merlet, and, most excitingly, Molly Hansen Read—Mary Hansen's niece. There would also be a tour single, later revealed as 'Cloud Land' / 'Flashes In The Afternoon', to be sold at the band's 2025 shows.

Instant Holograms On Metal Film, when it arrived, was an unexpectedly strong album—not *quite* a messianic comeback, but far better than I had dared to dream. The record wasn't *new* new, an *Emperor Tomato Ketchup*-style leap out into the future. But it was new enough, home to many of the familiar Stereolab tropes—jazzy chord sequences, looping bass, electronic texture, sonic collage, and French lyrics—arranged in ways we hadn't quite heard before.

In an interview with *Uncut* in 2025—one of few conversations around the new album—Sadier said that she had had 'much more musical input than before' on the new record, while Gane said that *Instant Holograms* features ideas he had been working on over the years, including 'sound ideas' from Cavern Of Anti-Matter's 2020 soundtrack to *In Fabric*, which show up on 'Flashes From Everywhere'.

Gane told the interviewer that he wasn't worried about how the album would be received: 'Music is just an exciting adventure, and I don't have any trepidation about doing it or presenting it to others,' he said. 'What comes out, comes out.'

Looking back at the fundamental qualities of Stereolab that I have examined in this book, *Instant Holograms On Metal Film* ticks numerous boxes, with moments of propulsion, groove, collage, populism, electronics, collaboration, harmony, and jazz, while the blocky, brightly coloured cover art screams retro-futurism. It's funny how a band that has changed so much over the years can still be so comforting in their familiarity.

Holograms, in other words, sounds a lot like Stereolab, without calling back to one specific era of the group's music, which feels like a smart way to return. That didn't stop fans tying themselves in knots trying to describe it in terms of other Stereolab records—*Cobra* meets *Fab Four Suture* seems to be a popular choice—but the comparisons never quite land.

If you're looking for novelty in the record, you could point to the fact that *Holograms* has a new producer in Cooper Crain, known for his work with Circuit Des Yeux and Ty Segall. It is also the Stereolab album that gives most space to the male voice, in this case the backing vocals of bassist Xavi Muñoz and keyboard player Joe Watson, which *should* perhaps sound radically different for the band, but somehow doesn't.*

For me, the album lacks something of the group's best vocal patchwork, but many of the melodies are excellent—on 'Flashes From Everywhere', say, or the earworm-ish 'If You Remember I Forgot How To Dream Pt 1'—and Laetitia's lyrics of capitalist despair feel more relevant than ever in the new Trump era. If Stereolab wanted to prove that they weren't just another 90s band on the reunion circuit—not an accusation many people have levelled at them, in all honesty—then *Instant Holograms On Metal Film* achieves that and much more.

Speaking to *Mojo* around the time of the album's release, Gane said that he felt he had achieved a balance between his obsession with musical puzzles 'and more classic songwriting styles, like picking up a guitar and playing it. . . . On this new record, I'm still really pushing myself by involving processes like cut-ups, random assembly of chords and other chance elements as a way to achieve something intriguing with the music,' he said.

Gane expanded on this when speaking to *Shindig!* magazine, noting how, while songs like 'Aerial Troubles' and 'Melodie Is A Wound' were the result of him playing chords on his guitar, others came about through 'elements of chance' and his use of cut-up techniques. 'I recorded a single note pulse, went through a scale of chords in every type (major, minor . . .), picked out the ones that had some interesting reaction with the single note and recorded them on an organ,' he explained. 'Sometimes I added note extensions to the chords to form drones and stuff like that. All the chords were then mixed up and picked out at random and assembled that way. After that, they formed into "songs" with melodies and riffs.'

Speaking to *Mojo*, Sadier said that the new album was optimistic

* Jean-Baptiste Garnero of the French band Spring is credited with backing vocals on *Mars Audiac Quintet*'s 'Transporté Sans Bouger', so this isn't an entirely new concept.

and empowering, coming back to the idea she has often expressed that people have the power to shape their own futures. 'I think that it is becoming more and more apparent to more and more people as the absurdity of the political situation intensifies that at some point—soon?—we will have to organise how society is run in radically different ways, based on radically different values, such as cooperation, as opposed to the current capitalist ideology of competition,' she said, adding that 'Aerial Troubles' tackles the concept of 'giving birth to/ creating a new existence as we experience the death of modernity.'

On the day before *Instant Holograms* was released, I attended an album-listening party at the Barcelona record store El Genio Equivocado, up in the fashionably twisted streets of Gràcia. By this point, most of the reviews of the new record had been published, along with a couple of small interviews with the band, but I wanted to see what the reaction to the album would be like in the real world, rather than in the online echo chamber. I wanted to *smell* the love of the Stereolab fans, because what is a band without fans?

About thirty people attended the party, a well-balanced mixture of ages, genders, and nationalities that made me feel pretty cheery about the Stereolab fan base. There were Felipe and Patricia from Brazil, for example: he likes the group's audiovisual side, their attitude, and their love of the avant-garde; she enjoys the band's connection with Brazil. 'The way Laetitia sings reminds me of MPB [Música popular brasileira] classics,' she explains.

There was Andreu, just twenty-two years old, who got into Stereolab after hearing them referenced by Spanish pop band La Casa Azul: he likes the band's noisier/shoegaze side, as well as their lounge/ bossa influences. There was Rafa, who likes the band because 'when you hear a song, you know it is Stereolab', and Daniel, who loves their melodies and their retro-futuristic sound. 'People used to complain that they always made the same record,' he tells me. 'But every record is really different.'

Reaction to the new album was universally strong. 'When I heard the first three songs, I was relieved,' explains Sacha Maxim, from the USA. 'It sounded like them. But not recycled.' Sara, from Barcelona, describes the *Instant Holograms* singles as probably the best new music of the year: perfect for walking around in the warm Catalan weather. Daniel says 'Melodie Is A Wound' is 'one hundred percent perfect'. And so on.

Two weeks later, I saw Stereolab live for the sixth time in my life at Primavera Sound 2025. I had been preparing for this, poring over setlists—'Peng'! '33'! 'The Way Will Be Opening'! No 'French Disko'?—and listening obsessively to *Instant Holograms* as I put the finishing touches to this book. The occasion threatened to be too much, but the gig was sublime. The new songs sounded fantastic live, especially 'If You Remember I Forgot How To Dream Pt 1', which might be on its way to becoming a new Stereolab anthem, and Laetitia looked delighted to be there, dancing around slightly nervously and jamming out on trombone. Tim was typically inscrutable, his record-collector-gone-good look only slightly spoiled by the appearance of a jaunty baseball cap.

In a way, it felt like nothing had changed since I first saw Stereolab back in 1993. Cliff was grimacing away from Andy Ramsay's bass drum like we were back in the pre-Britpop era, and the band played with an astounding force, locking into obscure grooves in the great textural rush that Stereolab were born to produce.

At the same time, so much had changed in the intervening years. Band members have come and gone, Mary Hansen is no longer with us, and Tim and Laetitia separated long ago. Stereolab no longer represent the youthful force of young love; they are older and slightly greying, and yet sublime in their maturity. The Primavera crowd, too, was very different from the three hundred people who watched Stereolab with me back in 1993. I don't remember Stereolab's audience being this diverse or this animated. There's dancing—a *lot* of dancing—and love.

The band ended the gig with 'Cybele's Reverie', and I almost wanted to cry, moved beyond reason by the song's bittersweet tale of lost youth and passing time. Stereolab have grown older; *I've* grown older, too, and I knew I would soon have to finish this book, disengage from the Stereolab world, and move on.

As I wandered away from the gig, overwhelmed, I wondered where Stereolab would go now. More than at any time since they reunited,

Stereolab feel like a living, breathing, *creating* monster, rather than a trawl-the-carcass-through-the-greatest-hits nostalgia act. In many ways, they're a normal band now, doing normal band things like releasing new albums and making videos. And yet, Stereolab could never, ever be normal.

So where would this most infinitely fascinating of bands venture after half a decade of reunion, seven album reissues, and one brand-new album?

The short answer is, I don't know, and I suspect they may not know either. Though three of their earlier albums remain to be reissued (*Peng!*, *Chemical Chords*, and *Not Music*), the band's catalogue of odds and sods has pretty much been picked dry. There are, of course, unreleased songs, alternative mixes, and demos—Jim O'Rourke told me about an hour-long version of 'Blue Milk' from *Cobra And Phases Group Play Voltage In The Milky Night*, the thought of which makes me froth with envy. But as manager Martin Pike said in a Facebook post in 2016, the quality might not be there. 'Rights aren't generally an issue. Some of the unreleased/uncompiled tracks aren't very good (subjective, I know) and we feel they should remain as they are—unreleased/uncompiled.'

Another new studio album, then? Tim wrote thirty songs for *Instant Holograms*, and the band have already released two new singles following its release: tour seven-inch 'Cloud Land' / 'Flashes In The Afternoon' and 'Fed Up With Your Job?' / 'Constant And Uniform Movement Unknown', which dropped out of nowhere in September 2025. I've heard from someone who was present at the *Instant Holograms* recording sessions that there is more to come beyond the two singles, so I guess we shall see. You may even be holding a new album in your hands as you read this.

Perhaps the more important question is whether the band will record together again. Both Laetitia Sadier and Tim Gane remain artistically active in their solo and band work, and they both remain curious about where music will take them. When I interviewed Laetitia in 2024, she talked about her vision of using the sampler as a base, 'and singing, playing guitar, playing trombone, just around it' with the admirable enthusiasm of someone who will almost certainly never get tired of making music. Could this become a Stereolab album one day, laden with trombones and samples? Who knows?

I would love to hear more Stereolab music, and I would love to see the band continue to tour, even at the inevitable risk of diminished returns. But I don't want to be greedy. Stereolab have already given us so much magnificent work that to demand more seems ungracious.

If there is no more, and Stereolab call it a day for a second time, drift off into gentle retirement, then that's fine, too. Like the Infinity Girl who gives her name to one of Stereolab's most loved songs, Gane and Sadier's music will go on racing hearts and opening minds inexorably, tracing their elegant rays of *Space Age Batchelor Pad Music* from now until forever.

BIBLIOGRAPHY

BOOKS

Anna Doble, *Connection Is A Song: Coming Up And Coming Out Through The Music Of The '90s* (Nine Eight Books, 2024)

Mick Houghton, *Fried & Justified: Hits, Myths, Break-Ups And Breakdowns In The Record Business 1978–98* (Faber, 2019)

ARTICLES

Camilla Aisa, 'Stereolab', *Shindig!* issue 164, June 2025

Albert Alcoz, 'Laetitia Sadier (Sala Vol, 23/05/24)', *Indie Lovers*, May 25, 2024

Cheri Amour, '10 Questions For The Avant-Pop Icons Stereolab', *The Arts Desk*, November 2, 2023

Toby Amies, 'Laetitia Sadier By Toby Amies', *Bomb Magazine*, March 15, 2024

Ben Beaumont-Thomas, 'Stereolab: There Was Craziness In Getting Lost And Dizzy', *The Guardian*, September 4, 2019

Billboard Staff, 'New Stereolab Album Stretches "Sound"', *Billboard*, June 21, 2001

Tom Breihan, 'Stereolab Go On Hiatus', *Pitchfork*, April 2, 2019

Eliot Van Buskirk, 'Stereolab's Tim Gane On Music, Business And Chemical Chords', *Wired*, August 5, 2008

Justin Colletti, 'Tim Gane: Stereolab And Beyond', *Tape Op*, November 2013

Shawn Conner, 'Changes Bring Stereolab Back To Familiar Ground', *Georgia Straight*, March 25, 2004

Clayton M Davis, 'The Goat Looks In', *Clay The Scribe*, March 4, 2016

Guy Debord, 'Report On The Construction Of Situations', July 1957

Nick Dwyer, 'Laetitia Sadier Interview', Red Bull Music Academy, 2015

Neil Durham, 'Gig Review: Stereolab At Sala Apolo, Barcelona', *Monstra Gigz*, November 9, 2022

John Everhart, 'Deerhunter vs. Stereolab: A Conversation Between Bradford Cox And Laetitia Sadier', *Under The Radar*, October 11, 2010

Trilby Foxx, 'Tim Gane, Leader Of Europe's Foremost "High-Concept Pop Group", Talks Us Through New Album *Chemical Chords*', *Fact*, 2009

Lestyn George, 'Cavern Of Anti-Matter: Raves From The Cave', *Electronic Sound*, April 13, 2018

Todd Gilchrist, 'Stereolab: Fab Four Suture', IGN, May 12, 2012

Carl Griffin, 'Tim Gane: Sky High', *Electronic Sound*, September 30, 2014

Tommy Gunnarsson, 'Miscellaneous—Interview With Tim Gane', *Penny Black Music*, June 23, 2006

Robert Ham, 'Stereolab: Pulse Of The Early Brain', *Pitchfork*, September 3, 2022

Jim Harrington, 'Stereolab Won't Let Hansen Be Forgotten', *Oakland Tribune*, April 1, 2004

Eric Harvey, 'Dots And Loops', *Pitchfork*, July 23, 2017

David Hidek, 'Laetitia Sadier & Tim Gane: Stereolab And Beyond', *Tape Op*, November 2013

H2O, 'Tim Gane (Duophonic/UHF Disks)', *Chunklet*, 2006

Alexander Iadarola, 'Cavern Of Anti-Matter's New Track Takes You Into A Psychedelic Techno Wormhole', *Vice*, September 7, 2016

Dave Jennings, 'Singles', *Melody Maker*, 1993
Mark Jenkins, 'Stereolab's Latest Experiment', *Washington Post*, November 4, 1999
Jason Josephes, 'Stereolab', *Pitchfork*, May 1996
Joshua Minsoo Kim, 'Tone Glow 124: Laetitia Sadier', *Tone Glow*, February 11, 2024
Cam Lindsay, 'Learning A New Language: Tim Gane On Leaving Stereolab Behind And For Cavern Of Anti-Matter', *Vice*, February 22, 2016
Colm McAuliffe, 'A Private Future: Tim Gane Discusses Cavern Of Anti-Matter', *The Quietus*, January 7, 2015
Craig McLean, 'Stereolab, Britain's Clever Post-Rock Innovators, Want To Capture Ears Again', *New York Times*, May 10, 2019
James McNair, 'Rock & Pop: Total Eclipse Of The Heart', The Independent, January 30, 2004
Hayden Merrick, 'Travels With Jenny: Stereolab's Transient Random—Noise Bursts With Announcements', *Bandcamp Daily*, February 23, 2023
'Michael', 'Stereolab/Unrest At The Grand, New York City', columbia.edu
Marta Moreira, 'Xavi Muñoz: Al Entrar En Stereolab He Confirmado Que No Existen Las Clases Medias En La Música', *Valencia Plaza*, July 8, 2020
Tom Murphy, 'Laetitia Sadier On How Music And Politics Go Hand In Hand, And How To Struggle Is To Live', *Westword*, October 10, 2012
Jim Newsom, 'Herbie Mann's New Groove', *Portfolio Weekly*, July 9, 2002
Sean O'Hagan, 'From The Desk Of The High Llamas' Sean O'Hagan: Turn On', *Magnet*, February 4, 2016
Adrian Pannett, 'Stereolab: Fab Four Suture', *Comes With A Smile*, April 2006
Pierre Perrone, 'Obituary: Mary Hansen', *The Independent*, December 13, 2002
Alexis Petridis, 'Stereolab Review: Art-Pop Pioneers Dance About Architecture', *The Guardian*, June 12, 2019
Tom Pinnock, 'Stereolab: We're Here To Create The World That We Desire', *Uncut*, January 2020
Ben Ratliff, 'Emperor Tomato Vinyl', *4Columns*, November 22, 2019
Simon Reynolds, 'Charles Long And Stereolab', *Artforum*, May 1995
Sam Richards, 'Laetitia Sadier And Tim Gane: Music Is Just An Exciting Adventure', *Uncut*, May 2025
Martin Schneider, 'The Intriguing Origins Of "Cliff", The Cartoon Character That's All Over Stereolab's Early Album Art', *Dangerous Minds*, April 27, 2017
Victoria Segal, 'Stereolab Interviewed: We Have To Organise How Society Is Run In Radically Different Ways, Based On Radically Different Values', *Mojo*, May 14, 2025
Jeff Stark, 'Stereolab On Philosophical Systems, The Economics Of Small Record Labels And Why You Shouldn't Have Sex To Barry White', *Salon*, September 22, 1999
Matthew Strauss, 'Stereolab's Laetitia Sadier Distances Herself From Jordan Peterson In New Statement', *Pitchfork*, August 7, 2018
Suzannah Tartan, 'The Method To The Madness', *Japan Times*, February 24, 2002
Jenny Toomey, 'Jim O'Rourke: Superchunk, Aluminum Group & More', *Tape Op*, March 2000
April Clare Welsh, 'Laetitia Sadier Finds Herself In A Hairy Situation', *Dazed*, August 13, 2013
Eleanor Whitney, 'Morgane Lhote Finds Her Disco-Drenched Place In The Sun With Hologram Teen', *Weird Sister*, April 24, 2018
Douglas Wolk, 'Living In Dual Mono', *Seattle Weekly*, October 9, 2006

– 'Analog Synth Summit With Bob Moog, Stereolab, Imperial Drag & Weezer', *Musician Magazine*, December 1997
– 'Funk And Fear: Hologram Teen Talks', *Ransom Note*, August 20, 2021
– 'Ghost Box Q&A', *Fact*, May 2006
– 'Interview With Malcolm Eden Of McCarthy', *Lacewings*, January 22, 2007
– 'Interview With Tim Gane Of McCarthy/Stereolab', *Lacewings*, October 3, 2006
– 'Interview With Tim Gane Of Stereolab', *Synth History*, November 30, 2023
– 'Julian House Interview,' *Soul Riot*, 2008
– 'Morgane Lhote—Not Just The Ex-Keyboardist From Stereolab', *Feminatronic*, June 10, 2016
– 'Painters Paint: The Definitive Career-Spanning Interview (To Date) With The High Llamas' Sean O'Hagan', *Popshifter*, January 30, 2011
– 'Stereolab: Koko, London', *The Line Of Best Fit*, December 23, 2008
– 'Tone Glow 127: David Lance Callahan (Moonshake, The Wolfhounds)', *Tone Glow*, February 27, 2024

SLEEVE NOTES

Tim Gane, *Transient Random-Noise Bursts With Announcements: Expanded Edition* (Duophonic/Warp, 2019)
Tim Gane, *Mars Audiac Quintet: Expanded Edition* (Duophonic/Warp, 2019)
Tim Gane, *Emperor Tomato Ketchup: Expanded Edition* (Duophonic/Warp, 2019)
Tim Gane, *Dots And Loops: Expanded Edition* (Duophonic/Warp, 2019)
Tim Gane, *Cobra And Phases Group Play Voltage In The Milky Night: Expanded Edition* (Duophonic/Warp, 2019)
Tim Gane, *Sound-Dust: Expanded Edition* (Duophonic/Warp, 2019)
Tim Gane, *Margerine Eclipse: Expanded Edition* (Duophonic/Warp, 2019)
Mike McGonigal, *Serene Velocity* (Elektra/Duophonic, 2006)

RADIO/PODCASTS/VIDEO

Nitsuh Abebe, 'Stereolab Interview', Pitchfork TV, January 2012
Ross Allen, 'J Dilla In Conversation With Ross Allen', NTS, 2001
Gilles Peterson, 'J Dilla Interview', BBC Radio One, 2001
Questlove, 'Black Music Month: James Poyser Part 2', *Questlove Supreme*, June 2024

WEBSITES

discogs.com/artist/388-Stereolab
forum.stereolab.co.uk/
forums.stevehoffman.tv
gearspace.com/board/
koly.com/stereolab/
maths.monash.edu.au/~rjh/stereolab/
reddit.com/r/stereolab
stereolab.co.uk/sleevenotes
stereolab.co.uk/lab-report
stereolab.co.uk/discography/

ALSO AVAILABLE FROM
JAWBONE PRESS

Riot On Sunset Strip: Rock'n'roll's Last Stand In Hollywood Domenic Priore

Million Dollar Bash: Bob Dylan, The Band, And The Basement Tapes Sid Griffin

Bowie In Berlin: A New Career In A New Town Thomas Jerome Seabrook

Hot Burritos: The True Story Of The Flying Burrito Brothers John Einarson with Chris Hillman

To Live Is To Die: The Life And Death Of Metallica's Cliff Burton Joel McIver

Jack Bruce Composing Himself: The Authorised Biography Harry Shapiro

Return Of The King: Elvis Presley's Great Comeback Gillian G. Gaar

Seasons They Change: The Story Of Acid And Psychedelic Folk Jeanette Leech

Becoming Elektra: The Incredible True Story Of Jac Holzman's Visionary Record Label Mick Houghton

A Wizard, A True Star: Todd Rundgren In The Studio Paul Myers

The Resurrection Of Johnny Cash: Hurt, Redemption, And American Recordings Graeme Thomson

Entertain Us: The Rise Of Nirvana Gillian G. Gaar

Adventures Of A Waterboy Mike Scott

Read & Burn: A Book About Wire Wilson Neate

Big Star: The Story Of Rock's Forgotten Band Rob Jovanovic

Recombo DNA: The Story Of Devo, Or How The 60s Became The 80s Kevin C. Smith

Neil Sedaka, Rock'n'roll Survivor: The Inside Story Of His Incredible Comeback Rich Podolsky

Touched By Grace: My Time With Jeff Buckley Gary Lucas

A Sense Of Wonder: Van Morrison's Ireland David Burke

Bathed In Lightning: John McLaughlin, The 60s And The Emerald Beyond Colin Harper

My Bloody Roots: From Sepultua To Soulfly And Beyond: The Autobiography Max Cavalera with Joel McIver

What's Exactly The Matter With Me? Memoirs Of A Life In Music P.F. Sloan and S.E. Feinberg

Who Killed Mister Moonlight? Bauhaus, Black Magick, And Benediction David J. Haskins

Confessions Of A Heretic: The Sacred & The Profane, Behemoth & Beyond Adam Nergal Darski with Mark Eglinton

Throwing Frisbees At The Sun: A Book About Beck Rob Jovanovic

Lee, Myself & I: Inside The Very Special World Of Lee Hazlewood Wyndham Wallace

Long Promised Road: Carl Wilson, Soul Of The Beach Boys Kent Crowley

Complicated Game: Inside The Songs Of XTC Andy Partridge and Todd Bernhardt

Seeing The Real You At Last: Life And Love On The Road With Bob Dylan Britta Lee Shain

Tragedy: The Ballad Of The Bee Gees Jeff Apter

The Monkees, Head, And The 60s Peter Mills

Perfect Day: An Intimate Portrait Of Life With Lou Reed Bettye Kronstad

Shredders! The Oral History Of Speed Guitar (And More) Greg Prato

I Scare Myself: A Memoir Dan Hicks

Shadows Across The Moon: Outlaws, Freaks, Shamans And The Making Of Ibiza Clubland Helen Donlon

Fearless: The Making Of Post-Rock Jeanette Leech

Staying Alive: The Disco Inferno Of The Bee Gees Simon Spence

Earthbound: David Bowie and The Man Who Fell To Earth Susan Compo

The Yacht Rock Book: The Oral History Of The Soft, Smooth Sounds Of The 70s And 80s Greg Prato

What's Big And Purple And Lives In The Ocean? The Moby Grape Story Cam Cobb

Swans: Sacrifice And Transcendence: The Oral History Nick Soulsby

Small Victories: The True Story Of Faith No More Adrian Harte

AC/DC 1973–1980: The Bon Scott Years Jeff Apter

King's X: The Oral History Greg Prato

Keep Music Evil: The Brian Jonestown Massacre Story Jesse Valencia

Lunch With The Wild Frontiers: A History Of Britpop And Excess In 13½ Chapters Phill Savidge

More Life With Deth David Ellefson with Thom Hazaert

Wilcopedia: A Comprehensive Guide To The Music Of America's Best Band Daniel Cook Johnson

Take It Off: KISS Truly Unmasked
Greg Prato

I Am Morbid: Ten Lessons Learned From Extreme Metal, Outlaw Country, And The Power Of Self-Determination
David Vincent with Joel McIver

Lydia Lunch: The War Is Never Over: A Companion To The Film By Beth B.
Nick Soulsby

Zeppelin Over Dayton: Guided By Voices Album By Album Jeff Gomez

What Makes The Monkey Dance: The Life And Music Of Chuck Prophet And Green On Red Stevie Simkin

So Much For The 30 Year Plan: Therapy? The Authorised Biography Simon Young

She Bop: The Definitive History Of Women In Popular Music Lucy O'Brien

Relax Baby Be Cool: The Artistry And Audacity Of Serge Gainsbourg
Jeremy Allen

Seeing Sideways: A Memoir Of Music And Motherhood Kristin Hersh

Two Steps Forward, One Step Back: My Life In The Music Business Miles A. Copeland III

It Ain't Retro: Daptone Records & The 21st-Century Soul Revolution Jessica Lipsky

Renegade Snares: The Resistance & Resilience Of Drum & Bass Ben Murphy and Carl Loben

Southern Man: Music And Mayhem In The American South Alan Walden with S.E. Feinberg

Frank & Co: Conversations With Frank Zappa 1977–1993 Co de Kloet

All I Ever Wanted: A Rock 'n' Roll Memoir
Kathy Valentine

Here They Come With Their Make-Up On: Suede, Coming Up ... And More Adventures Beyond The Wild Frontiers Jane Savidge

This Band Has No Past: How Cheap Trick Became Cheap Trick Brian J. Kramp

Gary Moore: The Official Biography
Harry Shapiro

Holy Ghost: The Life & Death Of Free Jazz Pioneer Albert Ayler Richard Koloda

Conform To Deform: The Weird & Wonderful World Of Some Bizzare
Wesley Doyle

Happy Forever: My Musical Adventures With The Turtles, Frank Zappa, T. Rex, Flo & Eddie, And More Mark Volman with John Cody

Johnny Thunders: In Cold Blood—The Official Biography, Revised & Updated
Nina Antonia

Absolute Beginner: Memoirs Of The World's Best Least-Known Guitarist Kevin Armstrong

Turn It Up! My Time Making Hit Records In The Glory Days Of Rock Music Tom Werman

Revolutionary Spirit: A Post-Punk Exorcism
Paul Simpson

Don't Dream It's Over: The Remarkable Life Of Neil Finn Jeff Apter

Chopping Wood: Thoughts & Stories Of A Legendary American Folksinger
Pete Seeger with David Bernz

Through The Crack In The Wall: The Secret History Of Josef K Johnnie Johnstone

Forever Changes: The Authorized Biography Of Arthur Lee & Love
John Einarson

I Wouldn't Say It If It Wasn't True: A Memoir Of Life, Music, And The Dream Syndicate
Steve Wynn

Gliders Over Hollywood: Airships, Airplay, And The Art Of Rock Promotion
Paul Rappaport

Jazz Revolutionary: The Life & Music Of Eric Dolphy Jonathon Grasse

Down On The Corner: Adventures In Busking & Street Music Cary Baker

Decade Of Dissent: How 1960s Bob Dylan Changed The World Sean Egan

Doing Time: Comedians Talk Stand-Up
JT Habersaat

Down River: In Search Of David Ackles
Mark Brend

Giant Steps: My Improbable Journey From Stage Lights To Executive Heights
Derek Shulman with Jon Wiederhorn

Turn My Head Into Sound: A History Of Kevin Shields And My Bloody Valentine
Andrew Perer

The Royal We: A Memoir Roddy Bottum